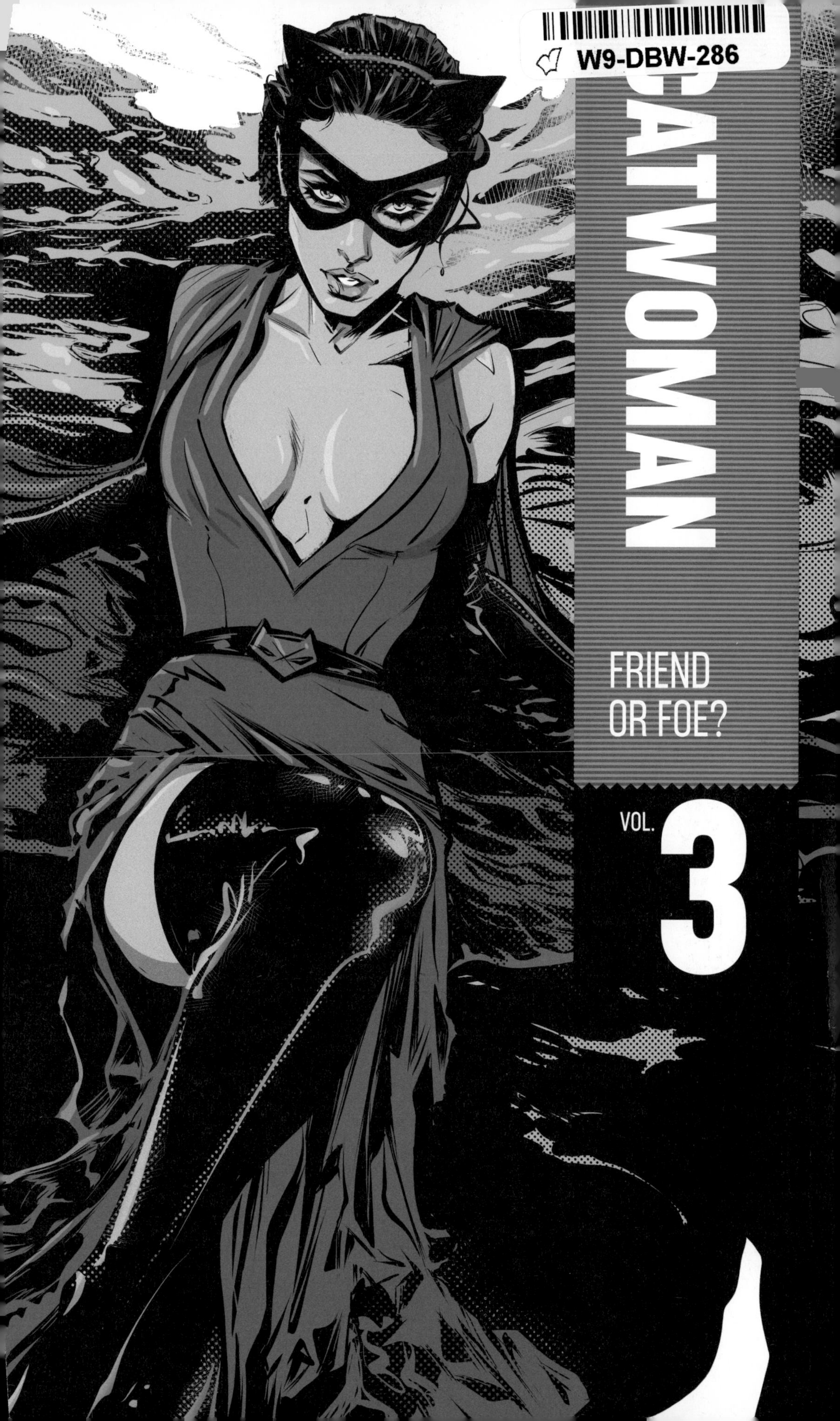

CATWOMAN

FRIEND
OR FOE?

VOL. 3

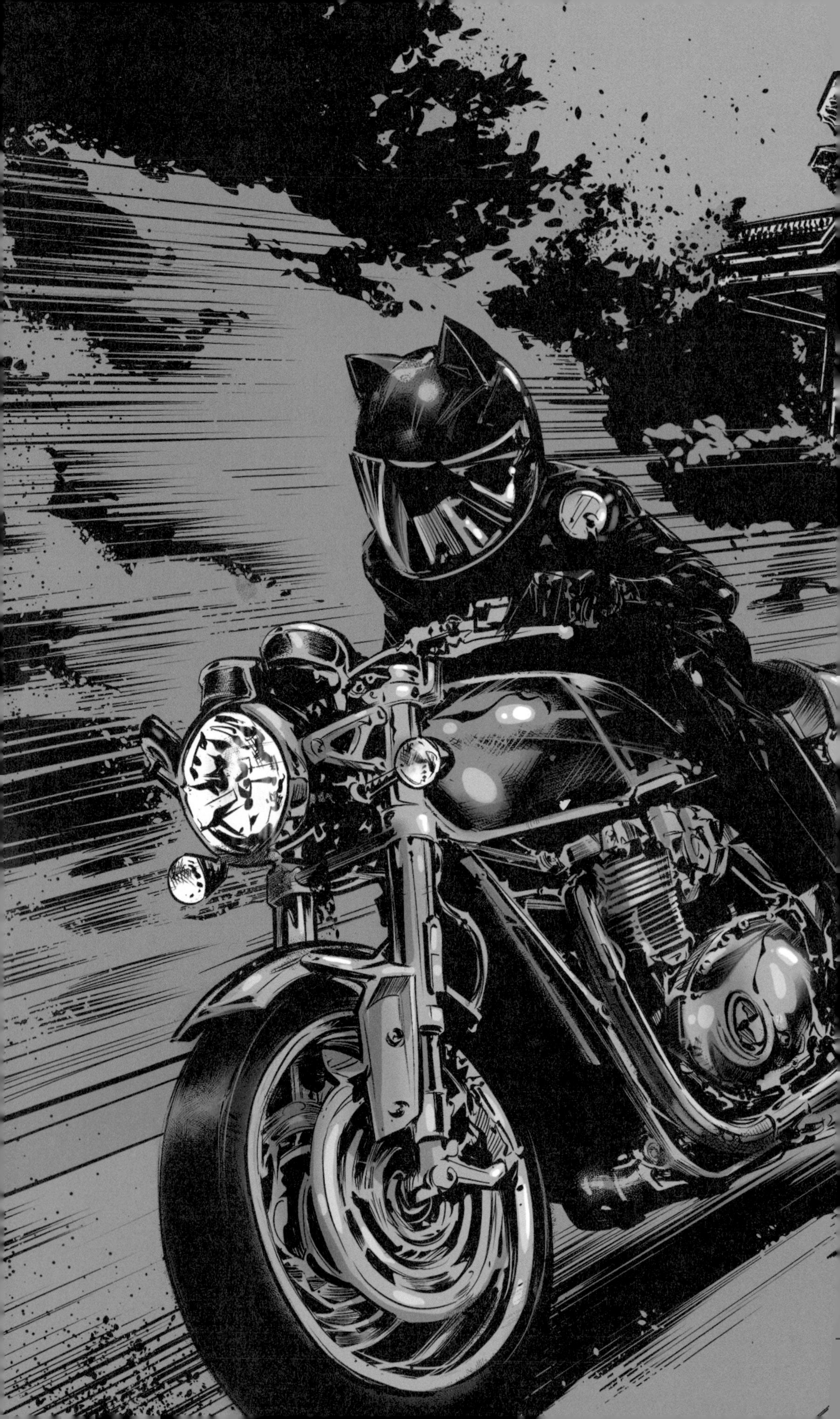

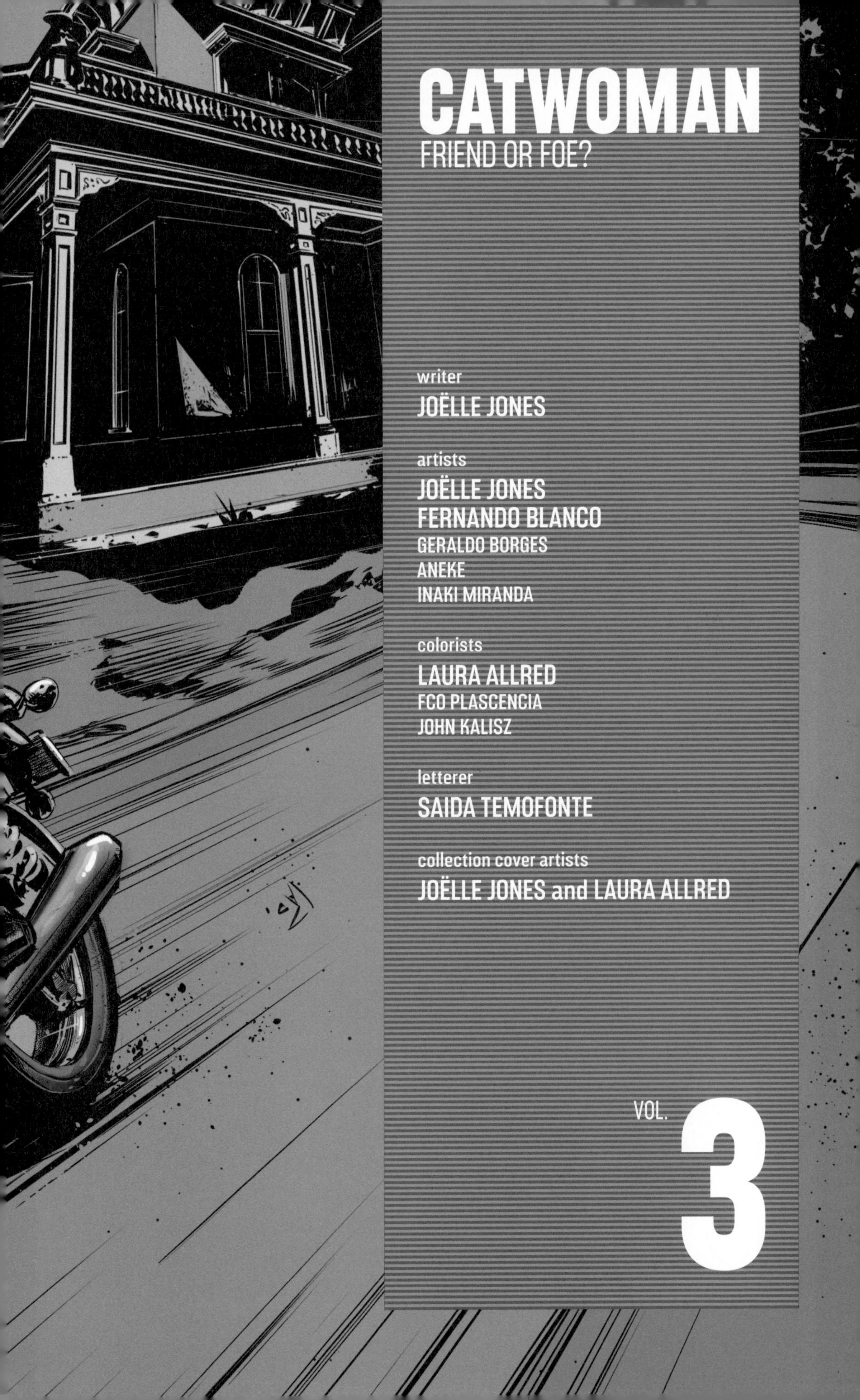

CATWOMAN

FRIEND OR FOE?

writer
JOËLLE JONES

artists
JOËLLE JONES
FERNANDO BLANCO
GERALDO BORGES
ANEKE
INAKI MIRANDA

colorists
LAURA ALLRED
FCO PLASCENCIA
JOHN KALISZ

letterer
SAIDA TEMOFONTE

collection cover artists
JOËLLE JONES and LAURA ALLRED

VOL. 3

JAMIE S. RICH, JESSICA CHEN Editors – Original Series
HARVEY RICHARDS Associate Editor – Original Series
BEN MEARES Assistant Editor – Original Series
JEB WOODARD Group Editor – Collected Editions
ROBIN WILDMAN Editor – Collected Edition
STEVE COOK Design Director – Books
MEGEN BELLERSEN Publication Design
CHRISTY SAWYER Publication Production

BOB HARRAS Senior VP – Editor-in-Chief, DC Comics

DAN DiDIO Publisher
JIM LEE Publisher & Chief Creative Officer
BOBBIE CHASE VP – New Publishing Initiatives
DON FALLETTI VP – Manufacturing Operations & Workflow Management
LAWRENCE GANEM VP – Talent Services
ALISON GILL Senior VP – Manufacturing & Operations
HANK KANALZ Senior VP – Publishing Strategy & Support Services
DAN MIRON VP – Publishing Operations
NICK J. NAPOLITANO VP – Manufacturing Administration & Design
NANCY SPEARS VP – Sales
JONAH WEILAND VP – Marketing & Creative Services
MICHELE R. WELLS VP & Executive Editor, Young Reader

CATWOMAN VOL. 3: FRIEND OR FOE?

Published by DC Comics. Compilation and all new material Copyright © 2020 DC Comics. All Rights Reserved.
Originally published in single magazine form in *Catwoman* 16-21. Copyright © 2019, 2020 DC Comics. All Rights
Reserved. All characters, their distinctive likenesses, and related elements featured in this publication are
trademarks of DC Comics. The stories, characters, and incidents featured in this publication are entirely
fictional. DC Comics does not read or accept unsolicited submissions of ideas, stories, or artwork.
DC – a WarnerMedia Company.

DC Comics, 2900 West Alameda Ave., Burbank, CA 91505
Printed by LSC Communications, Owensville, MO, USA. 5/8/20. First Printing.
ISBN: 978-1-4012-9976-7

Library of Congress Cataloging-in-Publication Data is available.

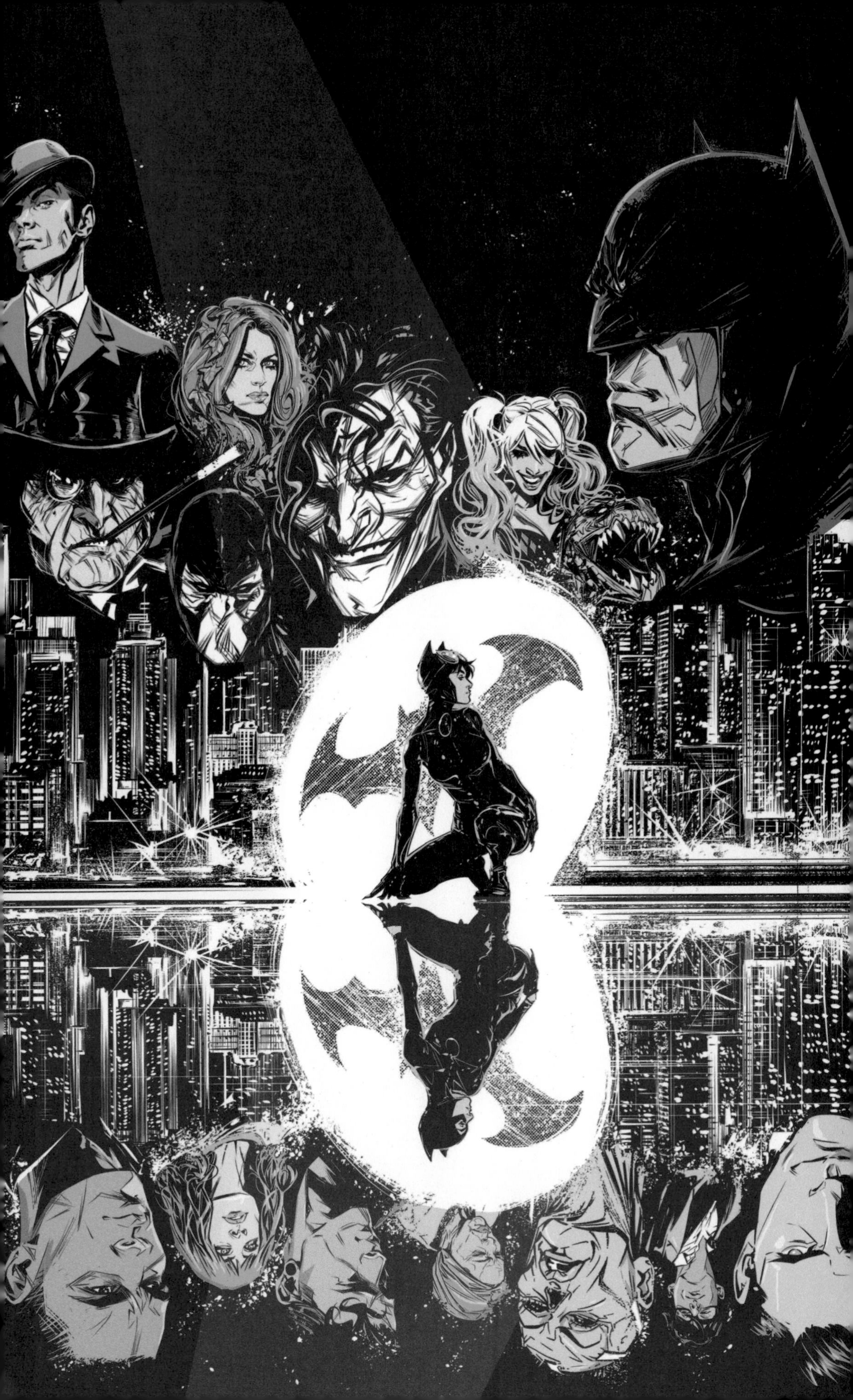

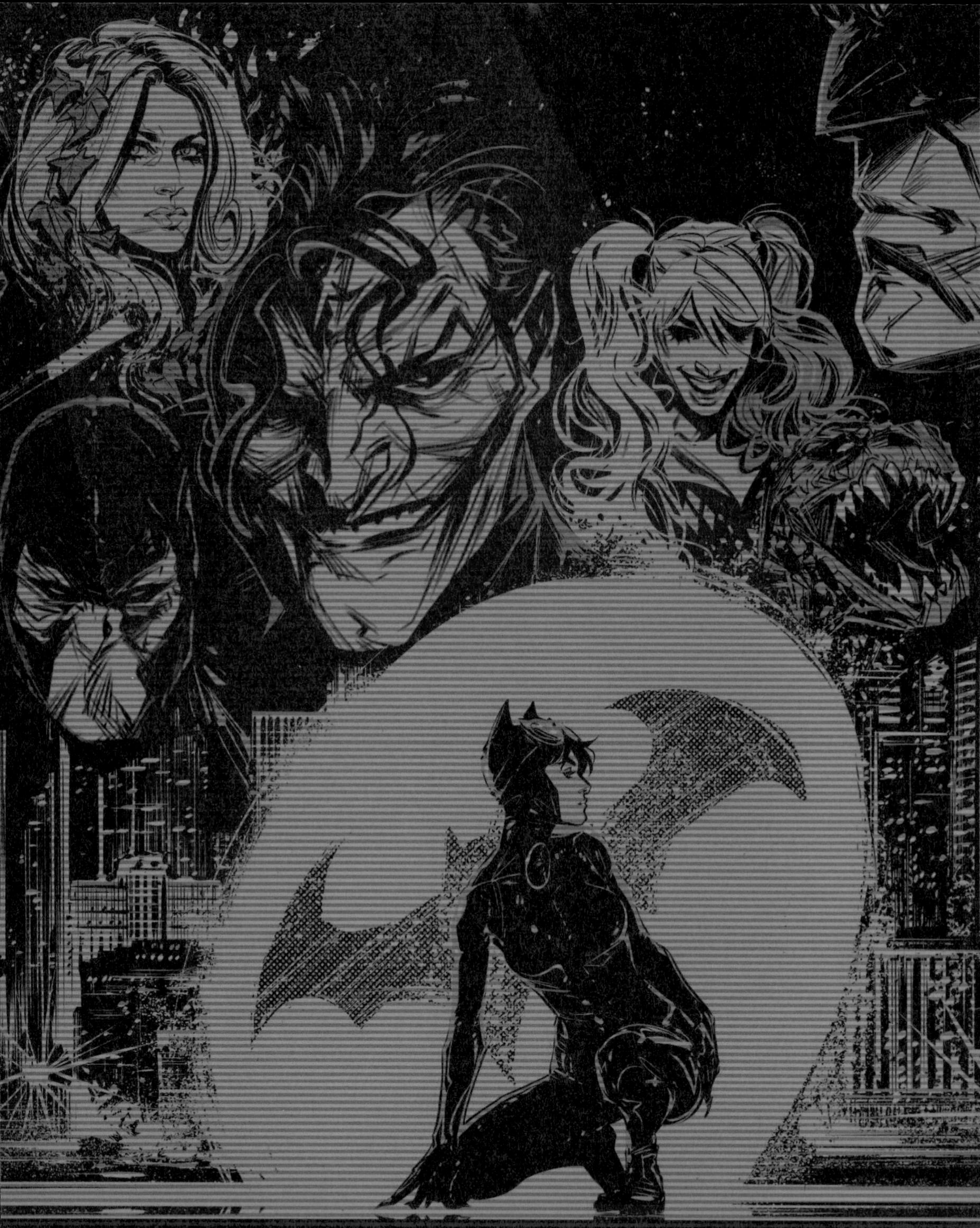

CATWOMAN
#16

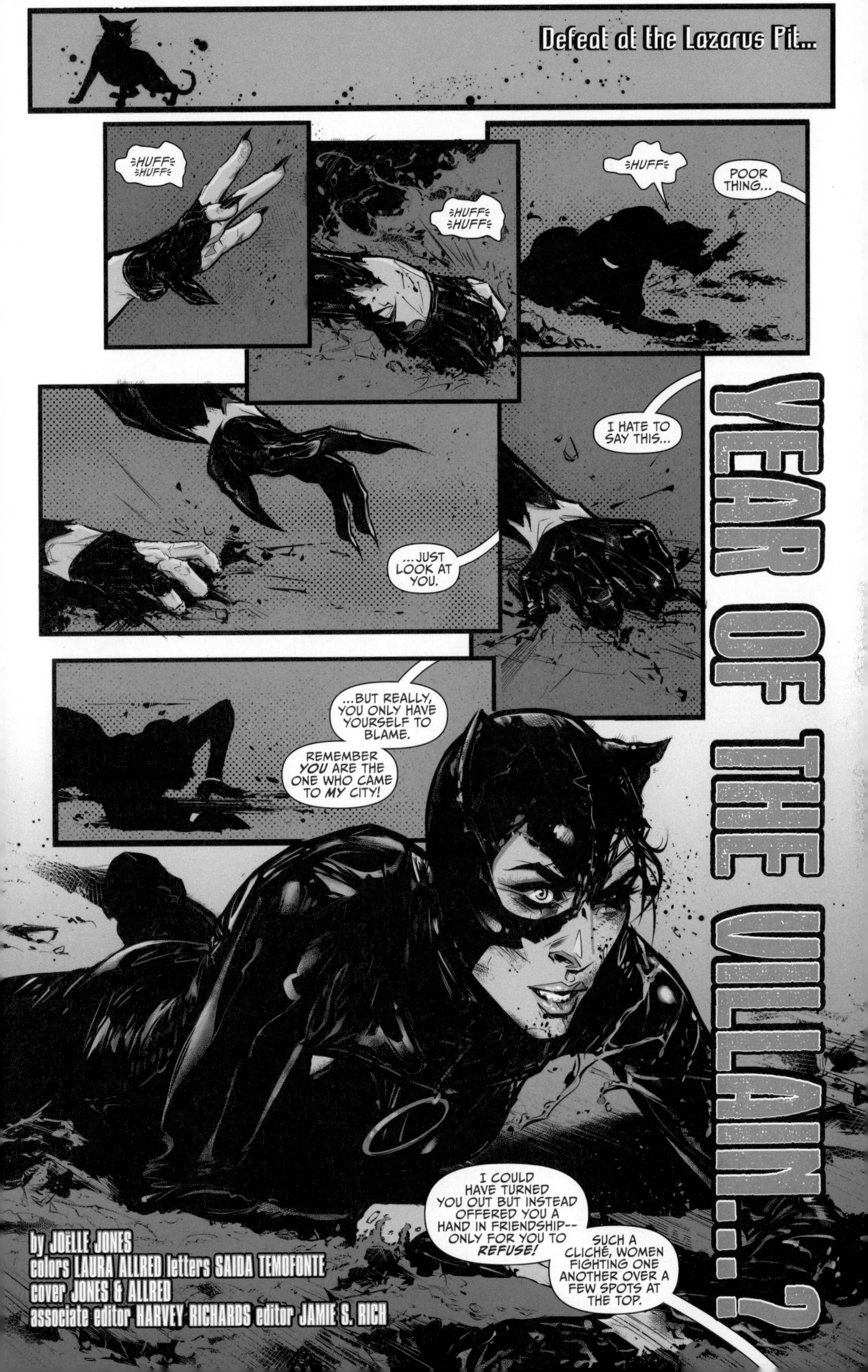
Defeat at the Lazarus Pit...
HUFF HUFF
HUFF HUFF
HUFF
POOR THING...
I HATE TO SAY THIS...
...JUST LOOK AT YOU.
...BUT REALLY, YOU ONLY HAVE YOURSELF TO BLAME.
REMEMBER YOU ARE THE ONE WHO CAME TO MY CITY!
YEAR OF THE VILLAIN...?
I COULD HAVE TURNED YOU OUT BUT INSTEAD OFFERED YOU A HAND IN FRIENDSHIP-- ONLY FOR YOU TO REFUSE!
SUCH A CLICHÉ, WOMEN FIGHTING ONE ANOTHER OVER A FEW SPOTS AT THE TOP.
by JOËLLE JONES
colors LAURA ALLRED letters SAIDA TEMOFONTE
cover JONES & ALLRED
associate editor HARVEY RICHARDS editor JAMIE S. RICH

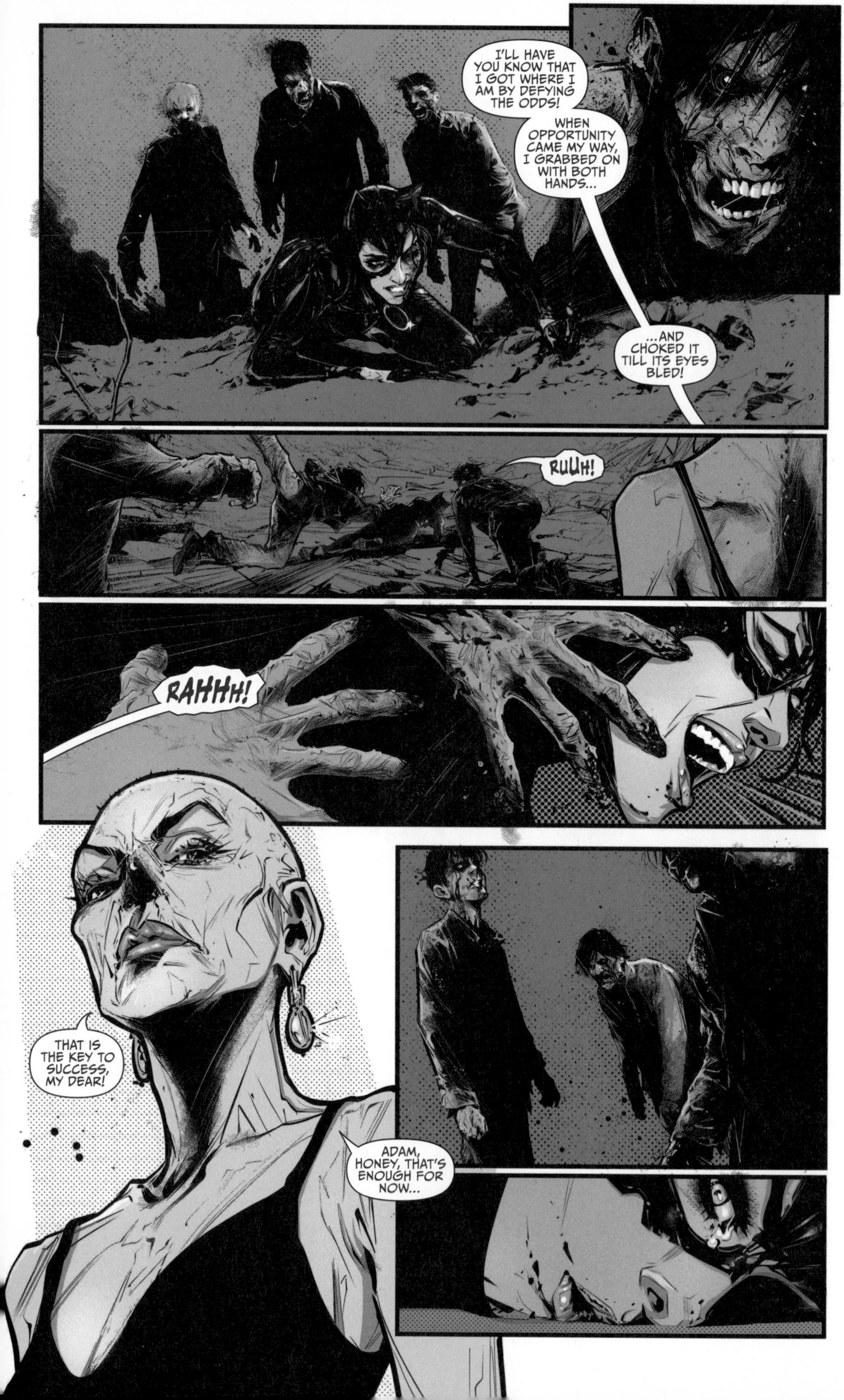

I'LL HAVE YOU KNOW THAT I GOT WHERE I AM BY DEFYING THE ODDS!
WHEN OPPORTUNITY CAME MY WAY, I GRABBED ON WITH BOTH HANDS...
...AND CHOKED IT TILL ITS EYES BLED!
RUUH!
RAHHH!
THAT IS THE KEY TO SUCCESS, MY DEAR!
ADAM, HONEY, THAT'S ENOUGH FOR NOW...

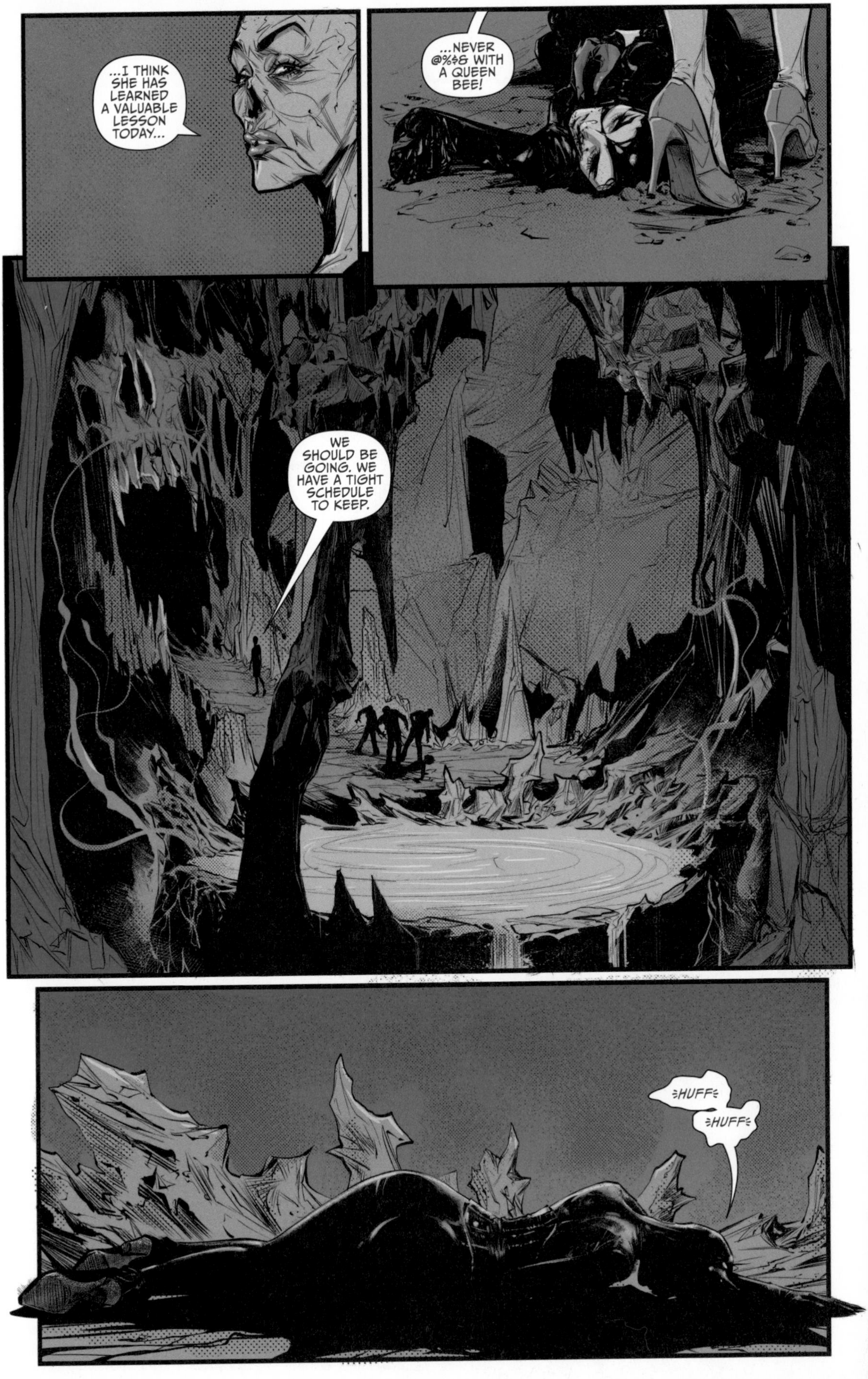
...I THINK SHE HAS LEARNED A VALUABLE LESSON TODAY...
...NEVER @%$& WITH A QUEEN BEE!
WE SHOULD BE GOING. WE HAVE A TIGHT SCHEDULE TO KEEP.
HUFF
HUFF

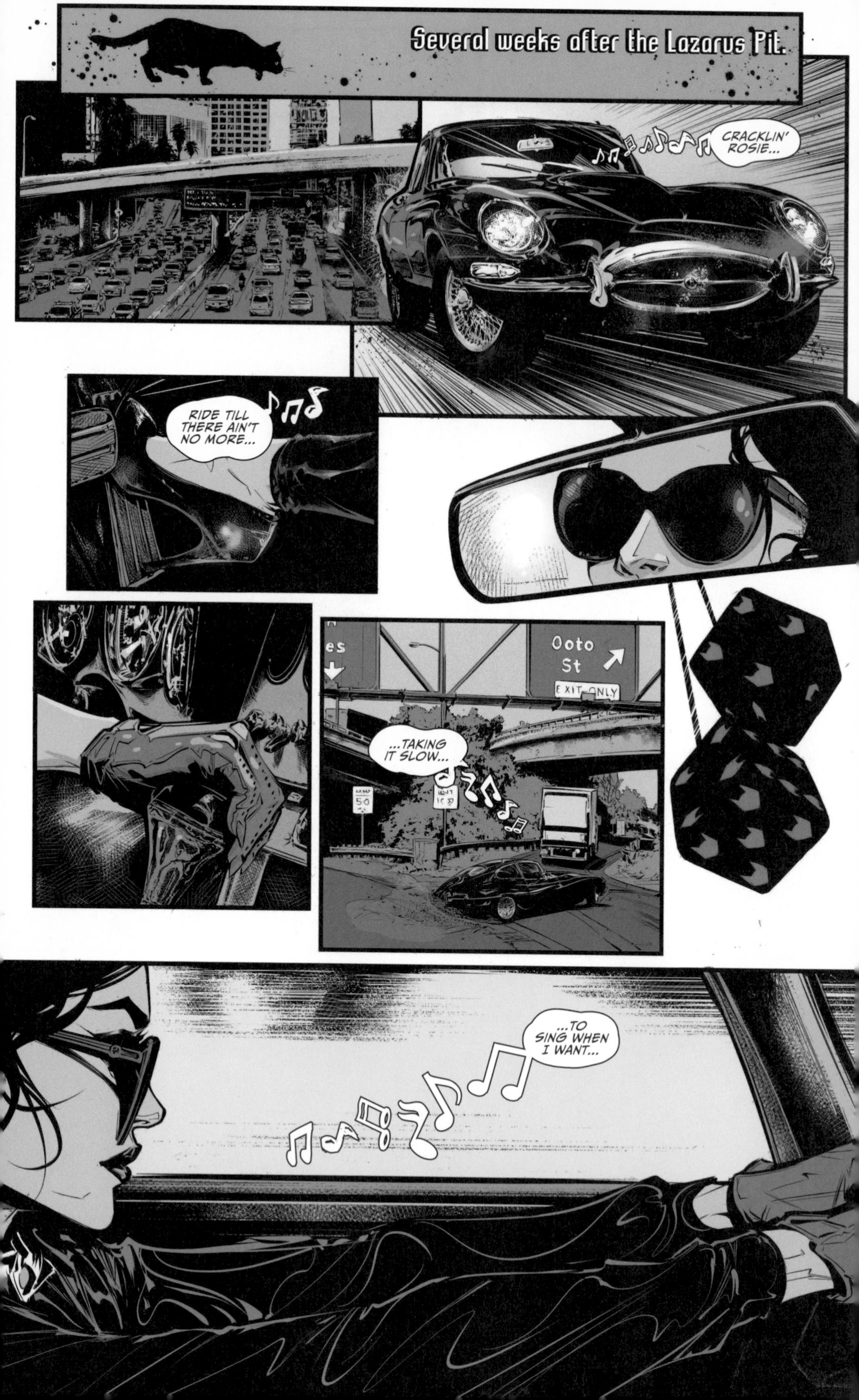
Several weeks after the Lazarus Pit.
CRACKLIN' ROSIE...
RIDE TILL THERE AIN'T NO MORE...
Ooto St
EXIT ONLY
50
...TAKING IT SLOW...
...TO SING WHEN I WANT...

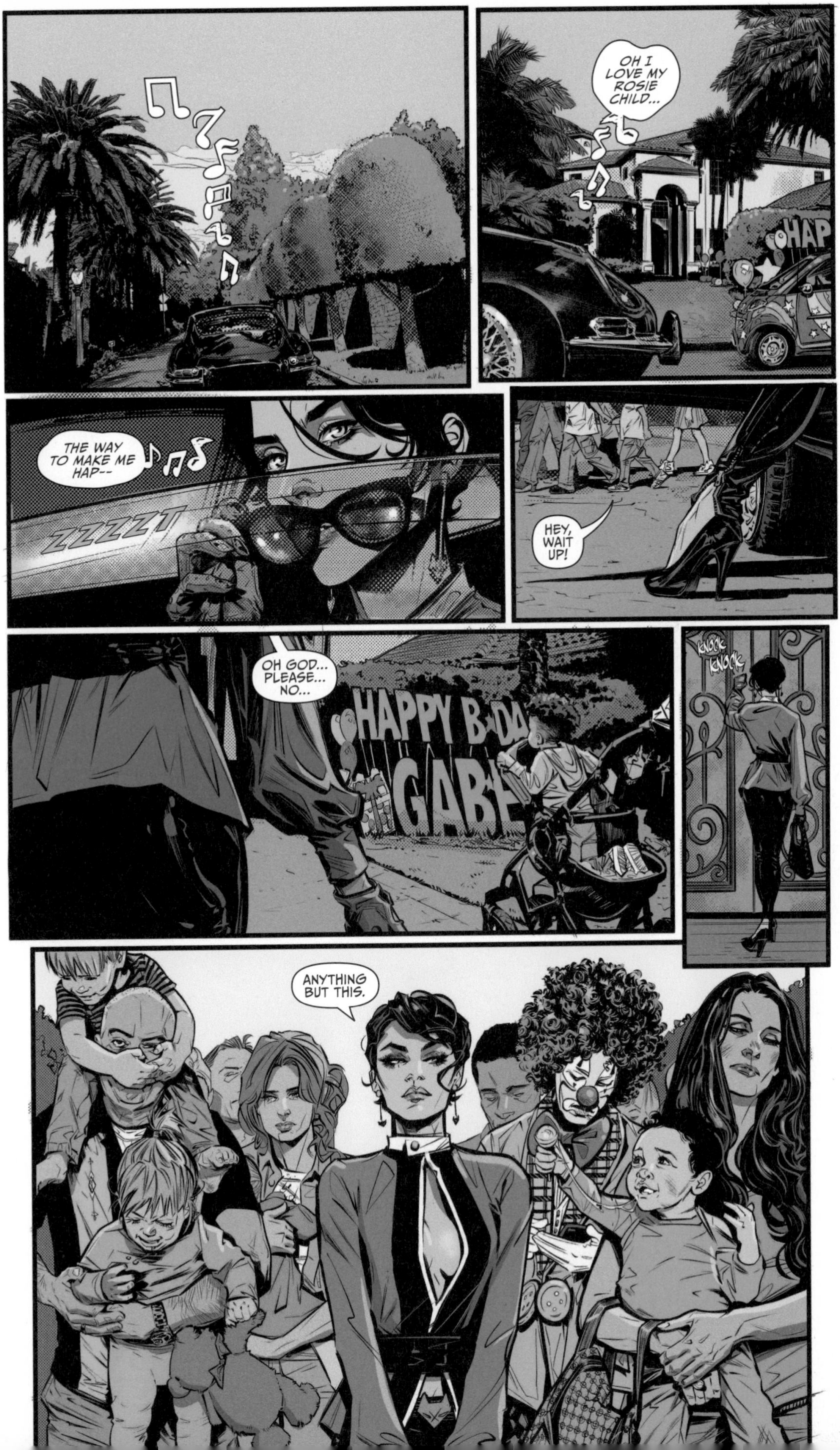
OH I LOVE MY ROSIE CHILD...
THE WAY TO MAKE ME HAP--
ZZZZZT
HEY, WAIT UP!
OH GOD... PLEASE... NO...
HAPPY B-DA
GABE
KNOCK KNOCK
ANYTHING BUT THIS.

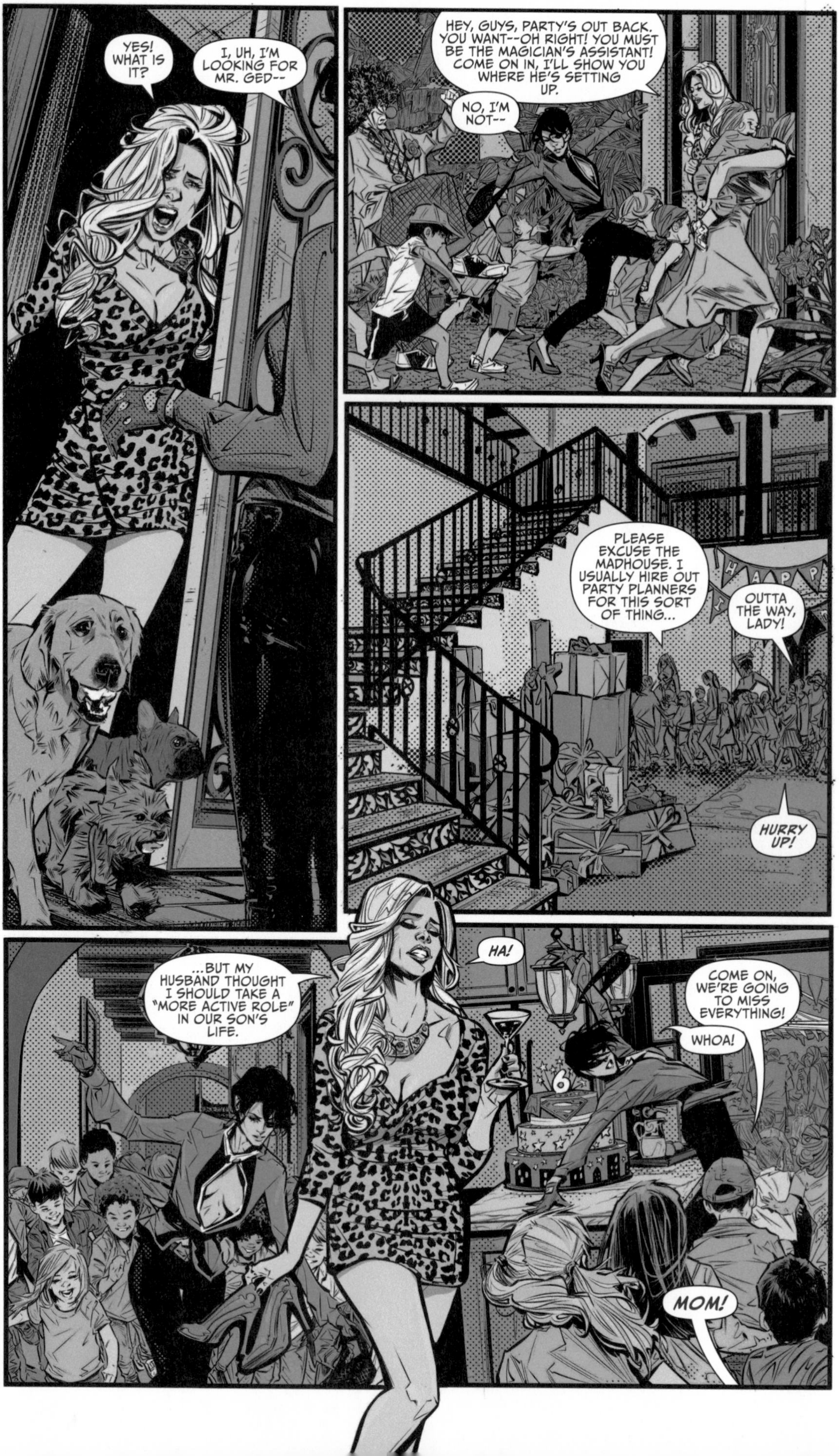
YES! WHAT IS IT?
I, UH, I'M LOOKING FOR MR. GED--
HEY, GUYS, PARTY'S OUT BACK. YOU WANT--OH RIGHT! YOU MUST BE THE MAGICIAN'S ASSISTANT! COME ON IN, I'LL SHOW YOU WHERE HE'S SETTING UP.
NO, I'M NOT--
PLEASE EXCUSE THE MADHOUSE. I USUALLY HIRE OUT PARTY PLANNERS FOR THIS SORT OF THING...
OUTTA THE WAY, LADY!
HURRY UP!
...BUT MY HUSBAND THOUGHT I SHOULD TAKE A "MORE ACTIVE ROLE" IN OUR SON'S LIFE.
HA!
COME ON, WE'RE GOING TO MISS EVERYTHING!
WHOA!
MOM!

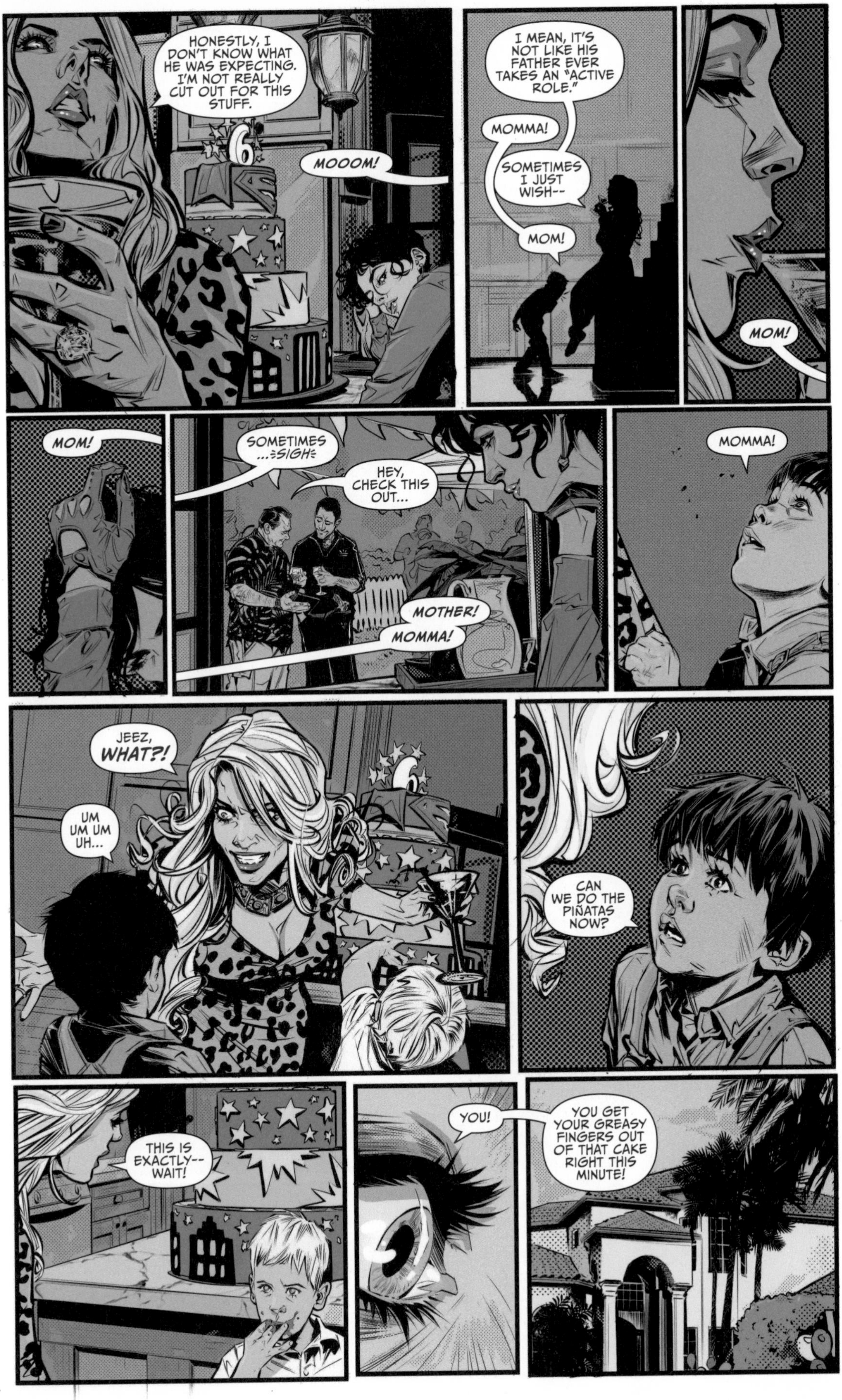
HONESTLY, I DON'T KNOW WHAT HE WAS EXPECTING. I'M NOT REALLY CUT OUT FOR THIS STUFF.
MOOOM!
I MEAN, IT'S NOT LIKE HIS FATHER EVER TAKES AN "ACTIVE ROLE."
MOMMA!
SOMETIMES I JUST WISH--
MOM!
MOM!
MOM!
SOMETIMES ...SIGH
HEY, CHECK THIS OUT...
MOTHER!
MOMMA!
MOMMA!
JEEZ, WHAT?!
UM UM UM UH...
CAN WE DO THE PIÑATAS NOW?
THIS IS EXACTLY-- WAIT!
YOU!
YOU GET YOUR GREASY FINGERS OUT OF THAT CAKE RIGHT THIS MINUTE!

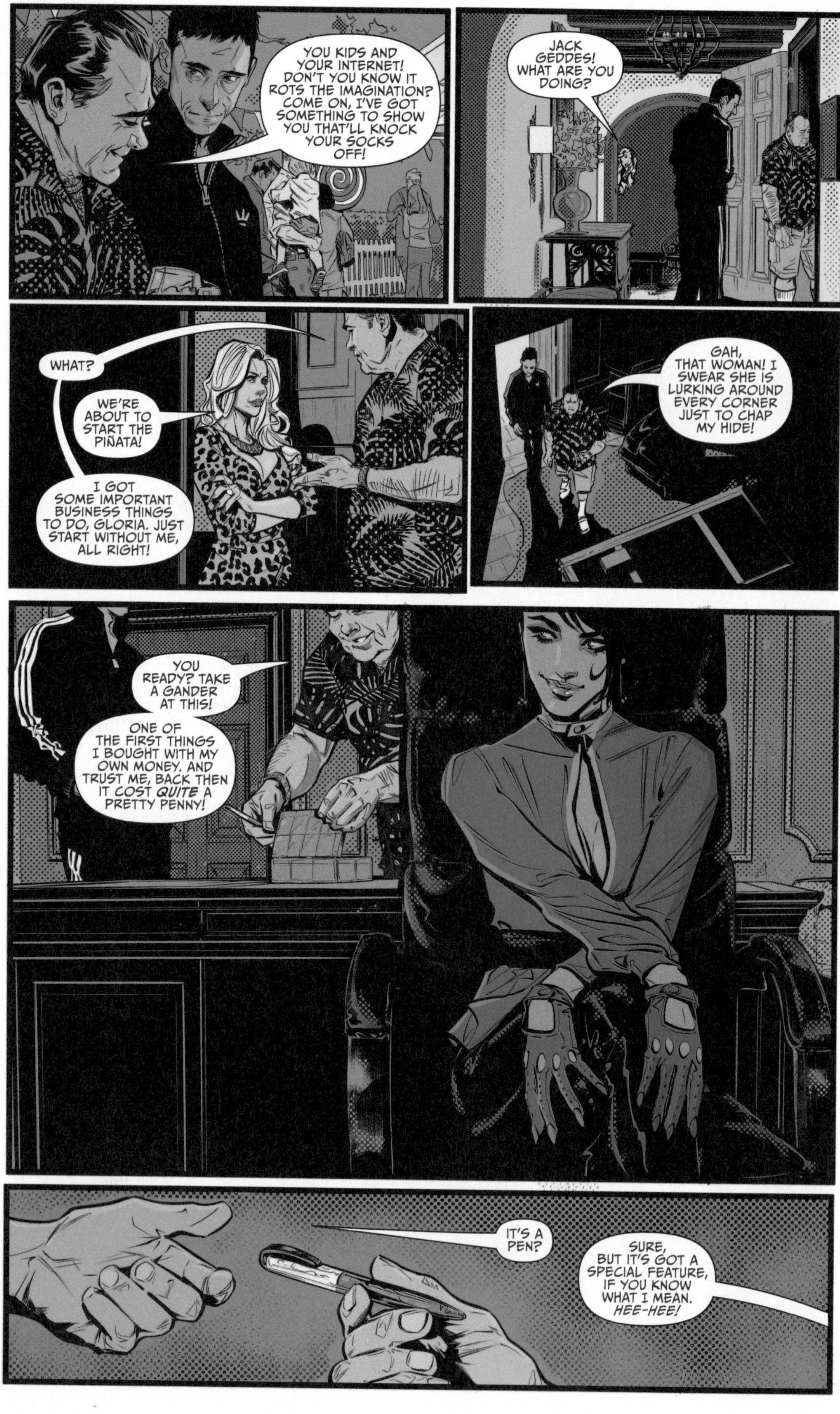
YOU KIDS AND YOUR INTERNET! DON'T YOU KNOW IT ROTS THE IMAGINATION? COME ON, I'VE GOT SOMETHING TO SHOW YOU THAT'LL KNOCK YOUR SOCKS OFF!
JACK GEDDES! WHAT ARE YOU DOING?
WHAT?
WE'RE ABOUT TO START THE PIÑATA!
I GOT SOME IMPORTANT BUSINESS THINGS TO DO, GLORIA. JUST START WITHOUT ME, ALL RIGHT!
GAH, THAT WOMAN! I SWEAR SHE IS LURKING AROUND EVERY CORNER JUST TO CHAP MY HIDE!
YOU READY? TAKE A GANDER AT THIS!
ONE OF THE FIRST THINGS I BOUGHT WITH MY OWN MONEY. AND TRUST ME, BACK THEN IT COST *QUITE* A PRETTY PENNY!
IT'S A PEN?
SURE, BUT IT'S GOT A SPECIAL FEATURE, IF YOU KNOW WHAT I MEAN. *HEE-HEE!*

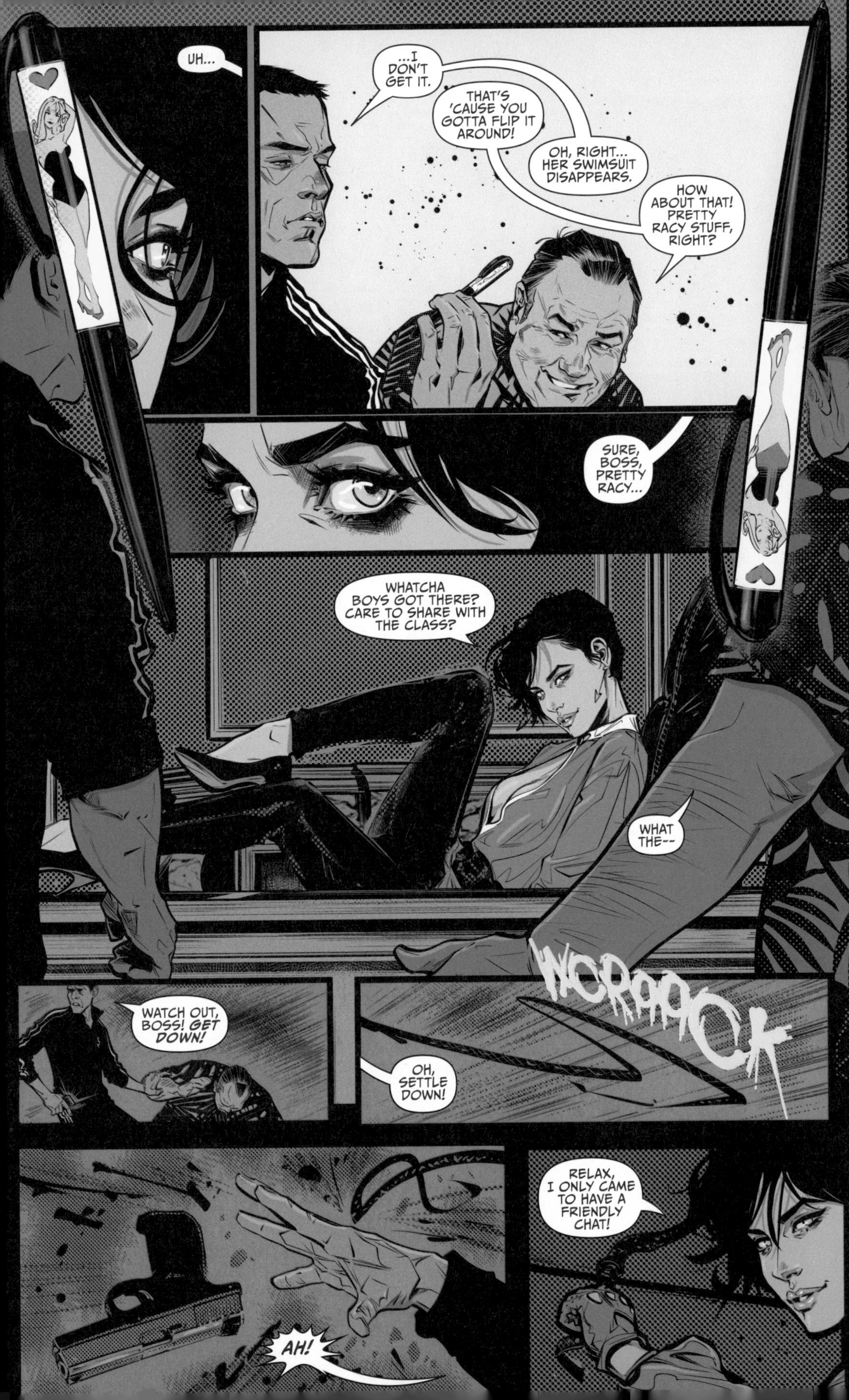

UH...
...I DON'T GET IT.
THAT'S 'CAUSE YOU GOTTA FLIP IT AROUND!
OH, RIGHT... HER SWIMSUIT DISAPPEARS.
HOW ABOUT THAT! PRETTY RACY STUFF, RIGHT?
SURE, BOSS, PRETTY RACY...
WHATCHA BOYS GOT THERE? CARE TO SHARE WITH THE CLASS?
WHAT THE--
WCRAAACK
WATCH OUT, BOSS! GET DOWN!
OH, SETTLE DOWN!
AH!
RELAX, I ONLY CAME TO HAVE A FRIENDLY CHAT!

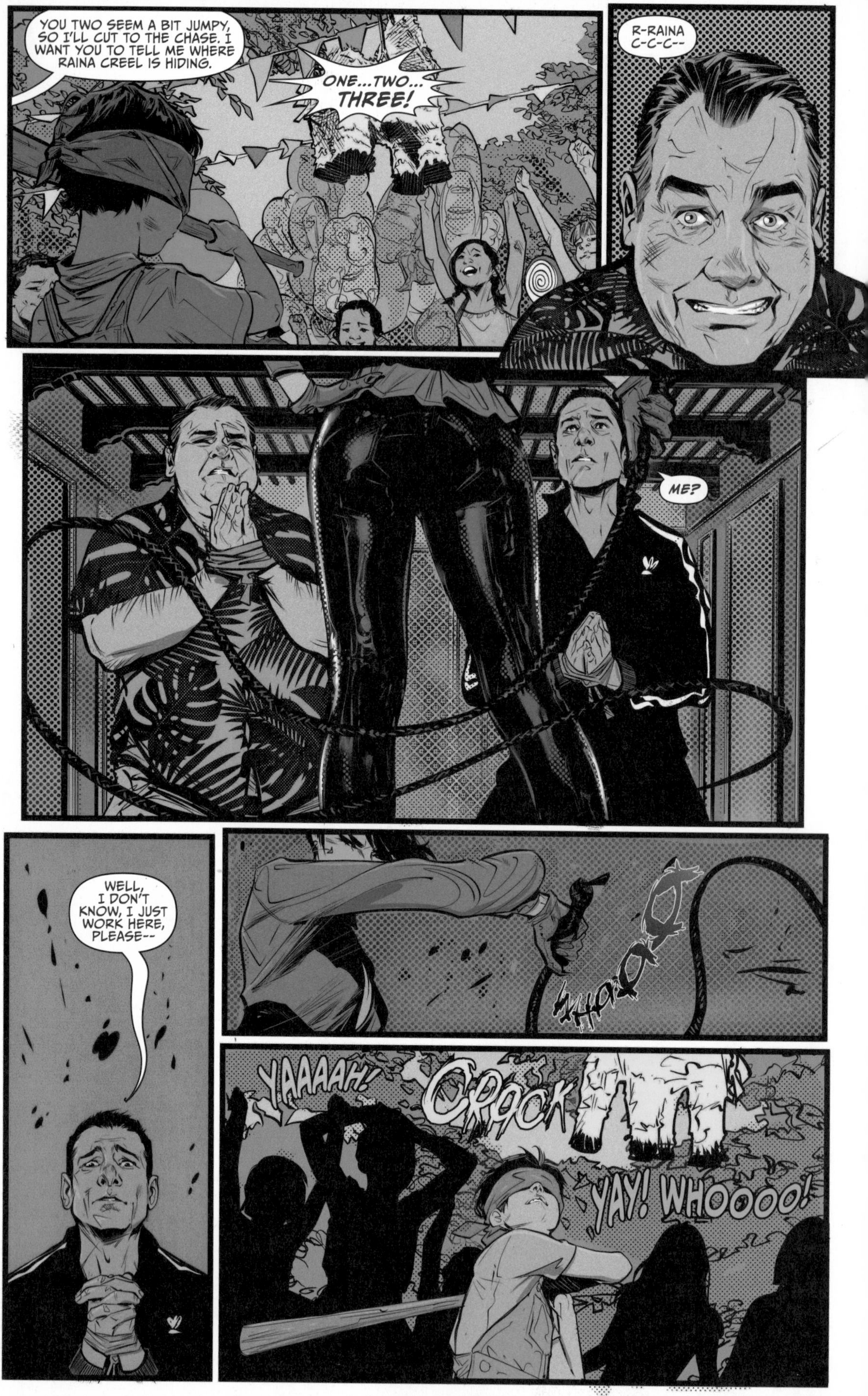

YOU TWO SEEM A BIT JUMPY, SO I'LL CUT TO THE CHASE. I WANT YOU TO TELL ME WHERE RAINA CREEL IS HIDING.
ONE...TWO... THREE!
R-RAINA C-C-C--
ME?
WELL, I DON'T KNOW, I JUST WORK HERE, PLEASE--
YAAAAH!
CRACK
YAY! WHOOOO!

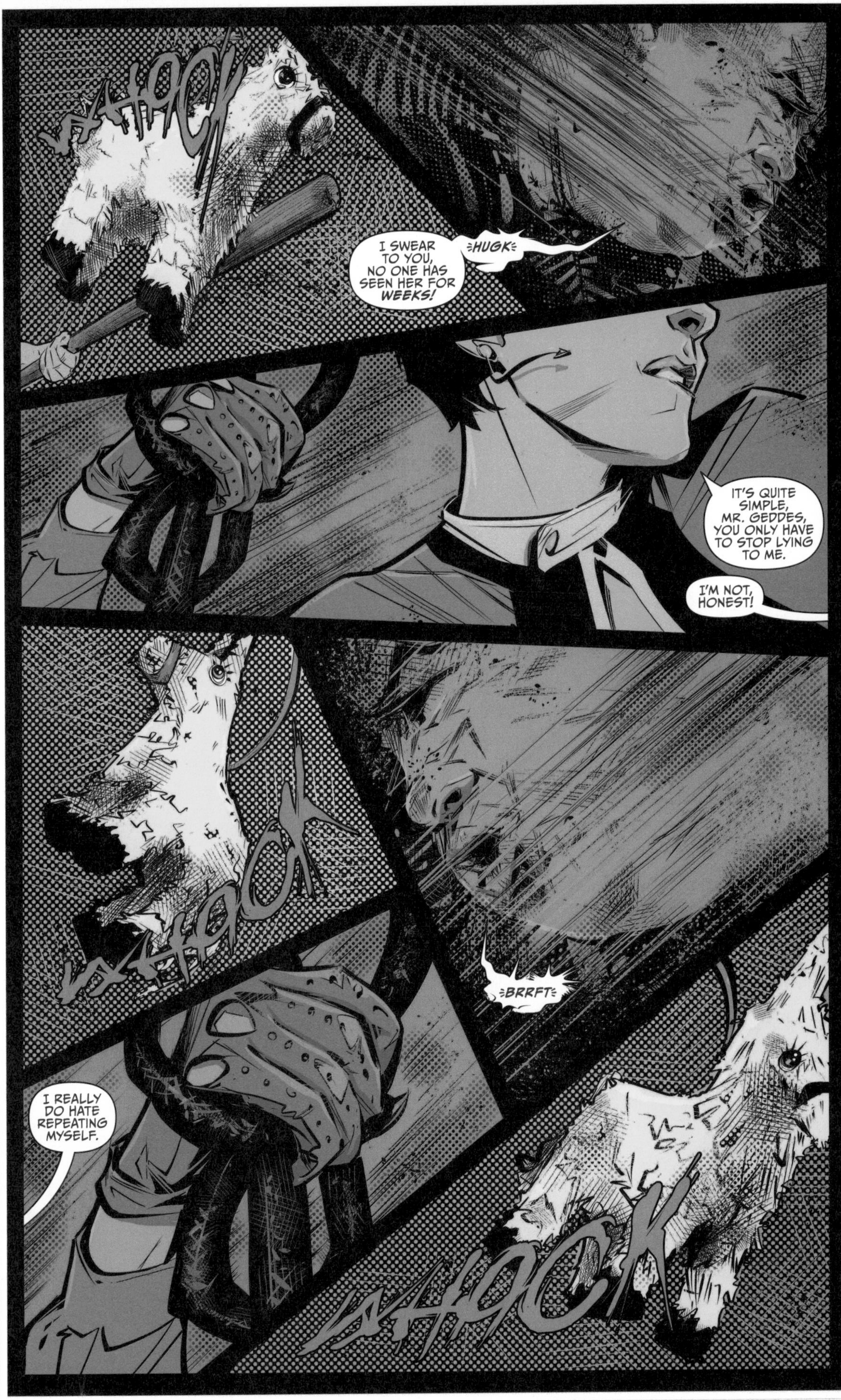
I SWEAR TO YOU, NO ONE HAS SEEN HER FOR WEEKS!
HUGK
IT'S QUITE SIMPLE, MR. GEDDES, YOU ONLY HAVE TO STOP LYING TO ME.
I'M NOT, HONEST!
BRRFT
I REALLY DO HATE REPEATING MYSELF.
WHOCK

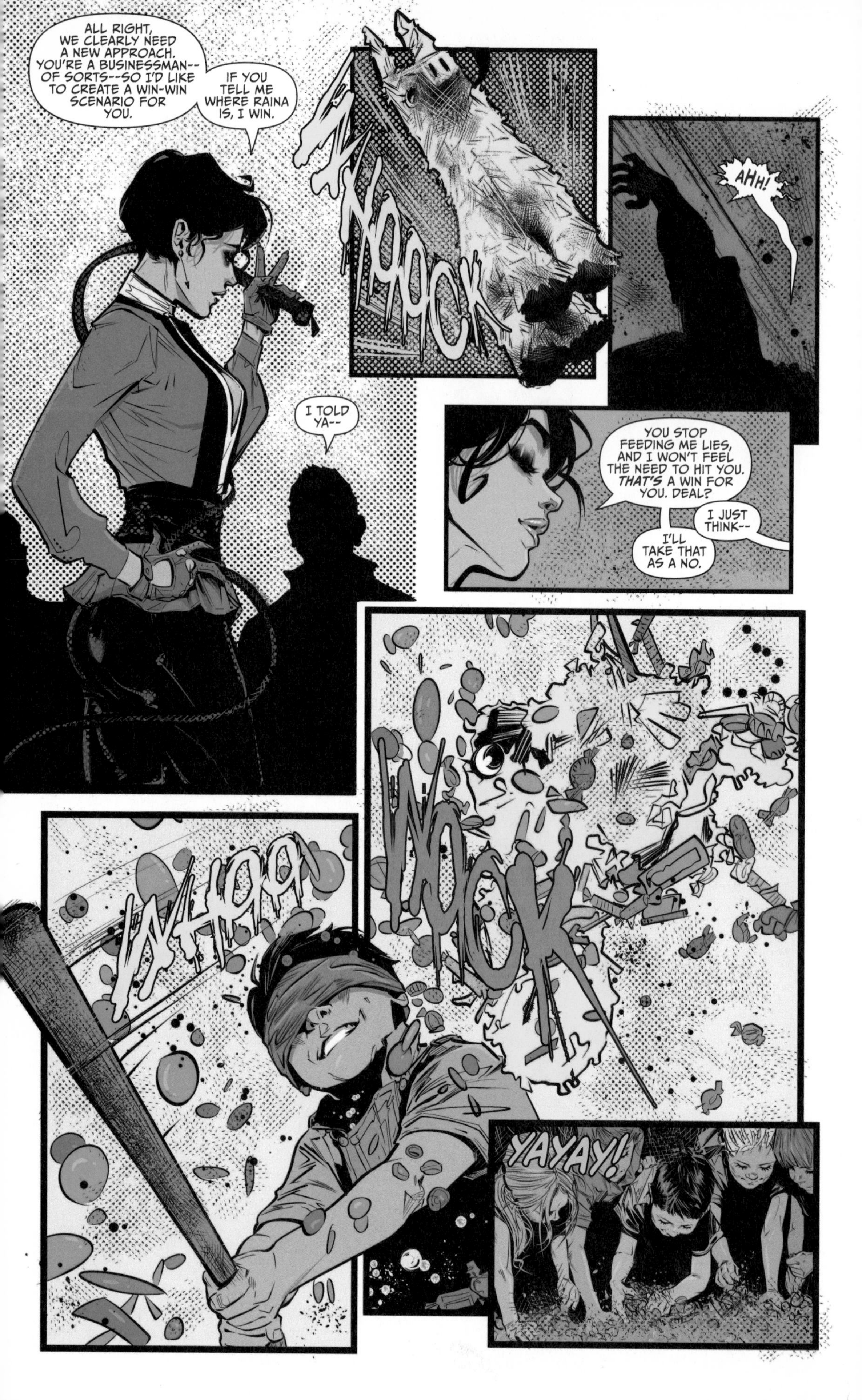
ALL RIGHT, WE CLEARLY NEED A NEW APPROACH. YOU'RE A BUSINESSMAN--OF SORTS--SO I'D LIKE TO CREATE A WIN-WIN SCENARIO FOR YOU.
IF YOU TELL ME WHERE RAINA IS, I WIN.
I TOLD YA--
WHOOCK
AHH!
YOU STOP FEEDING ME LIES, AND I WON'T FEEL THE NEED TO HIT YOU. THAT'S A WIN FOR YOU. DEAL?
I JUST THINK--
I'LL TAKE THAT AS A NO.
WHOOO
WOOCK
YAYAY!

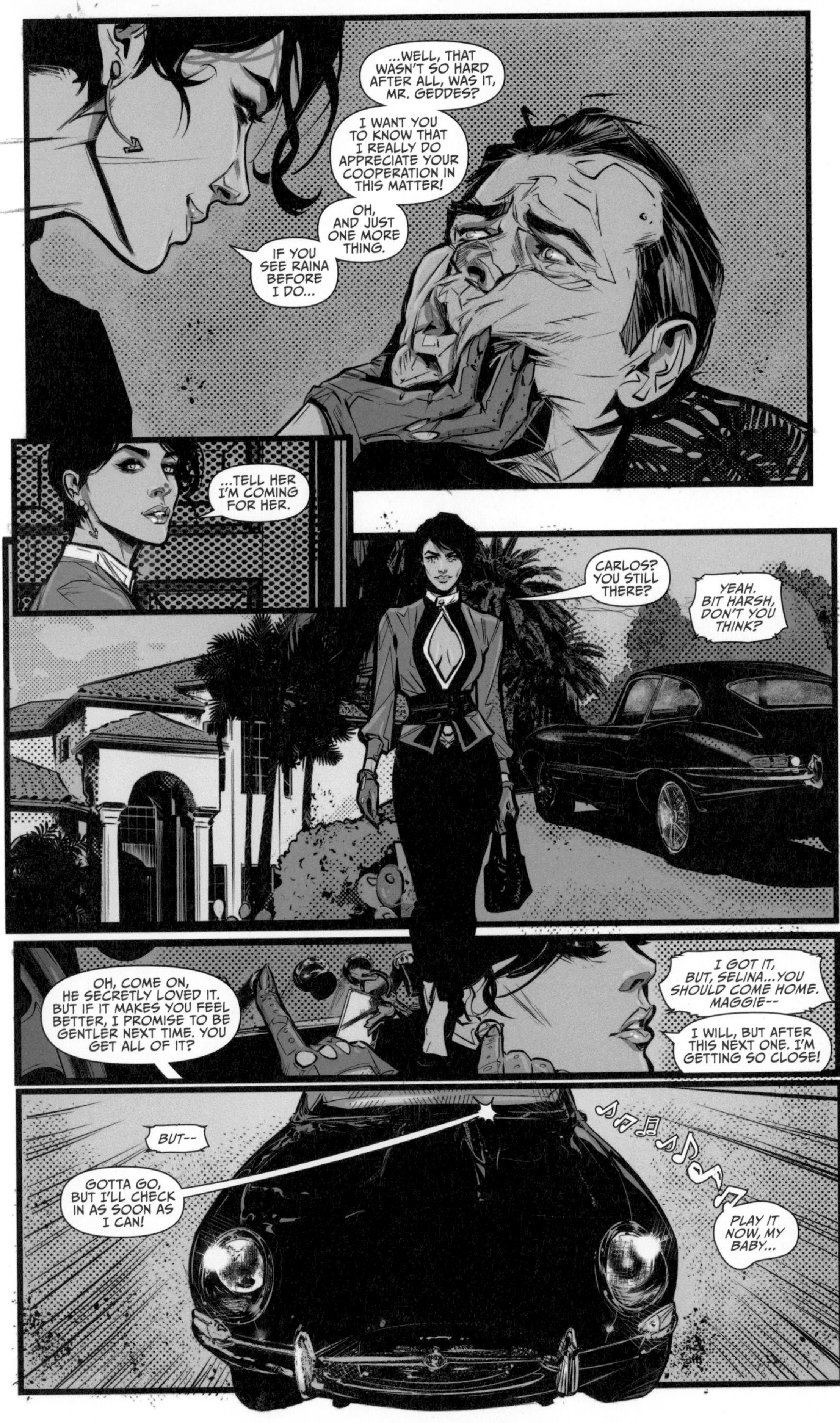
...WELL, THAT WASN'T SO HARD AFTER ALL, WAS IT, MR. GEDDES?
I WANT YOU TO KNOW THAT I REALLY DO APPRECIATE YOUR COOPERATION IN THIS MATTER!
OH, AND JUST ONE MORE THING.
IF YOU SEE RAINA BEFORE I DO...
...TELL HER I'M COMING FOR HER.
CARLOS? YOU STILL THERE?
YEAH. BIT HARSH, DON'T YOU THINK?
OH, COME ON, HE SECRETLY LOVED IT. BUT IF IT MAKES YOU FEEL BETTER, I PROMISE TO BE GENTLER NEXT TIME. YOU GET ALL OF IT?
I GOT IT, BUT, SELINA...YOU SHOULD COME HOME. MAGGIE--
I WILL, BUT AFTER THIS NEXT ONE. I'M GETTING SO CLOSE!
BUT--
GOTTA GO, BUT I'LL CHECK IN AS SOON AS I CAN!
PLAY IT NOW, MY BABY...

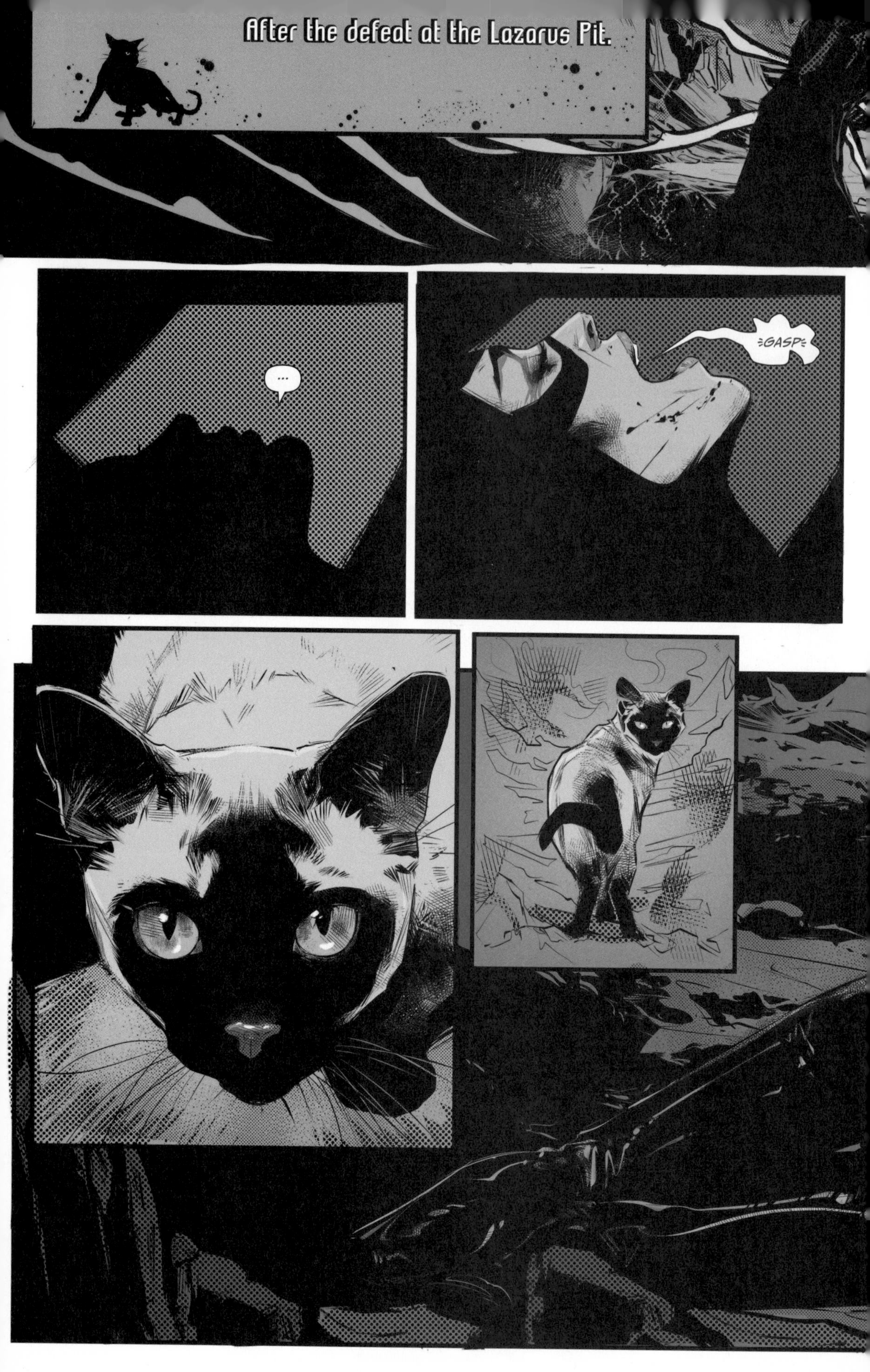

After the defeat at the Lazarus Pit.
...
GASP

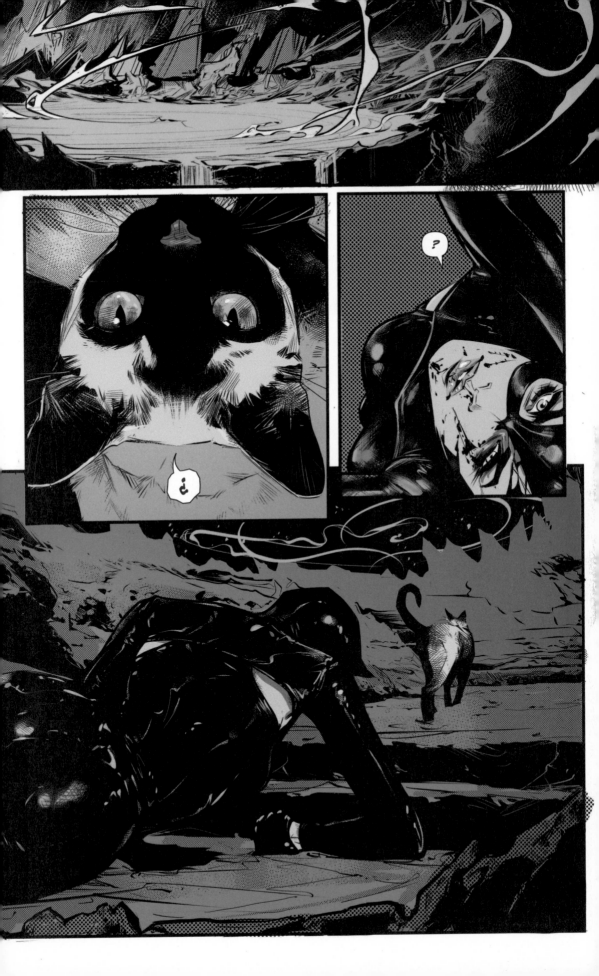

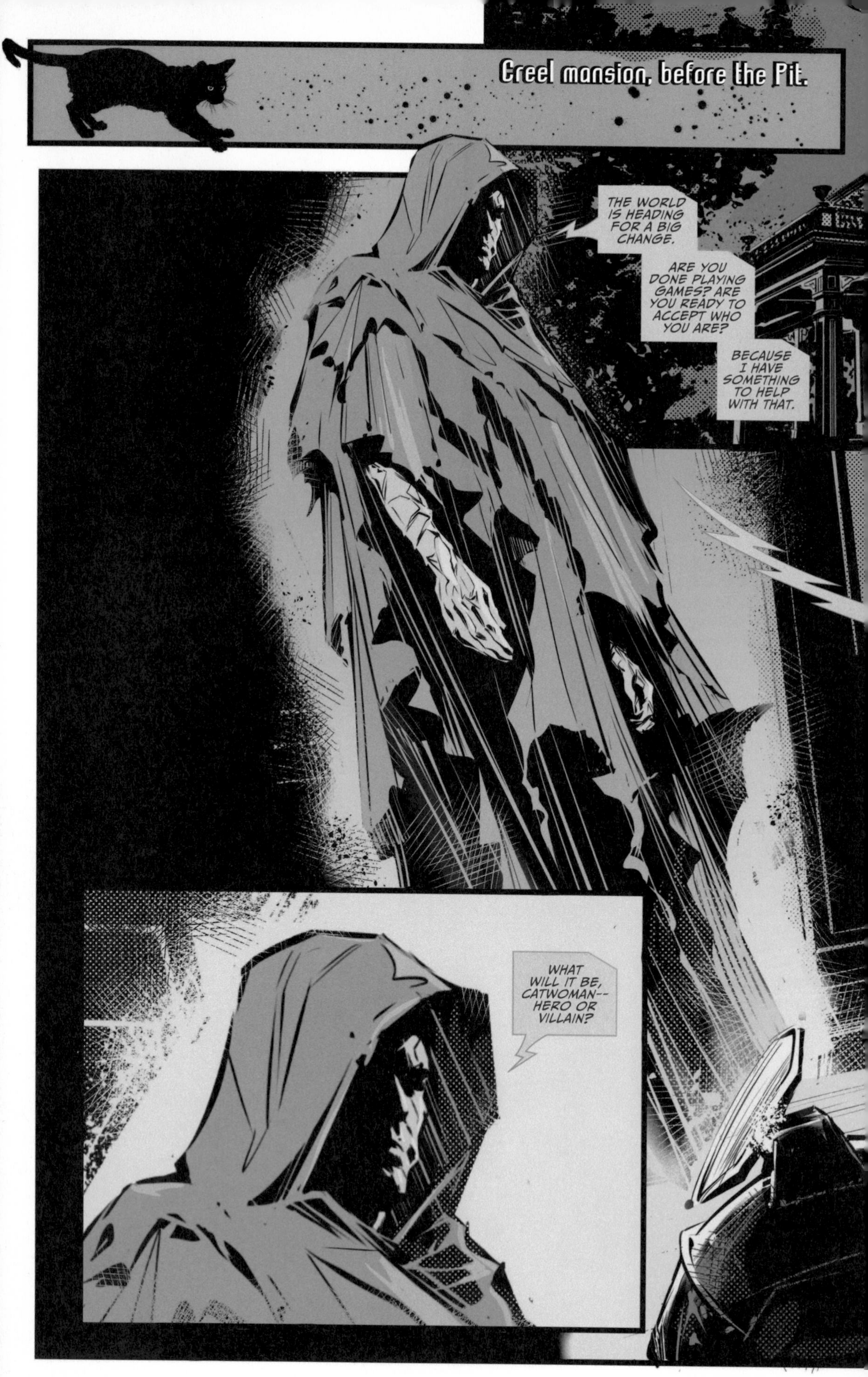
Creel mansion, before the Pit.
THE WORLD IS HEADING FOR A BIG CHANGE.
ARE YOU DONE PLAYING GAMES? ARE YOU READY TO ACCEPT WHO YOU ARE?
BECAUSE I HAVE SOMETHING TO HELP WITH THAT.
WHAT WILL IT BE, CATWOMAN-- HERO OR VILLAIN?

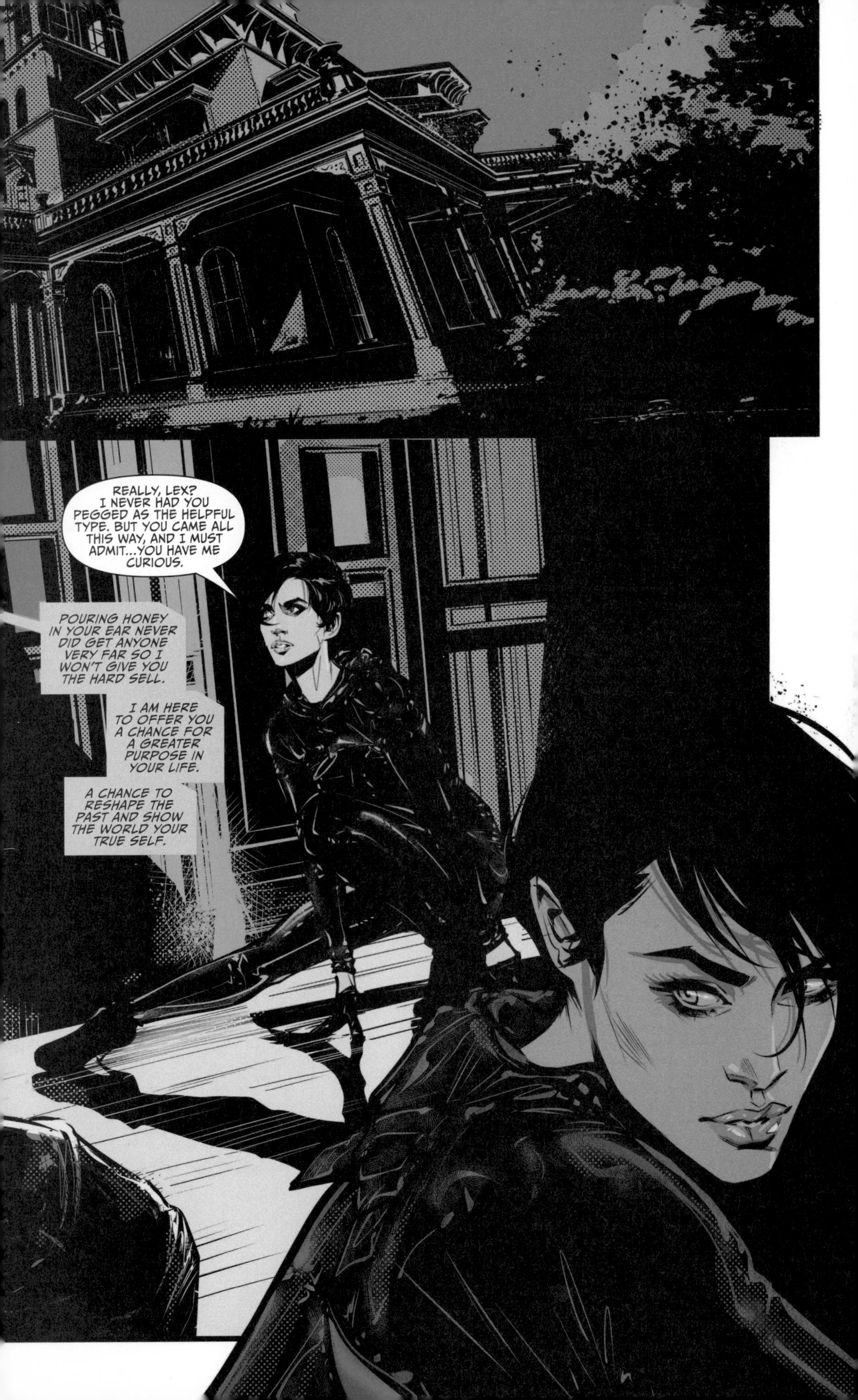
REALLY, LEX? I NEVER HAD YOU PEGGED AS THE HELPFUL TYPE. BUT YOU CAME ALL THIS WAY, AND I MUST ADMIT...YOU HAVE ME CURIOUS.
POURING HONEY IN YOUR EAR NEVER DID GET ANYONE VERY FAR SO I WON'T GIVE YOU THE HARD SELL.
I AM HERE TO OFFER YOU A CHANCE FOR A GREATER PURPOSE IN YOUR LIFE.
A CHANCE TO RESHAPE THE PAST AND SHOW THE WORLD YOUR TRUE SELF.

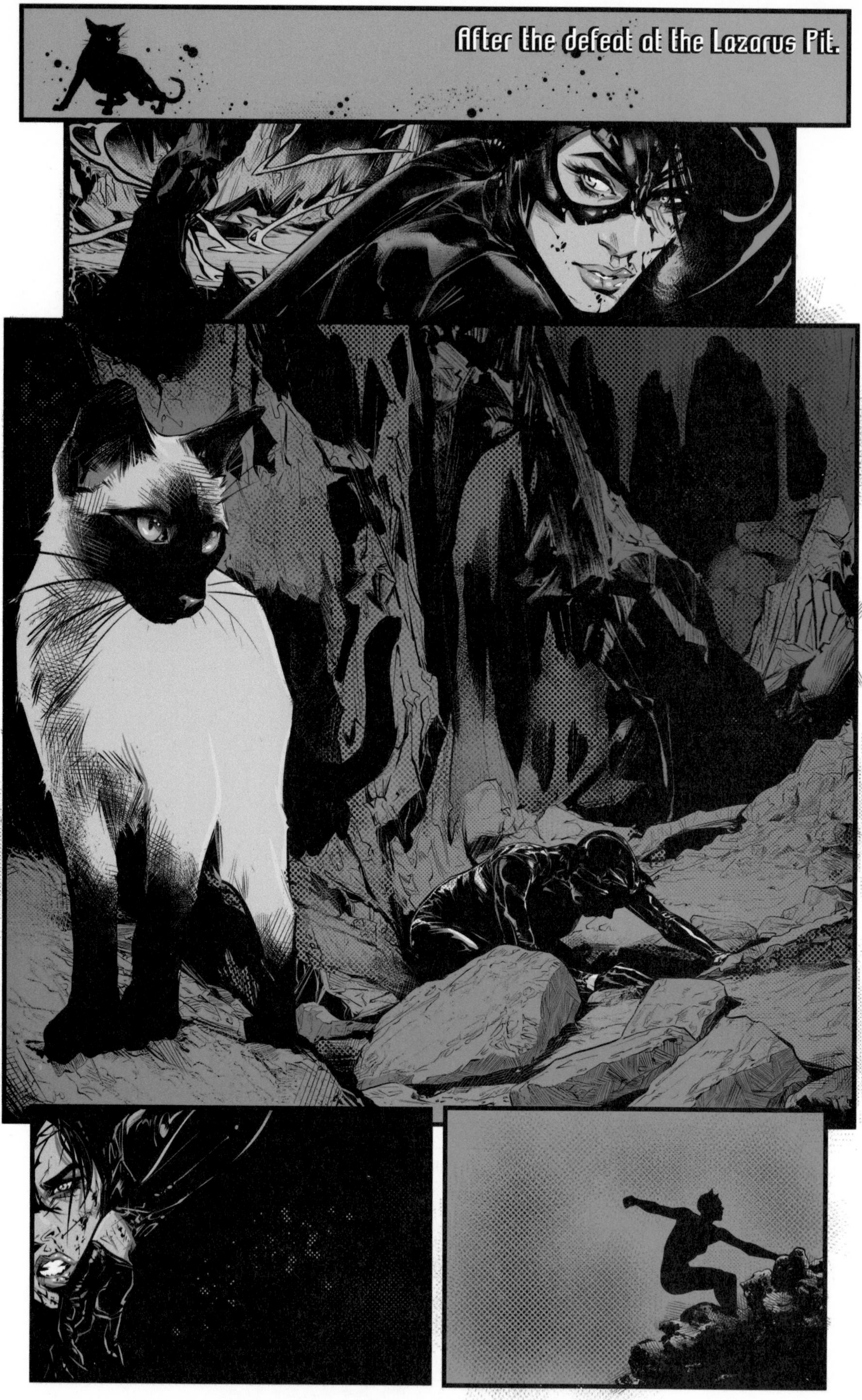
After the defeat at the Lazarus Pit.

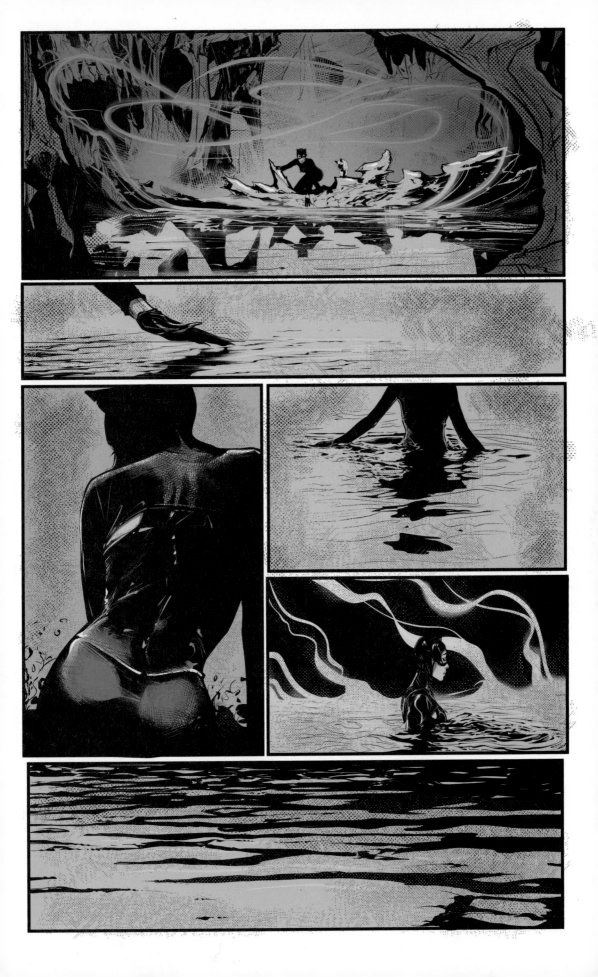

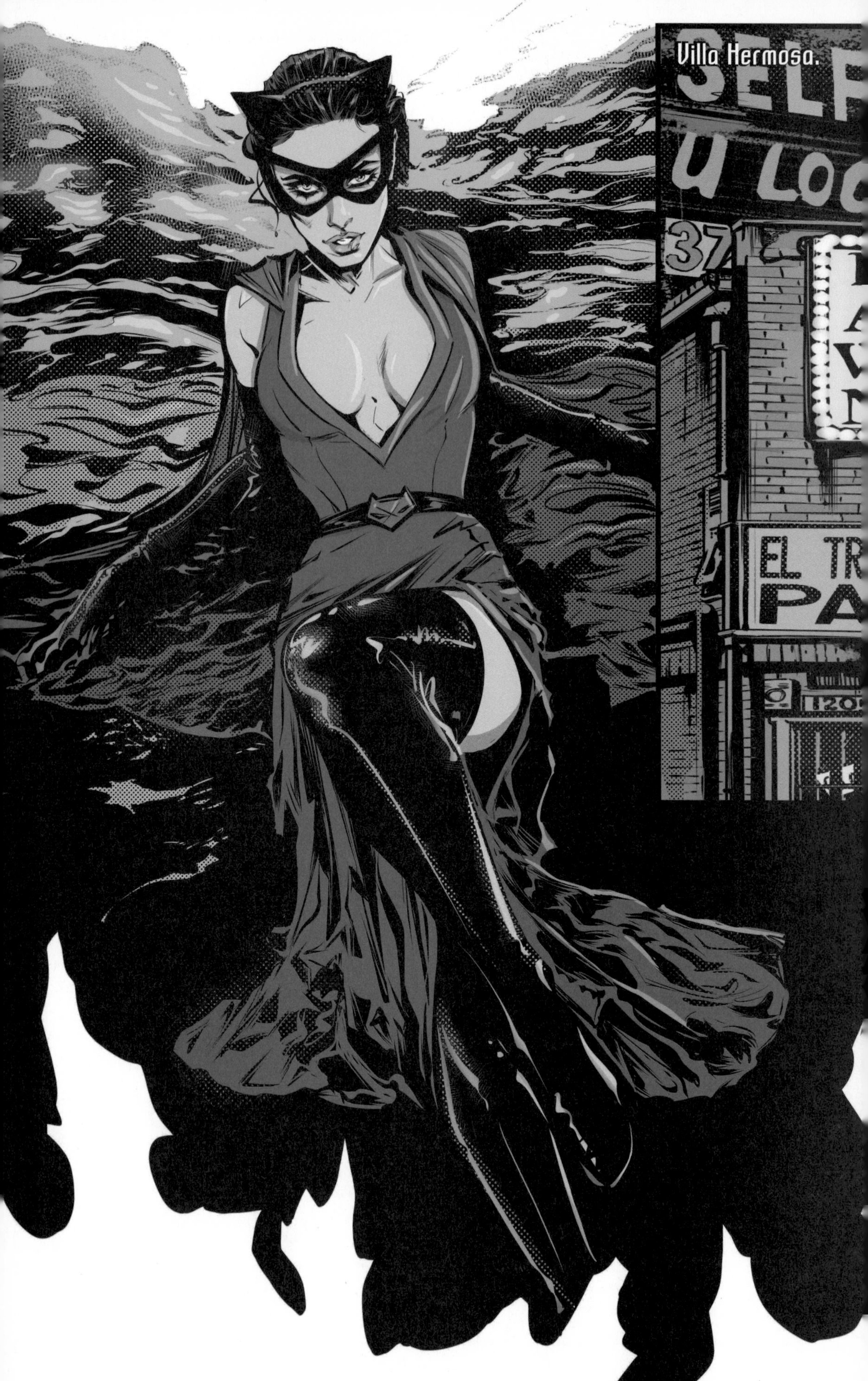
Villa Hermosa.
SELF
U LOC
37
EL TR
PA

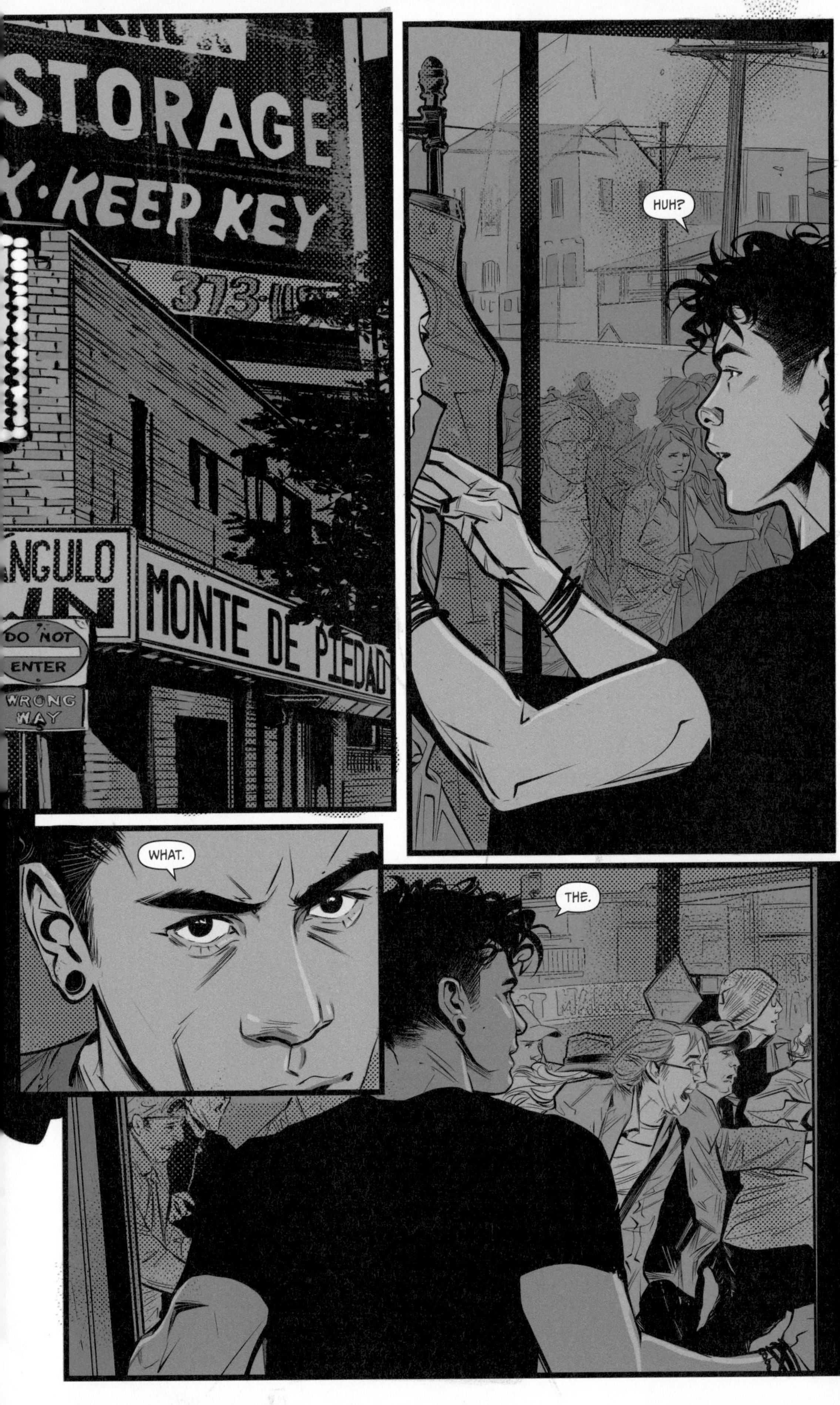
STORAGE
KEEP KEY
MONTE DE PIEDAD
DO NOT ENTER
WRONG WAY
HUH?
WHAT.
THE.

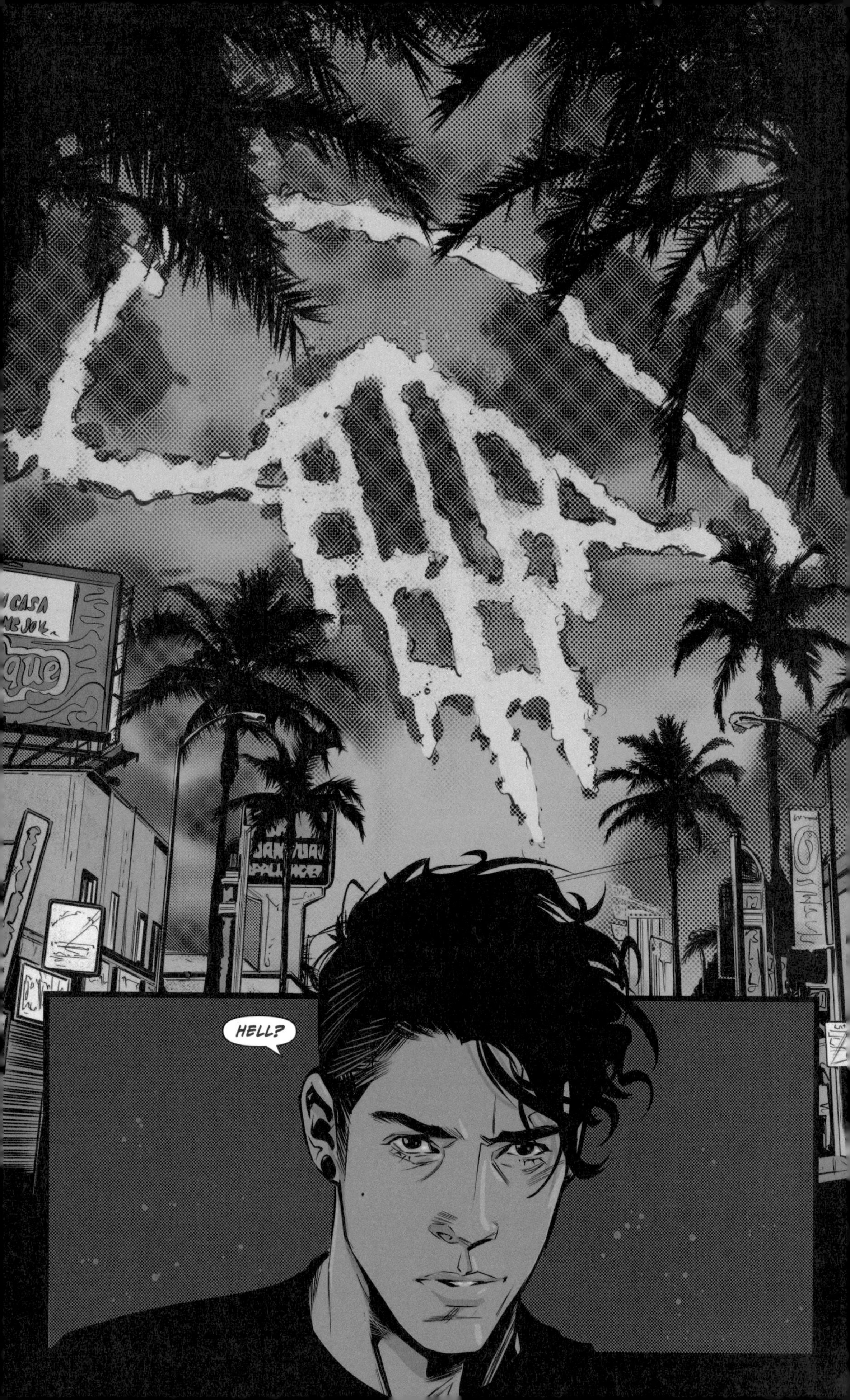
HELL?

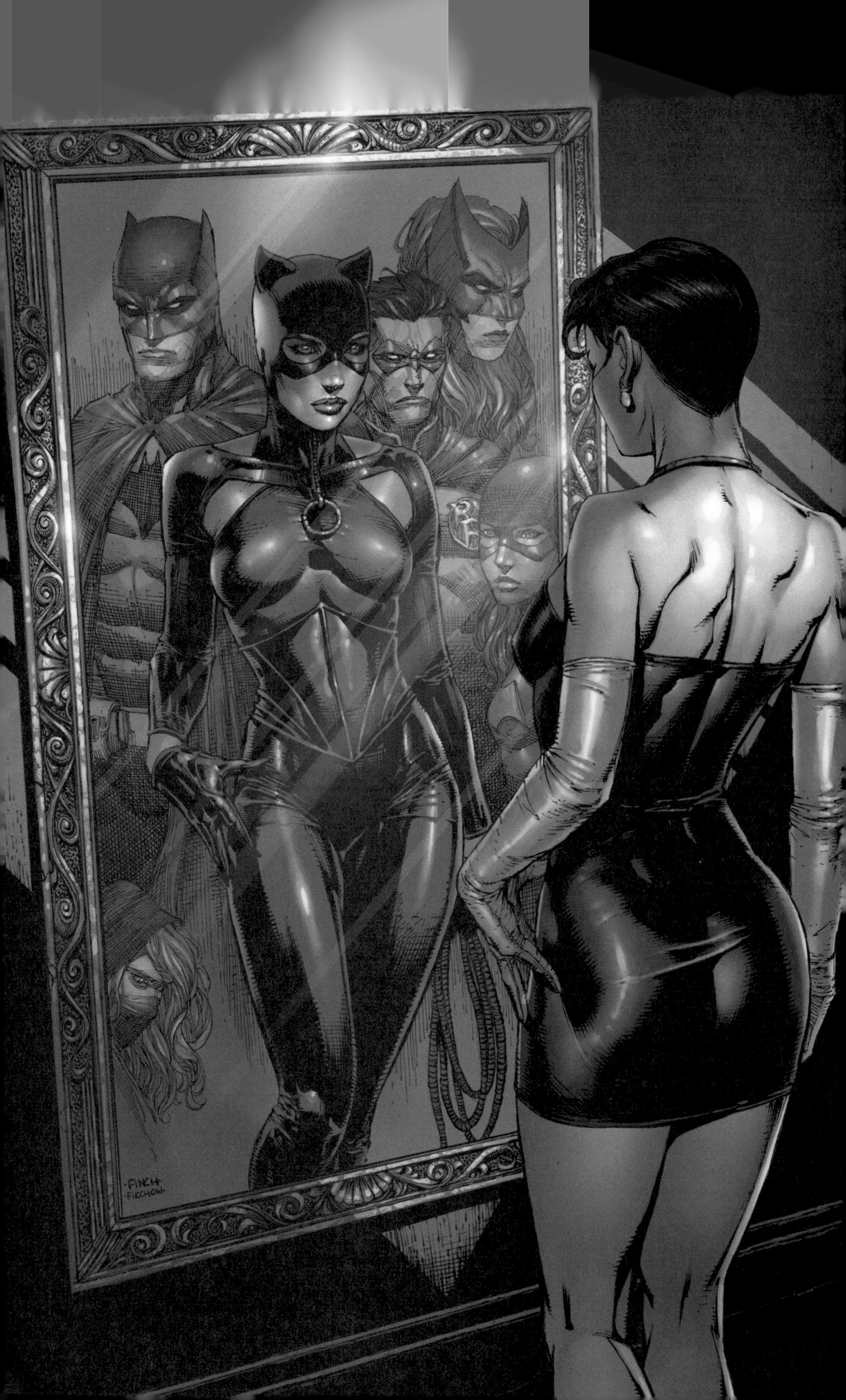
FINCH

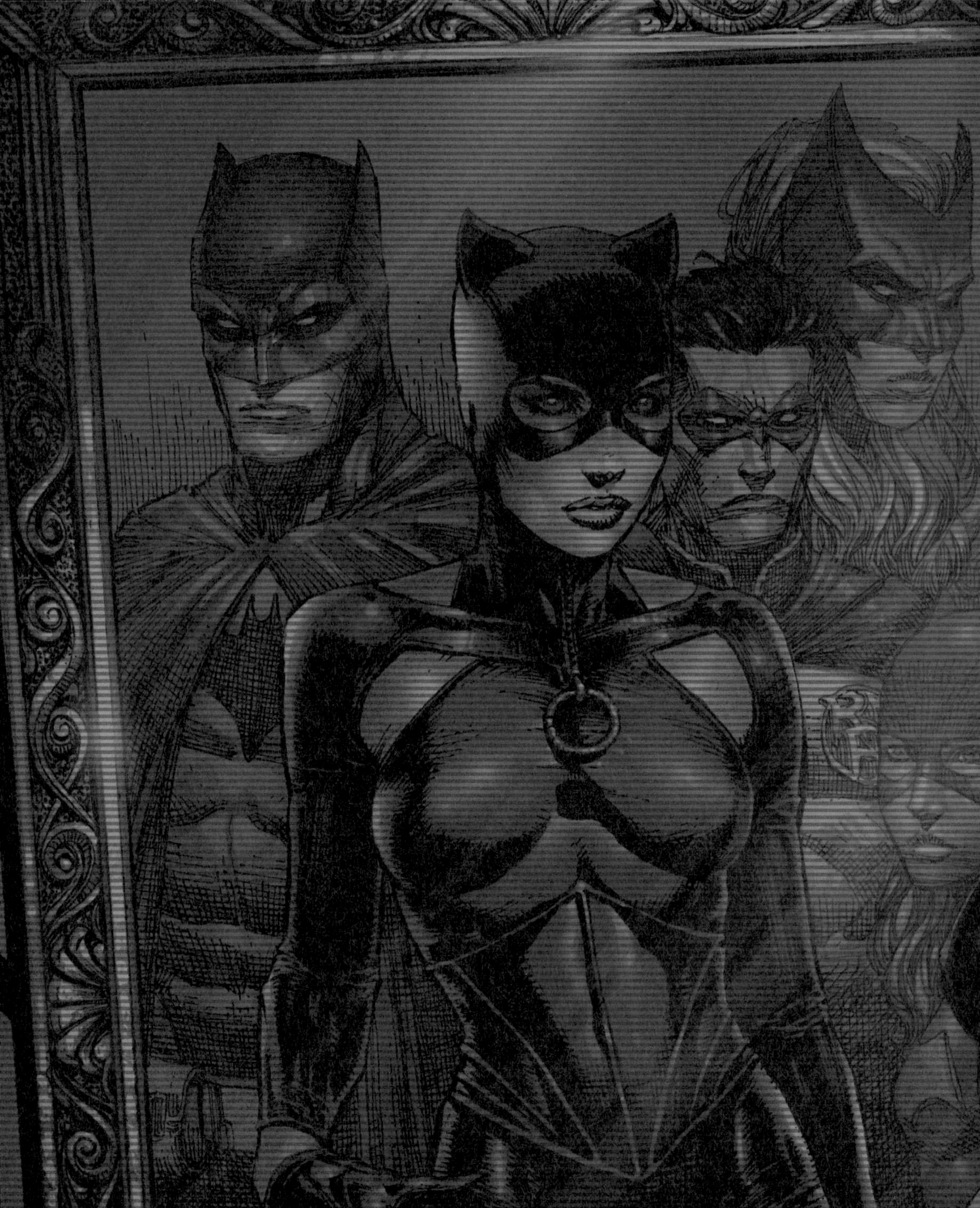

CATWOMAN

#17

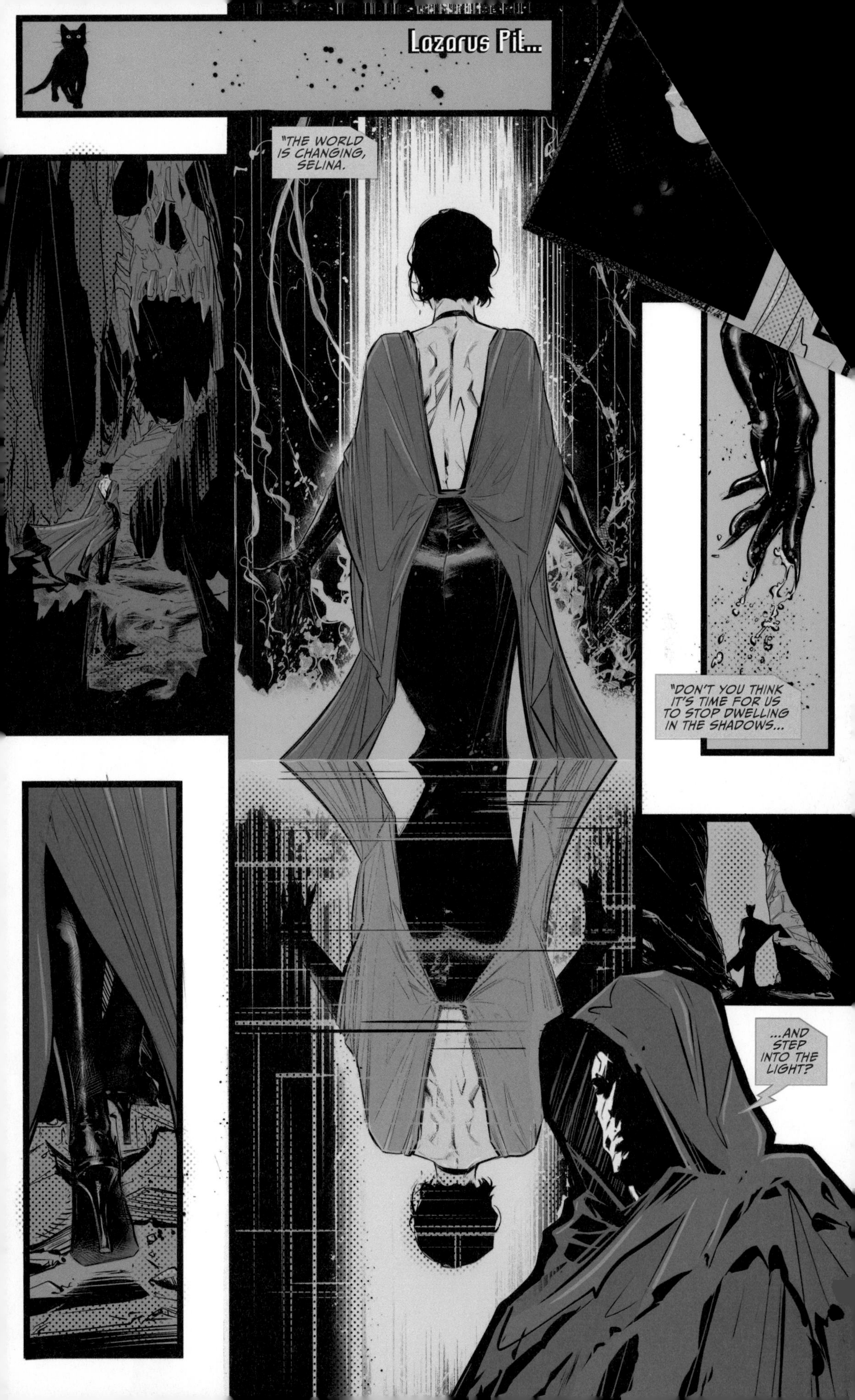
Lazarus Pit...
"THE WORLD IS CHANGING, SELINA.
"DON'T YOU THINK IT'S TIME FOR US TO STOP DWELLING IN THE SHADOWS...
...AND STEP INTO THE LIGHT?

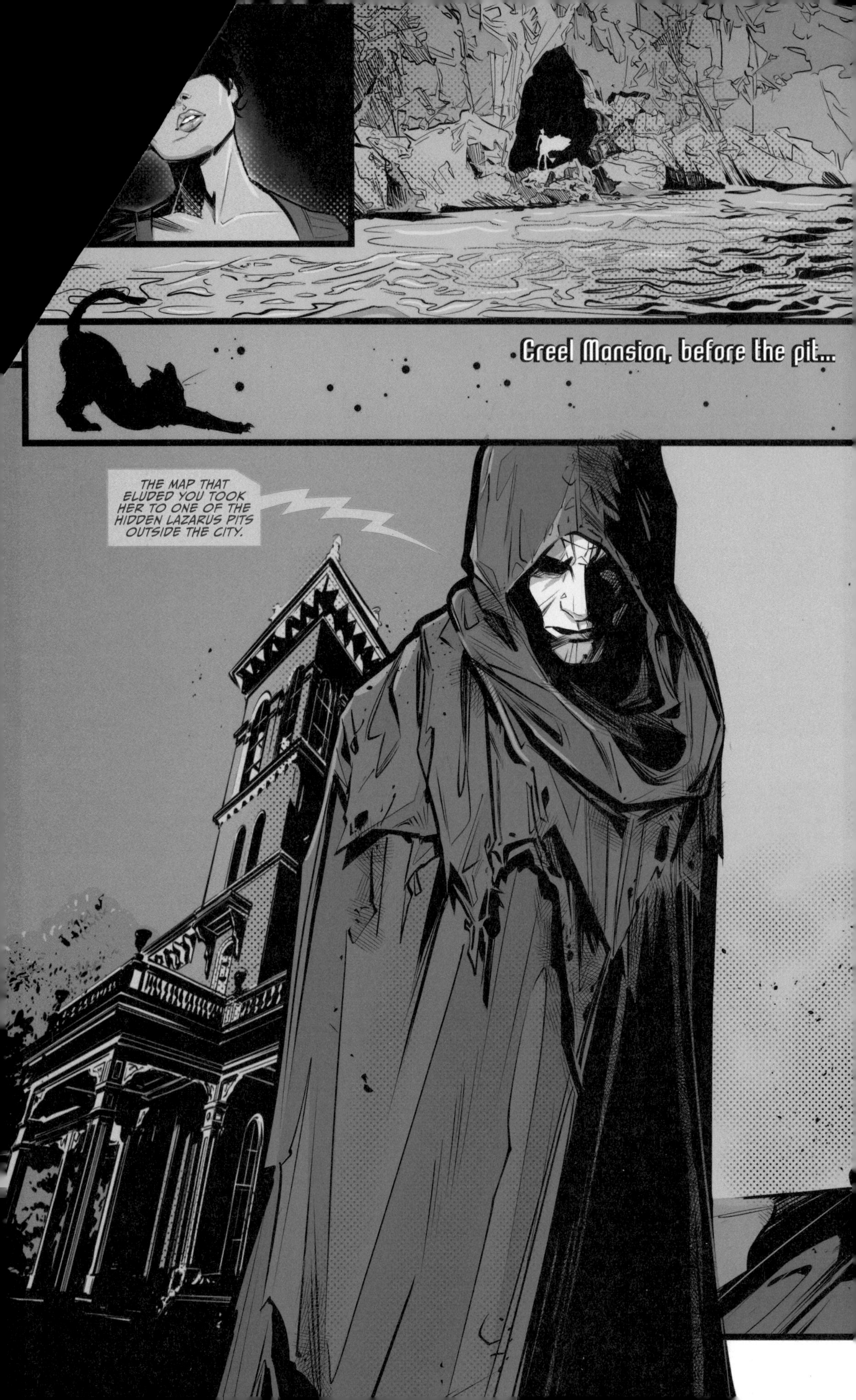
Creel Mansion, before the pit...
THE MAP THAT ELUDED YOU TOOK HER TO ONE OF THE HIDDEN LAZARUS PITS OUTSIDE THE CITY.

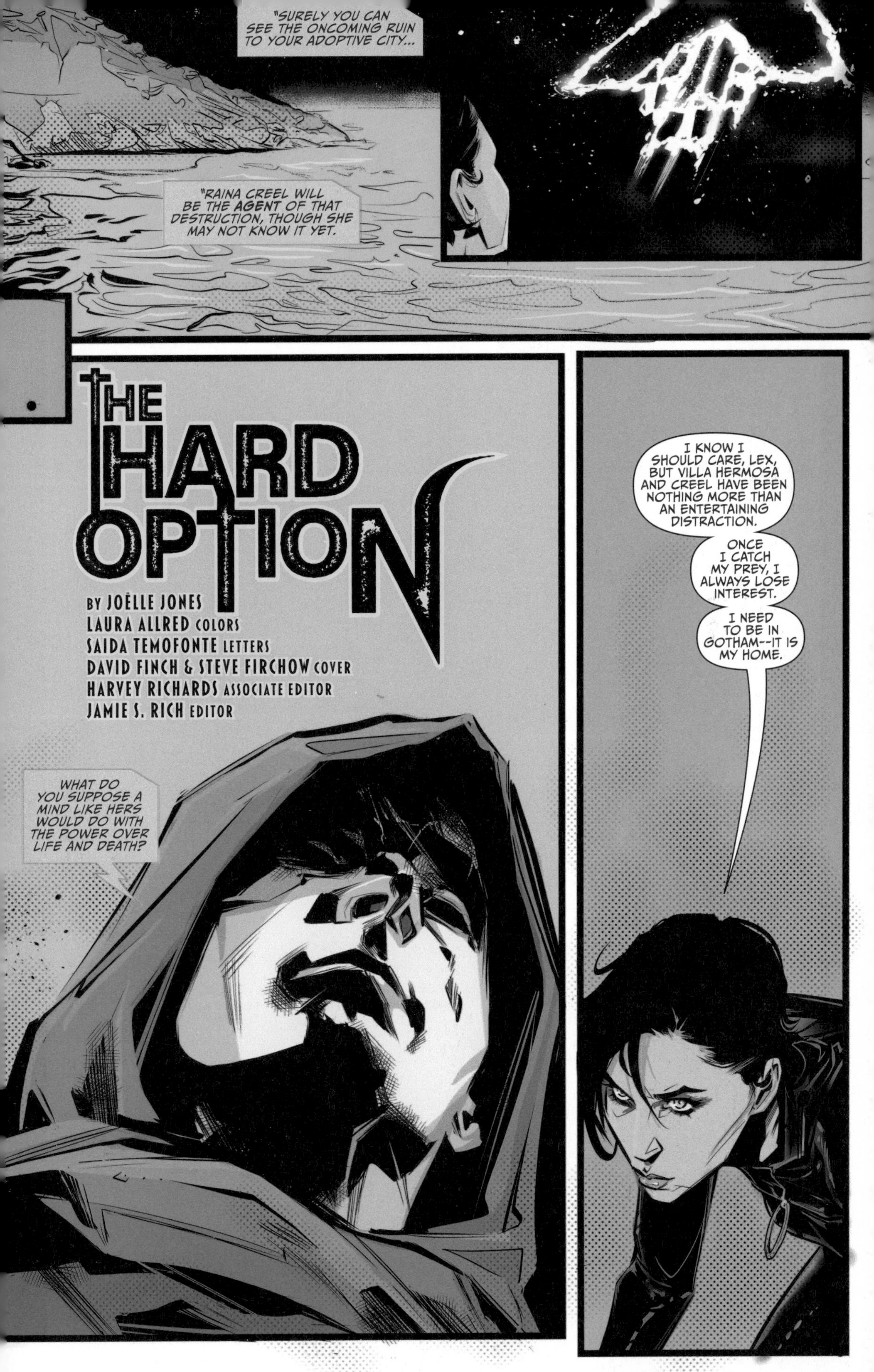
"SURELY YOU CAN SEE THE ONCOMING RUIN TO YOUR ADOPTIVE CITY...
"RAINA CREEL WILL BE THE AGENT OF THAT DESTRUCTION, THOUGH SHE MAY NOT KNOW IT YET.
THE HARD OPTION
BY JOËLLE JONES
LAURA ALLRED COLORS
SAIDA TEMOFONTE LETTERS
DAVID FINCH & STEVE FIRCHOW COVER
HARVEY RICHARDS ASSOCIATE EDITOR
JAMIE S. RICH EDITOR
WHAT DO YOU SUPPOSE A MIND LIKE HERS WOULD DO WITH THE POWER OVER LIFE AND DEATH?
I KNOW I SHOULD CARE, LEX, BUT VILLA HERMOSA AND CREEL HAVE BEEN NOTHING MORE THAN AN ENTERTAINING DISTRACTION.
ONCE I CATCH MY PREY, I ALWAYS LOSE INTEREST.
I NEED TO BE IN GOTHAM--IT IS MY HOME.

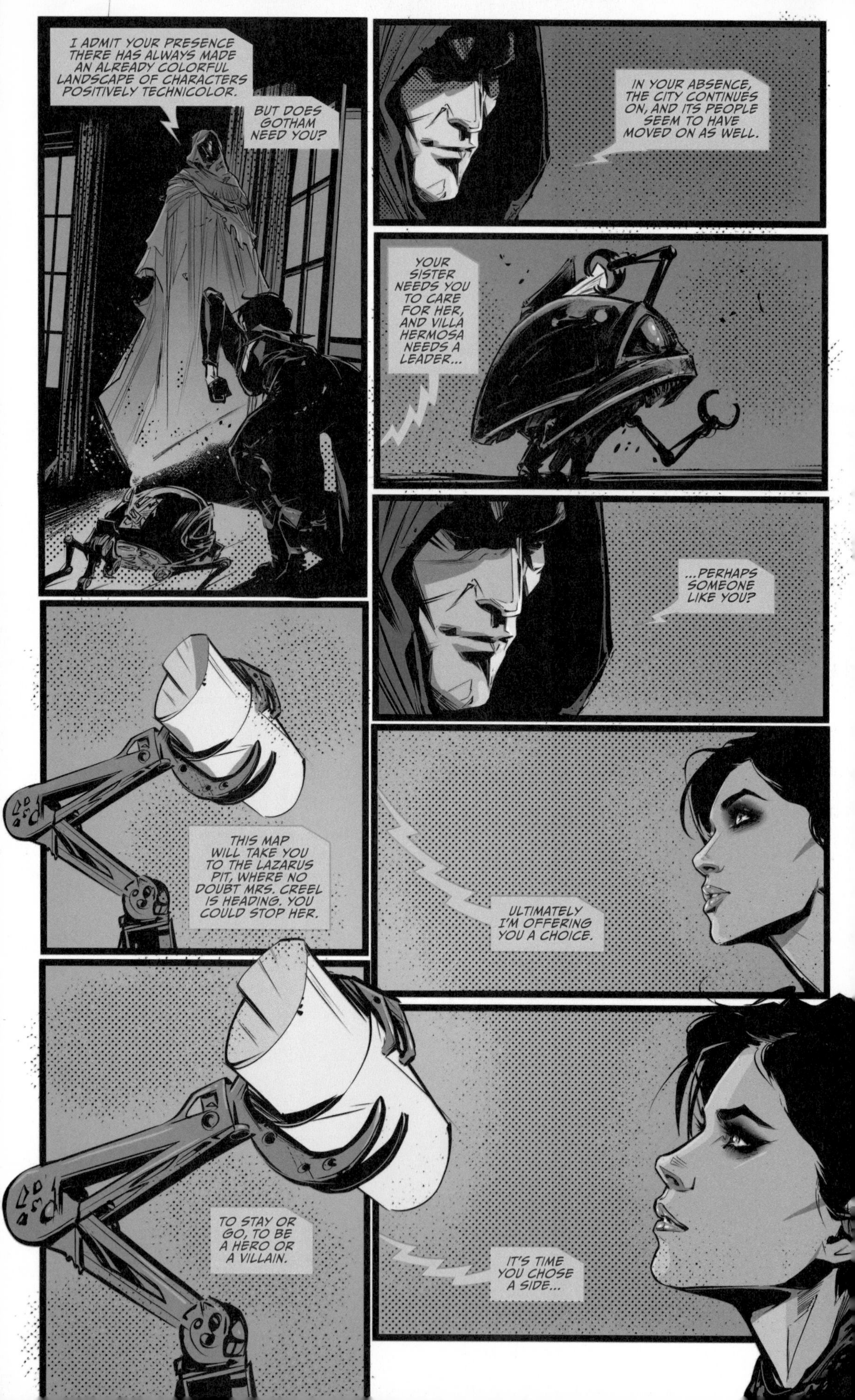
I ADMIT YOUR PRESENCE THERE HAS ALWAYS MADE AN ALREADY COLORFUL LANDSCAPE OF CHARACTERS POSITIVELY TECHNICOLOR.
BUT DOES GOTHAM NEED YOU?
IN YOUR ABSENCE, THE CITY CONTINUES ON, AND ITS PEOPLE SEEM TO HAVE MOVED ON AS WELL.
YOUR SISTER NEEDS YOU TO CARE FOR HER, AND VILLA HERMOSA NEEDS A LEADER...
...PERHAPS SOMEONE LIKE YOU?
THIS MAP WILL TAKE YOU TO THE LAZARUS PIT, WHERE NO DOUBT MRS. CREEL IS HEADING. YOU COULD STOP HER.
ULTIMATELY I'M OFFERING YOU A CHOICE.
TO STAY OR GO, TO BE A HERO OR A VILLAIN.
IT'S TIME YOU CHOSE A SIDE...

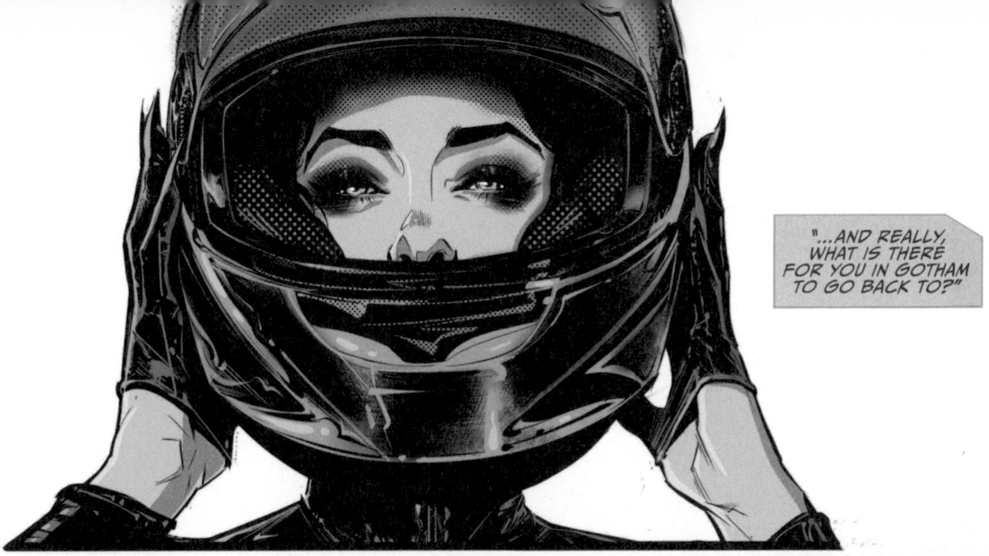
"...AND REALLY, WHAT IS THERE FOR YOU IN GOTHAM TO GO BACK TO?"

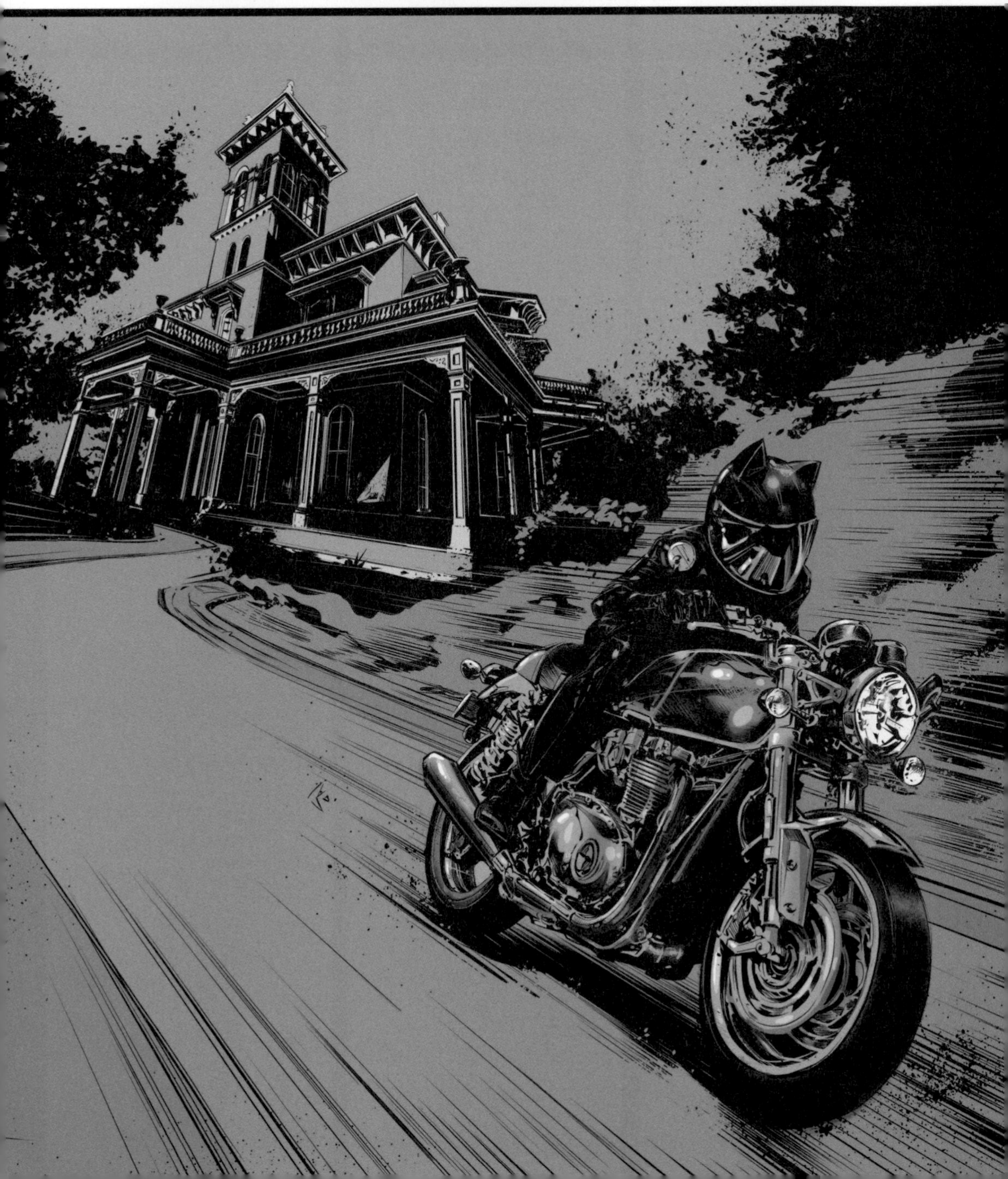

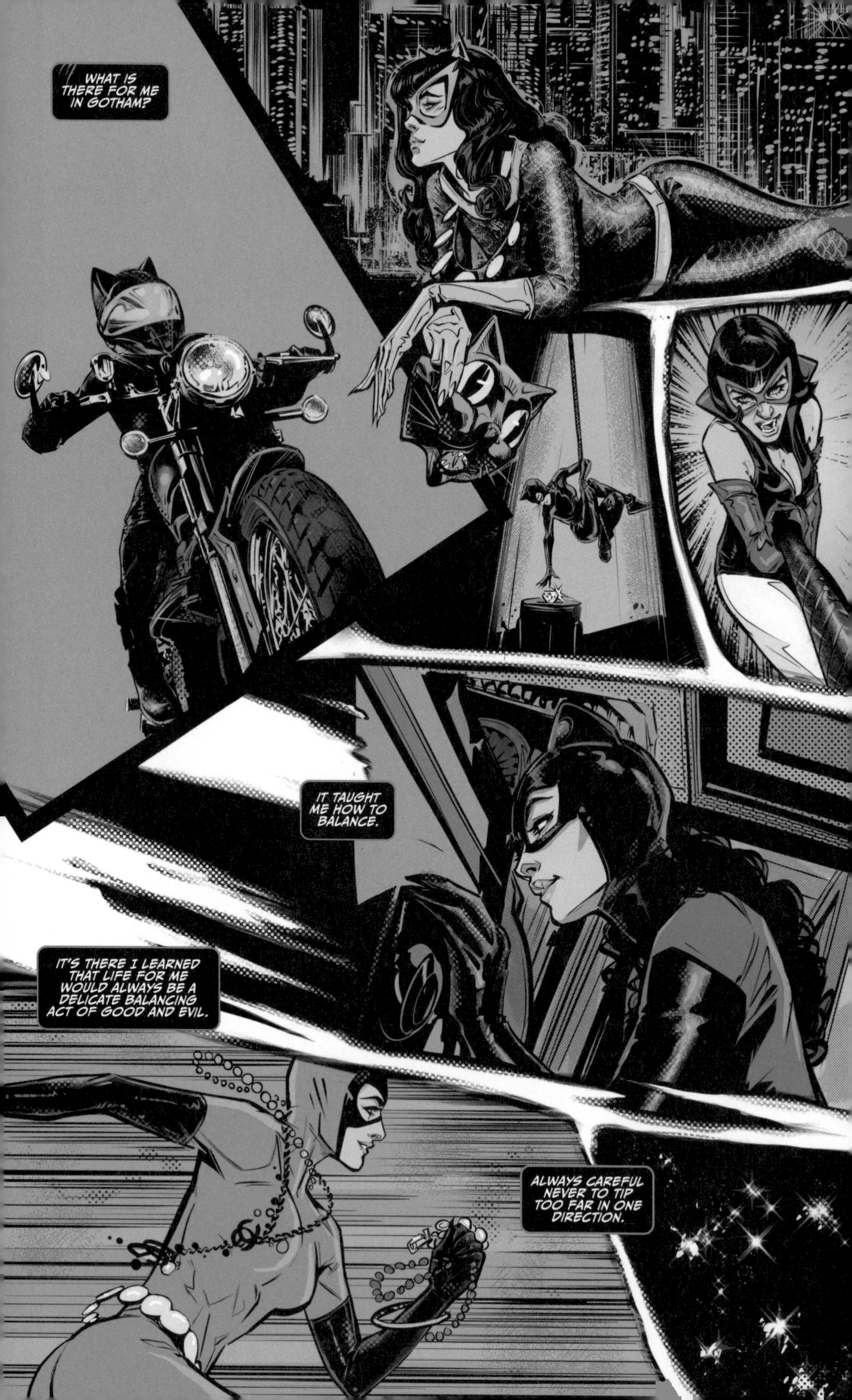
WHAT IS THERE FOR ME IN GOTHAM?
IT TAUGHT ME HOW TO BALANCE.
IT'S THERE I LEARNED THAT LIFE FOR ME WOULD ALWAYS BE A DELICATE BALANCING ACT OF GOOD AND EVIL.
ALWAYS CAREFUL NEVER TO TIP TOO FAR IN ONE DIRECTION.

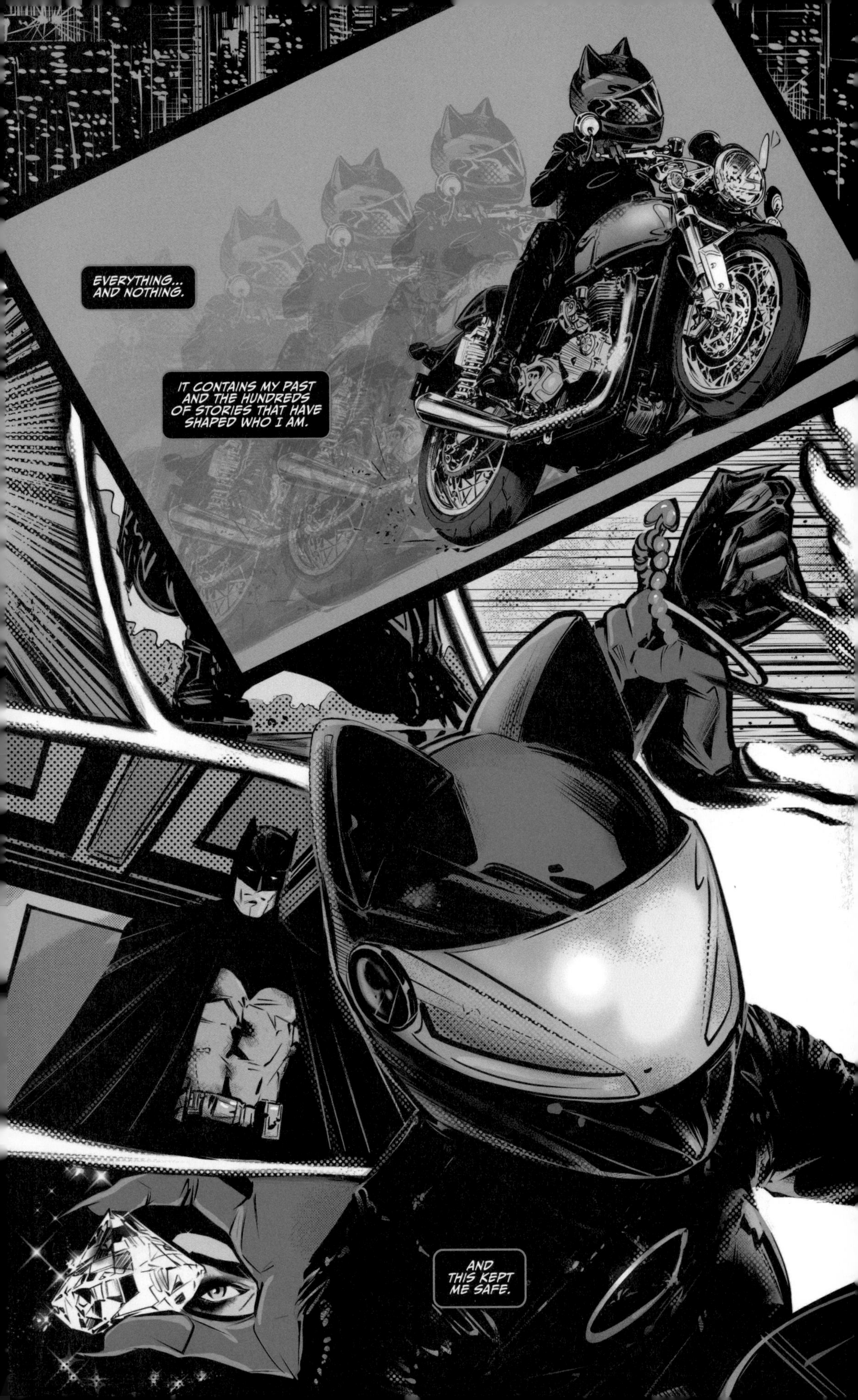
EVERYTHING... AND NOTHING.
IT CONTAINS MY PAST AND THE HUNDREDS OF STORIES THAT HAVE SHAPED WHO I AM.
AND THIS KEPT ME SAFE.

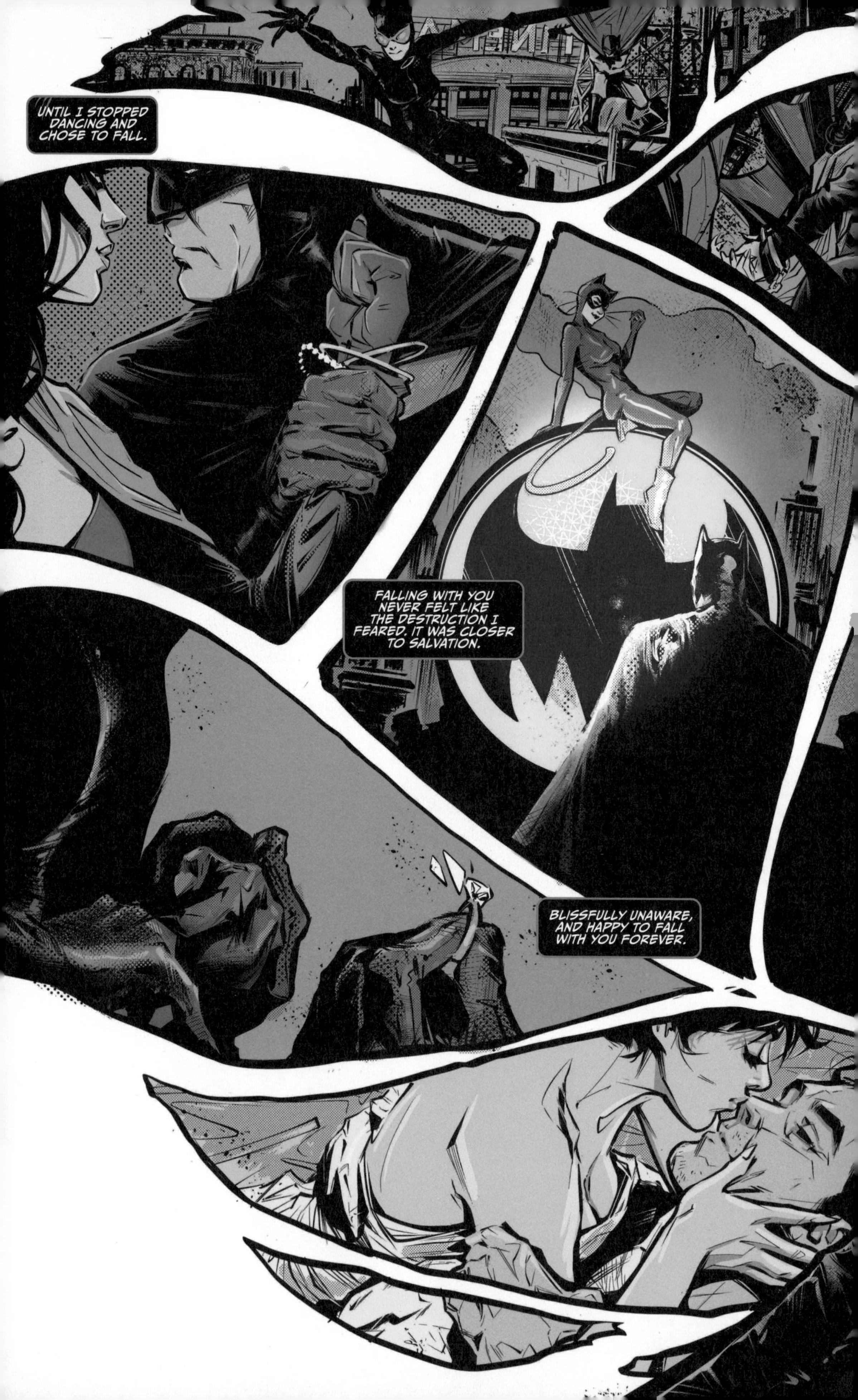
UNTIL I STOPPED DANCING AND CHOSE TO FALL.
FALLING WITH YOU NEVER FELT LIKE THE DESTRUCTION I FEARED. IT WAS CLOSER TO SALVATION.
BLISSFULLY UNAWARE, AND HAPPY TO FALL WITH YOU FOREVER.

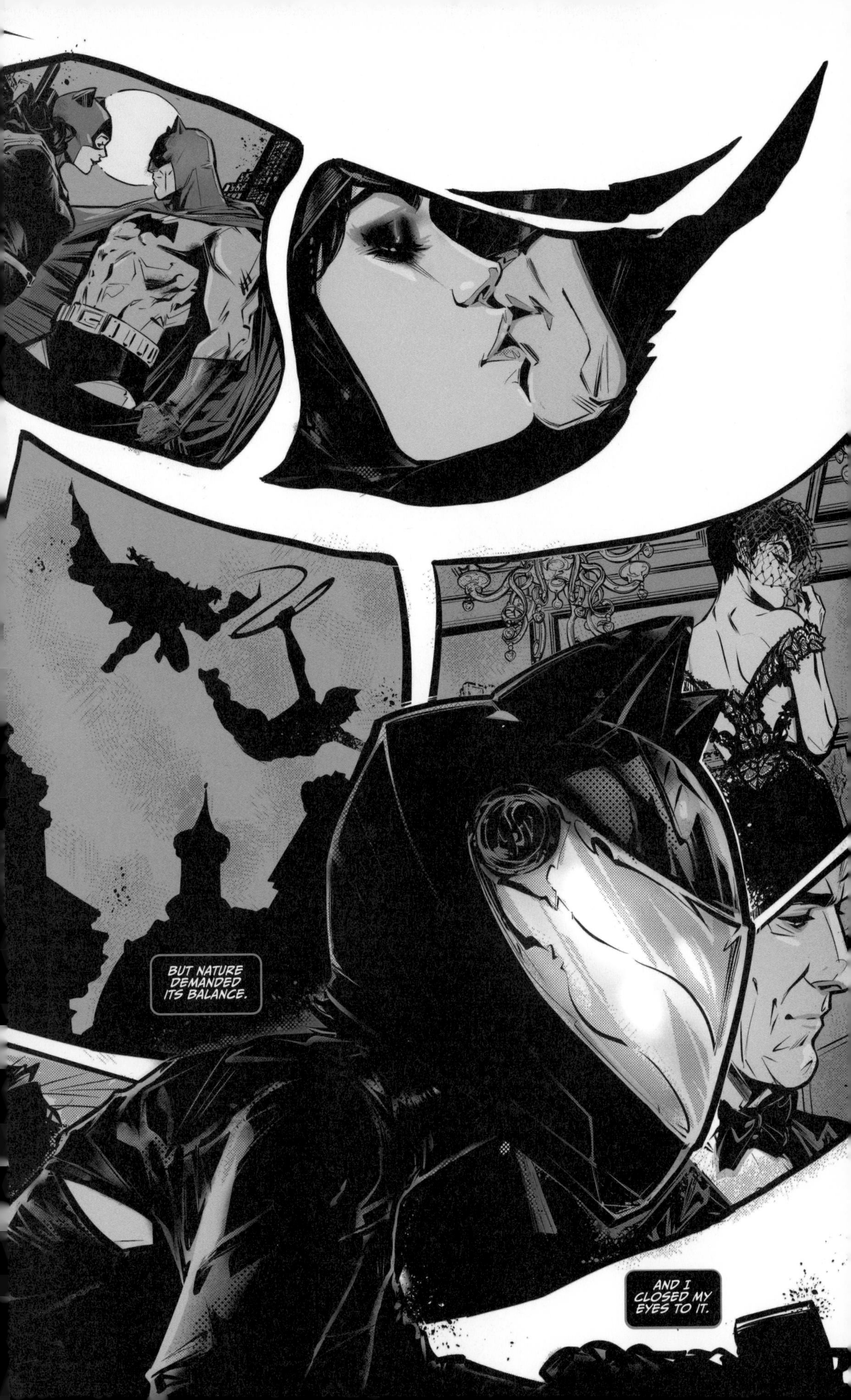
BUT NATURE DEMANDED ITS BALANCE.
AND I CLOSED MY EYES TO IT.

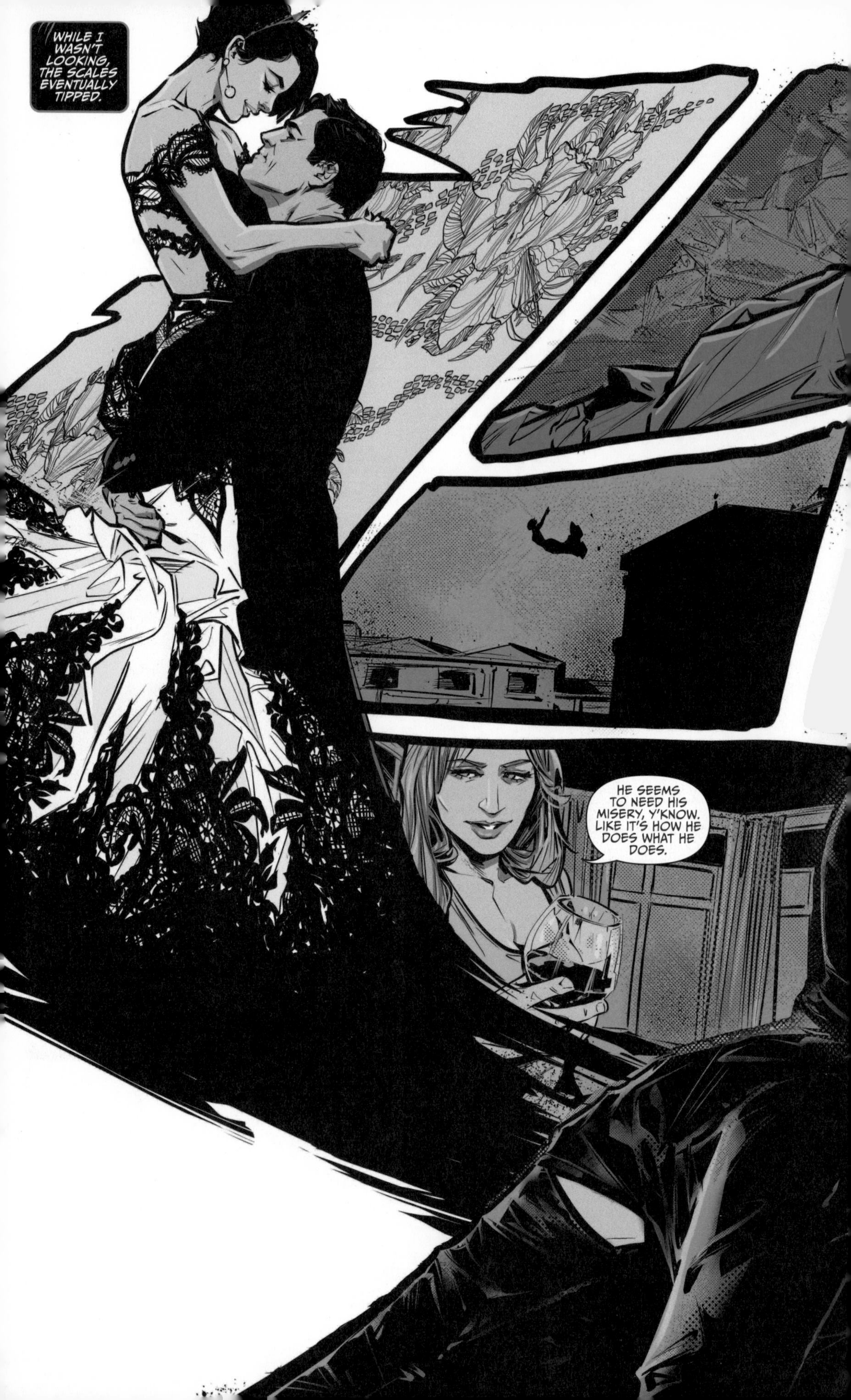
WHILE I WASN'T LOOKING, THE SCALES EVENTUALLY TIPPED.
HE SEEMS TO NEED HIS MISERY, Y'KNOW. LIKE IT'S HOW HE DOES WHAT HE DOES.

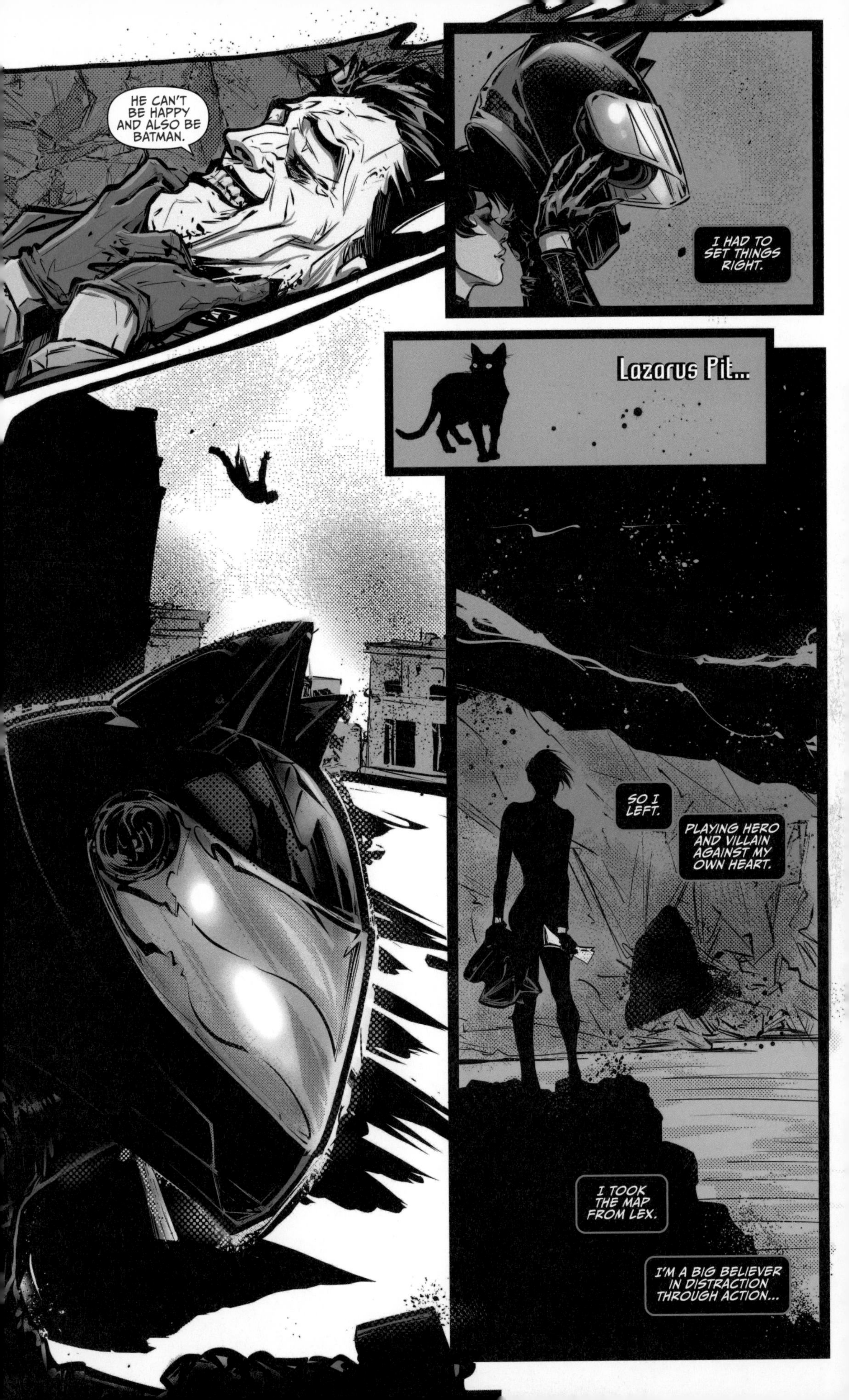
HE CAN'T BE HAPPY AND ALSO BE BATMAN.
I HAD TO SET THINGS RIGHT.
Lazarus Pit...
SO I LEFT.
PLAYING HERO AND VILLAIN AGAINST MY OWN HEART.
I TOOK THE MAP FROM LEX.
I'M A BIG BELIEVER IN DISTRACTION THROUGH ACTION...

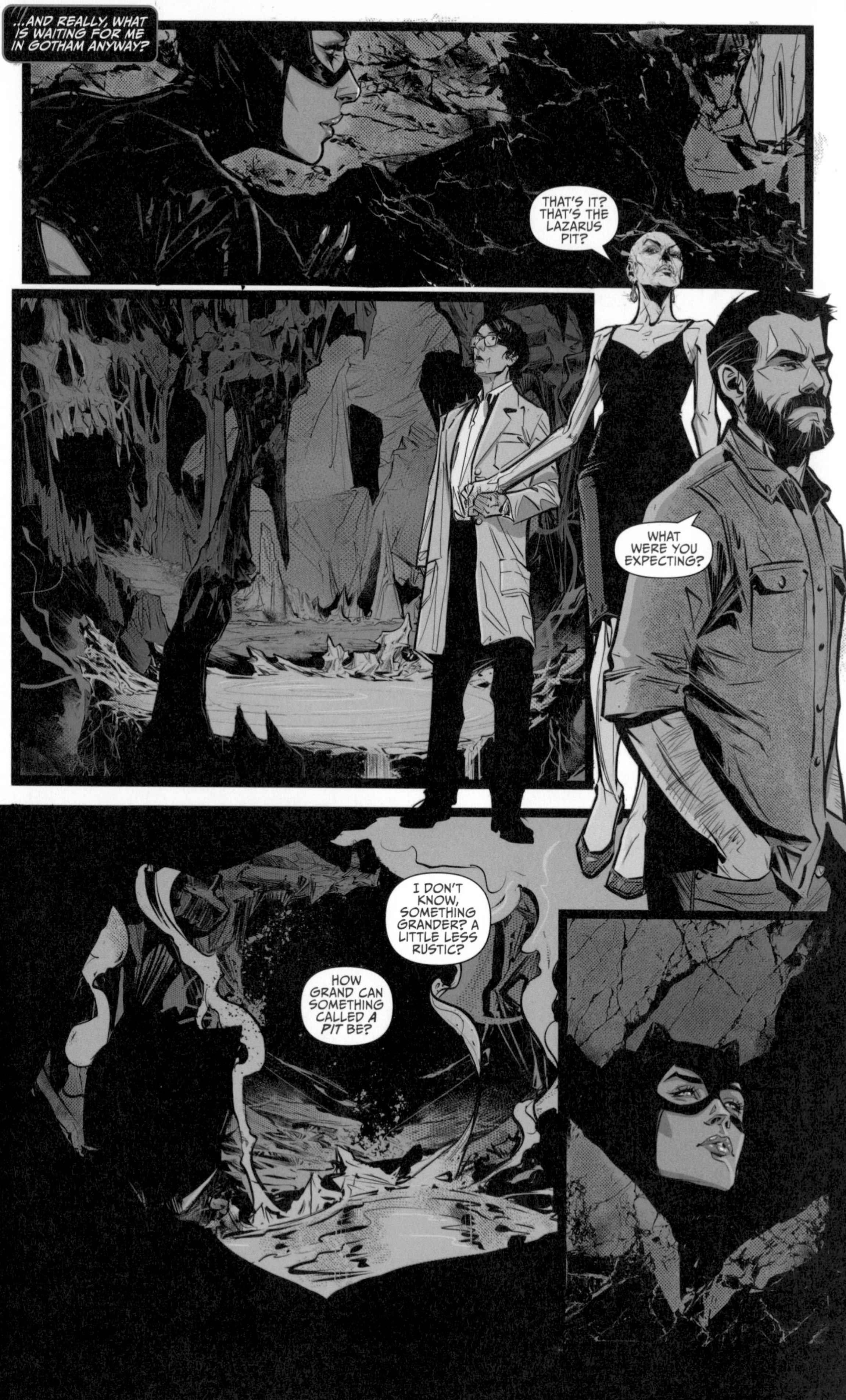
...AND REALLY, WHAT IS WAITING FOR ME IN GOTHAM ANYWAY?
THAT'S IT? THAT'S THE LAZARUS PIT?
WHAT WERE YOU EXPECTING?
I DON'T KNOW, SOMETHING GRANDER? A LITTLE LESS RUSTIC?
HOW GRAND CAN SOMETHING CALLED *A PIT* BE?

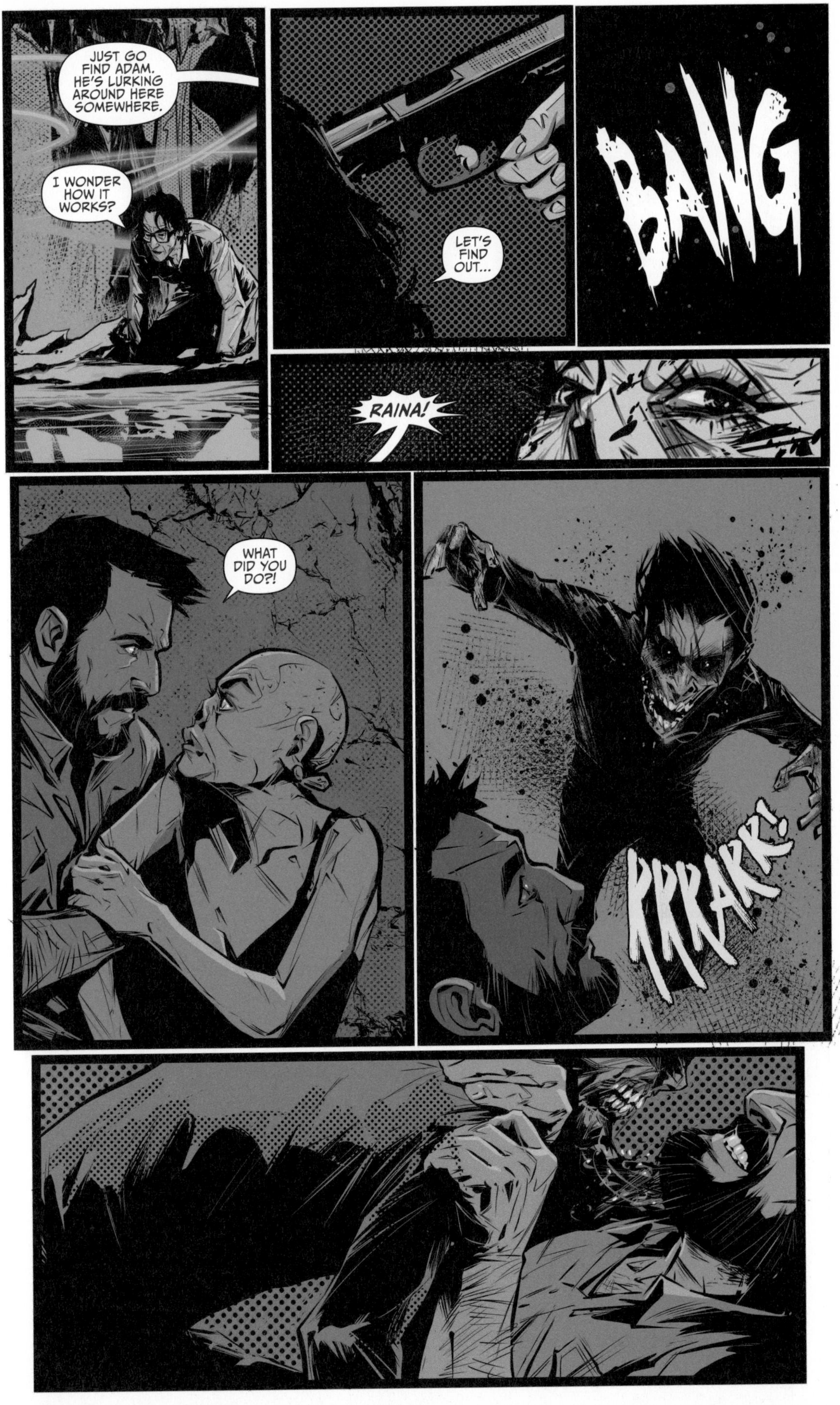
JUST GO FIND ADAM. HE'S LURKING AROUND HERE SOMEWHERE.
I WONDER HOW IT WORKS?
LET'S FIND OUT...
BANG
RAINA!
WHAT DID YOU DO?!
KRRAKK!

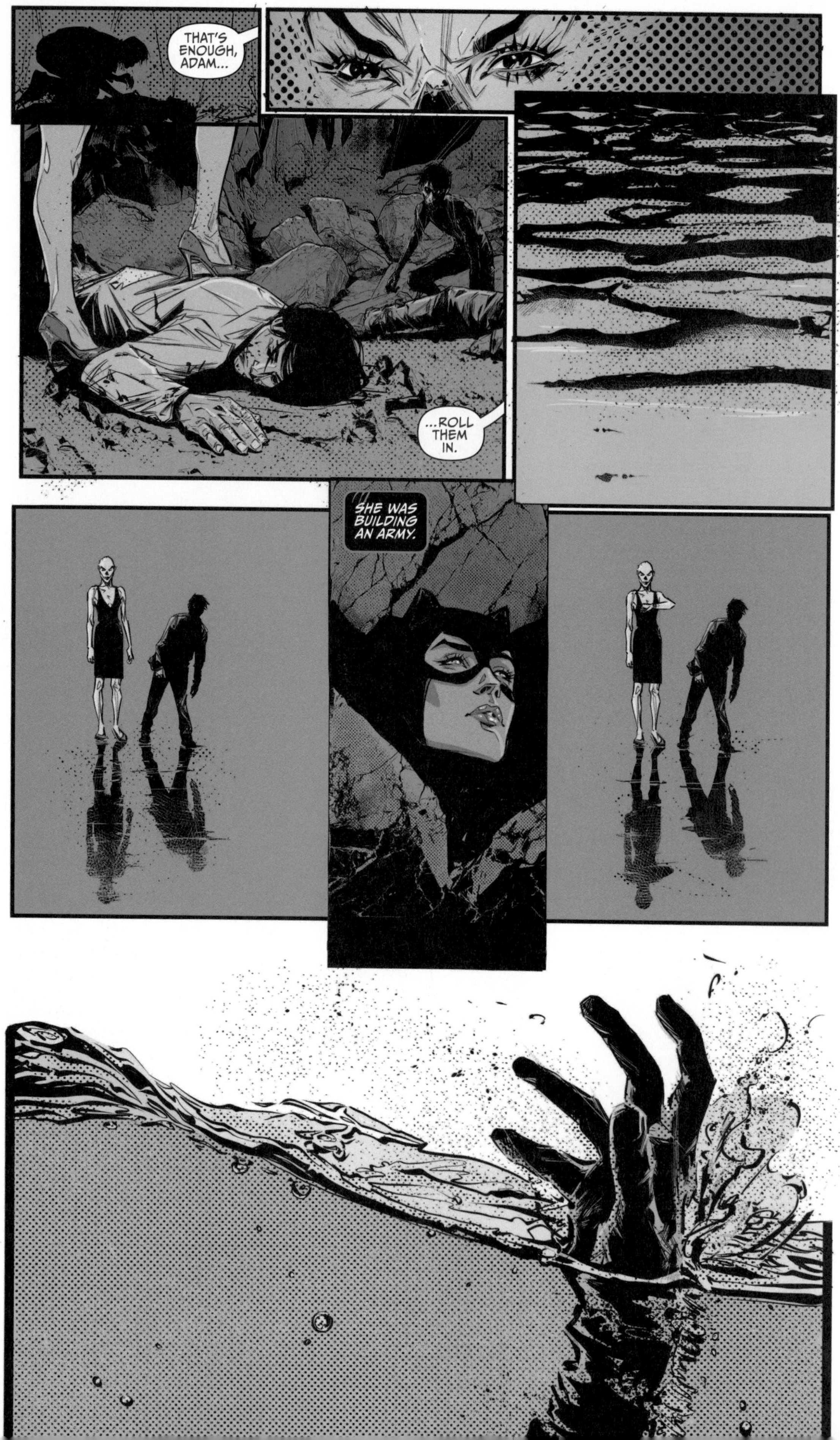
THAT'S ENOUGH, ADAM...
...ROLL THEM IN.
SHE WAS BUILDING AN ARMY.

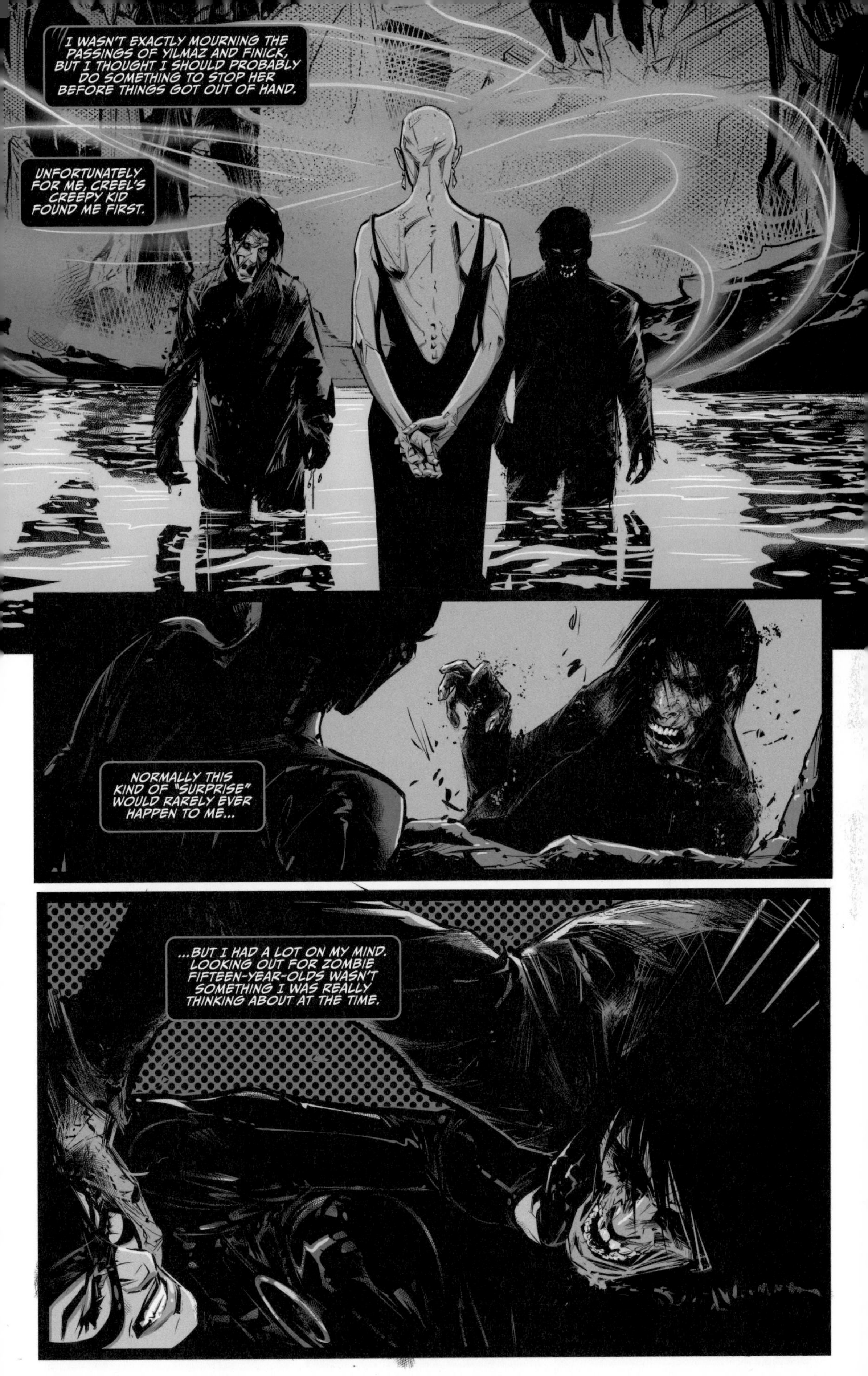
I WASN'T EXACTLY MOURNING THE PASSINGS OF YILMAZ AND FINICK, BUT I THOUGHT I SHOULD PROBABLY DO SOMETHING TO STOP HER BEFORE THINGS GOT OUT OF HAND.
UNFORTUNATELY FOR ME, CREEL'S CREEPY KID FOUND ME FIRST.
NORMALLY THIS KIND OF "SURPRISE" WOULD RARELY EVER HAPPEN TO ME...
...BUT I HAD A LOT ON MY MIND. LOOKING OUT FOR ZOMBIE FIFTEEN-YEAR-OLDS WASN'T SOMETHING I WAS REALLY THINKING ABOUT AT THE TIME.

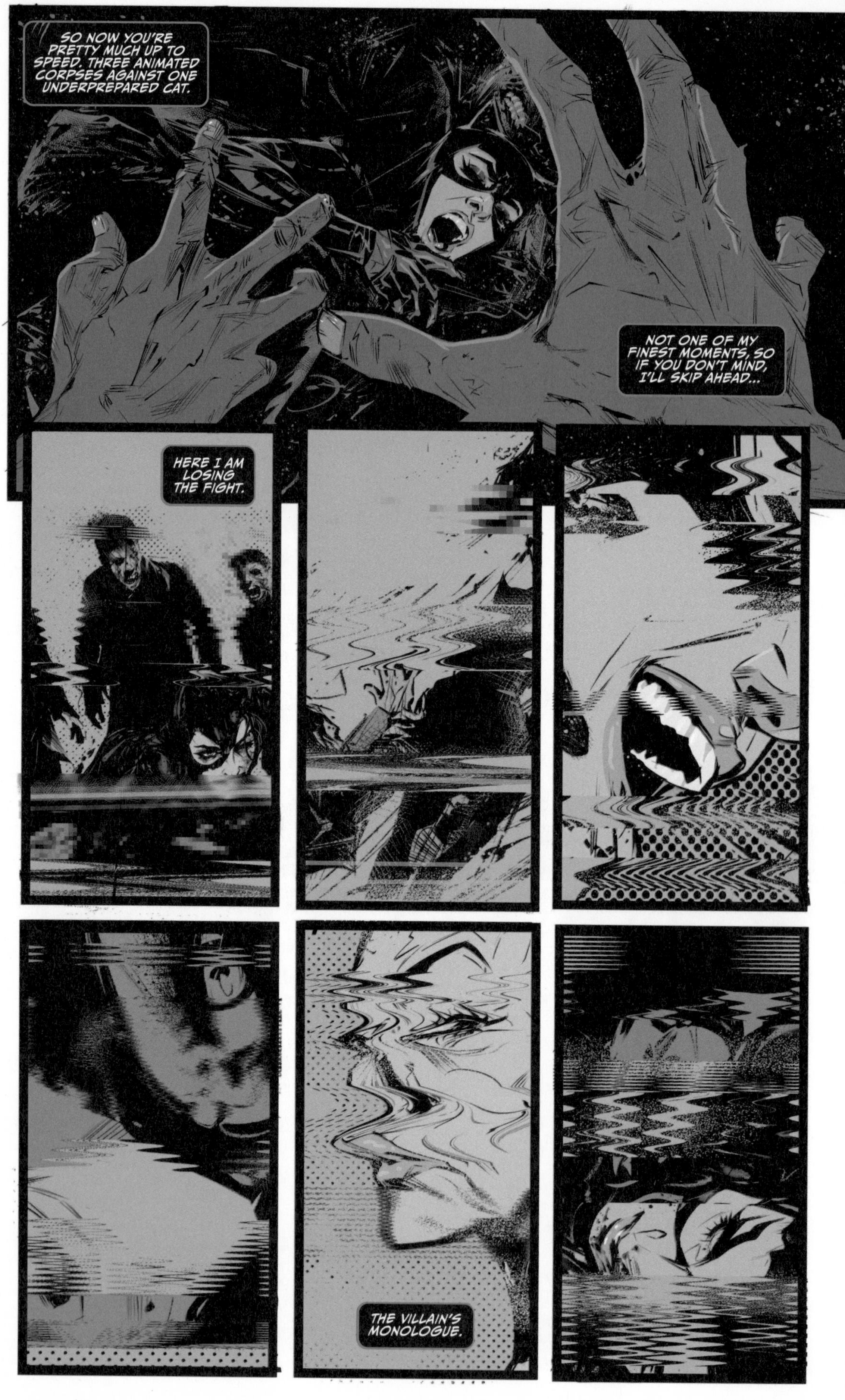
SO NOW YOU'RE PRETTY MUCH UP TO SPEED. THREE ANIMATED CORPSES AGAINST ONE UNDERPREPARED CAT.
NOT ONE OF MY FINEST MOMENTS, SO IF YOU DON'T MIND, I'LL SKIP AHEAD...
HERE I AM LOSING THE FIGHT.
THE VILLAIN'S MONOLOGUE.

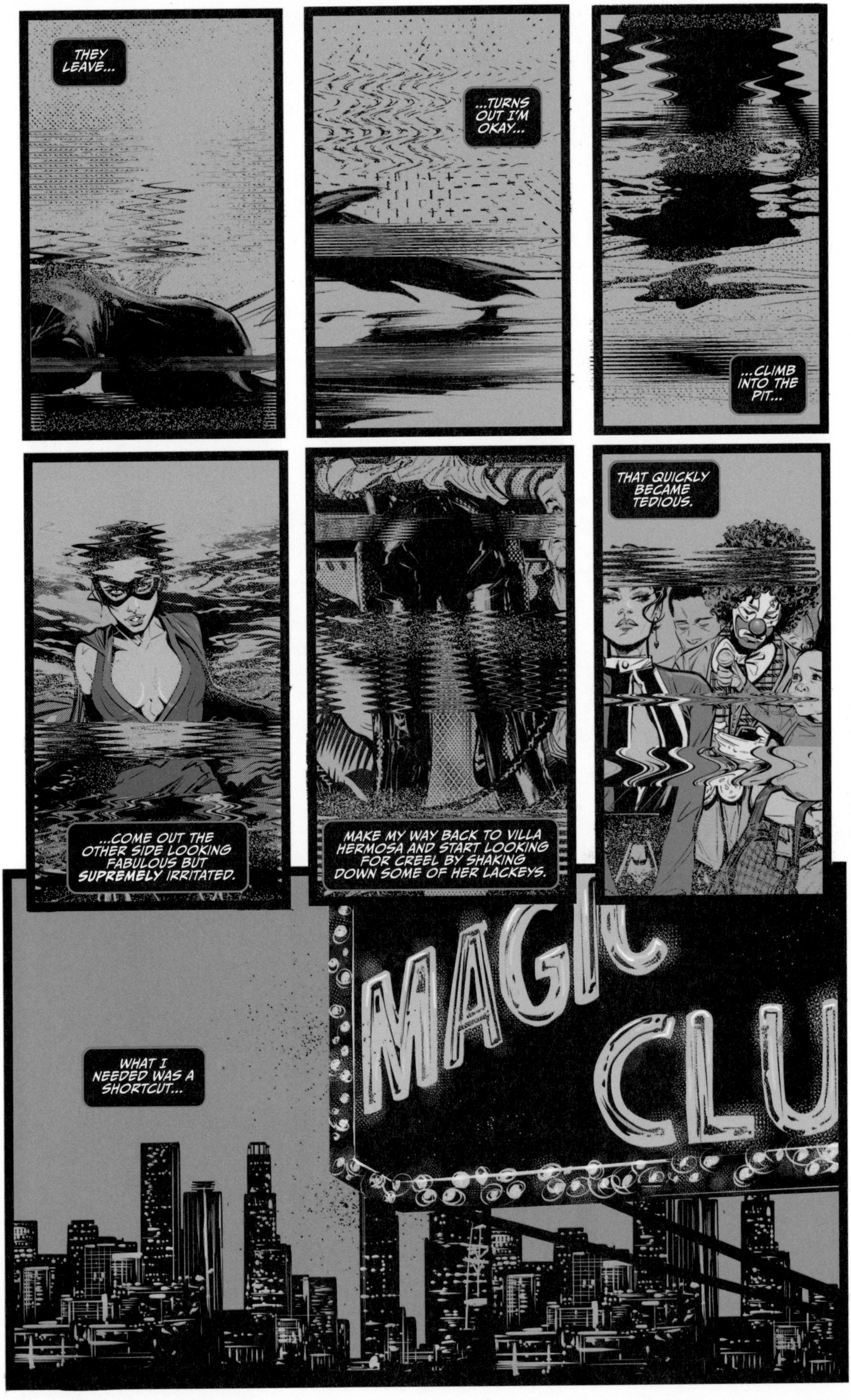
THEY LEAVE...
...TURNS OUT I'M OKAY...
...CLIMB INTO THE PIT...
...COME OUT THE OTHER SIDE LOOKING FABULOUS BUT SUPREMELY IRRITATED.
MAKE MY WAY BACK TO VILLA HERMOSA AND START LOOKING FOR CREEL BY SHAKING DOWN SOME OF HER LACKEYS.
THAT QUICKLY BECAME TEDIOUS.
WHAT I NEEDED WAS A SHORTCUT...
MAGIC
CLU

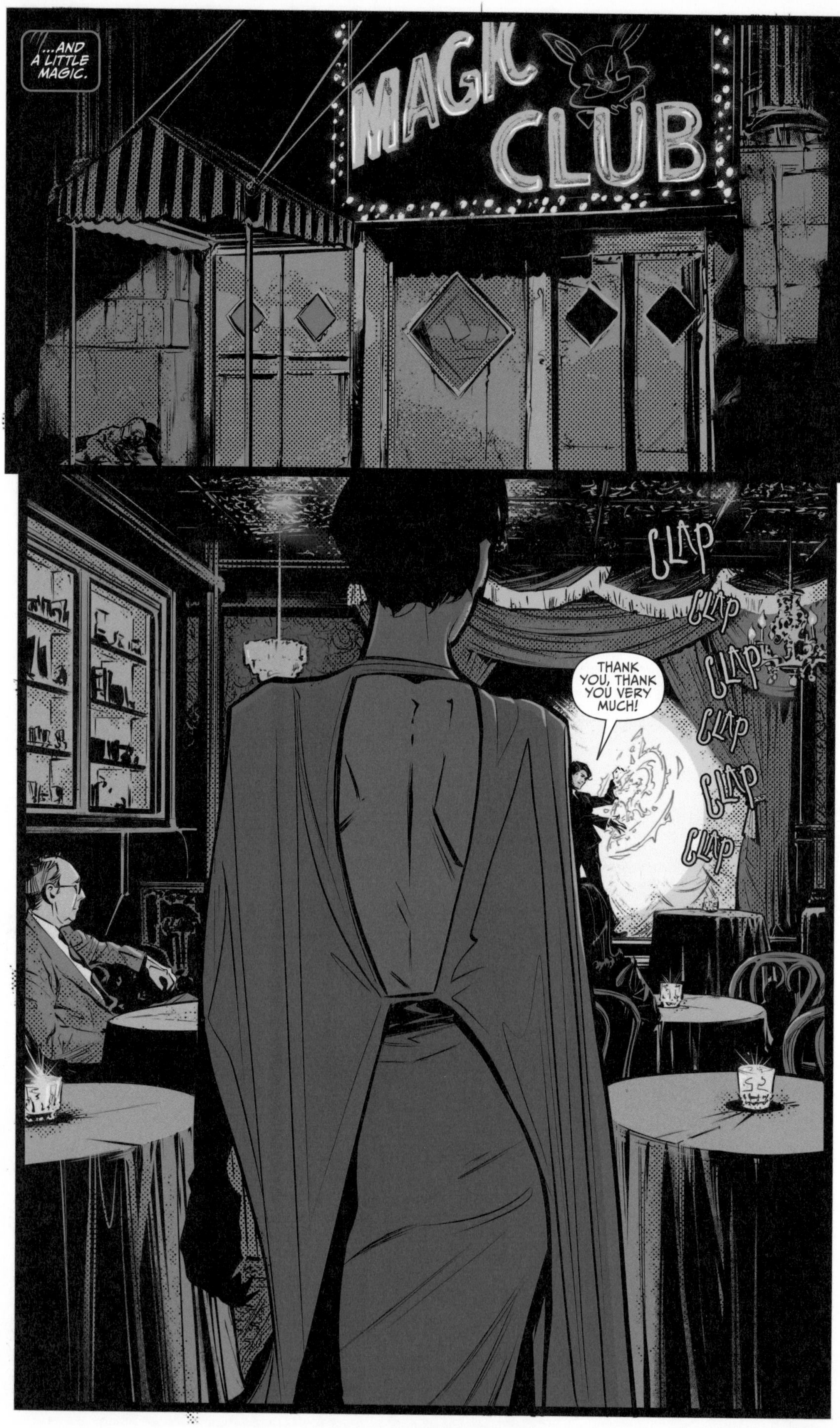
...AND A LITTLE MAGIC.
MAGIC CLUB
CLAP
CLAP
CLAP
CLAP
CLAP
CLAP
THANK YOU, THANK YOU VERY MUCH!

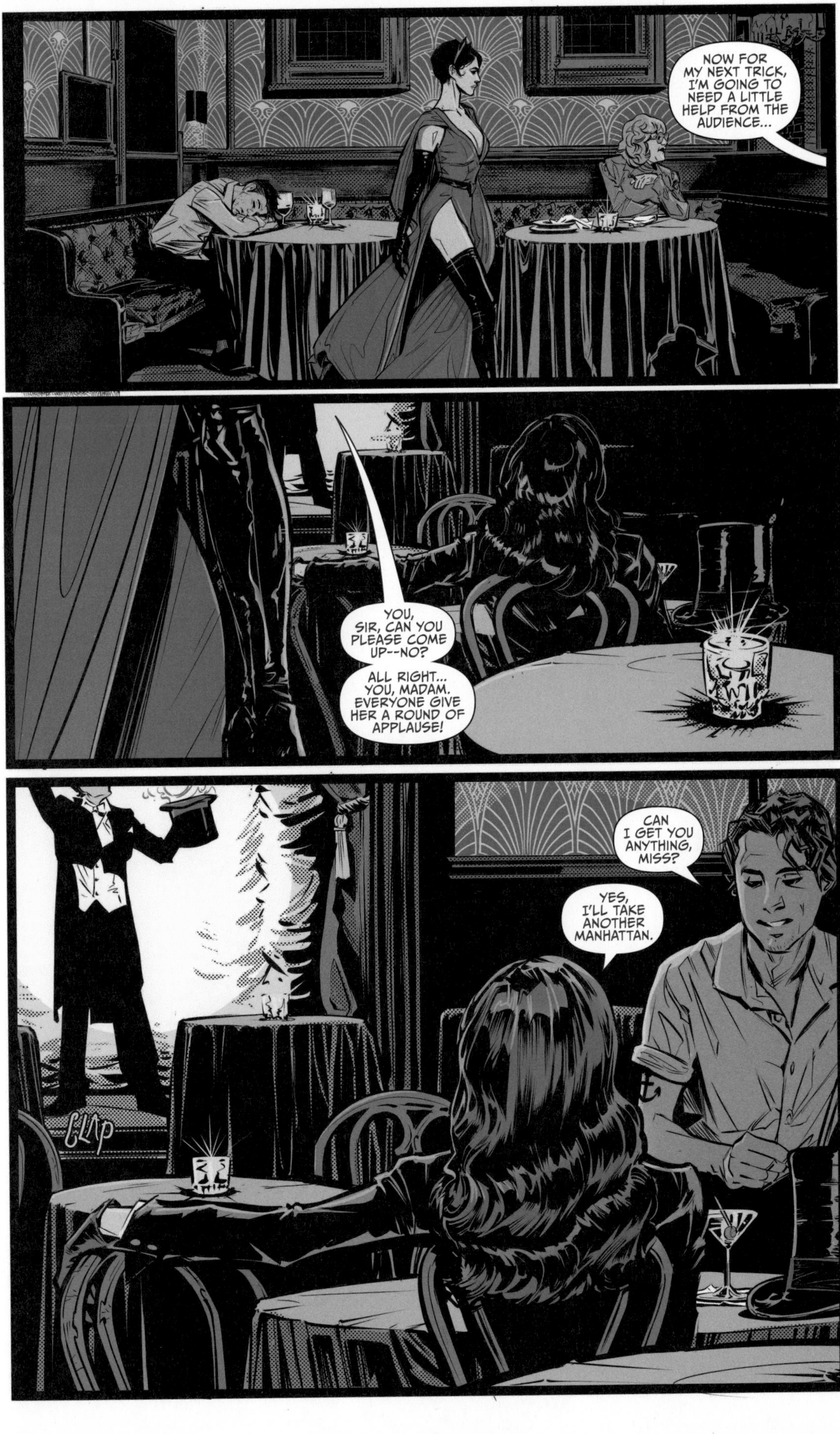
NOW FOR MY NEXT TRICK, I'M GOING TO NEED A LITTLE HELP FROM THE AUDIENCE...
YOU, SIR, CAN YOU PLEASE COME UP--NO?
ALL RIGHT... YOU, MADAM. EVERYONE GIVE HER A ROUND OF APPLAUSE!
CLAP
CAN I GET YOU ANYTHING, MISS?
YES, I'LL TAKE ANOTHER MANHATTAN.

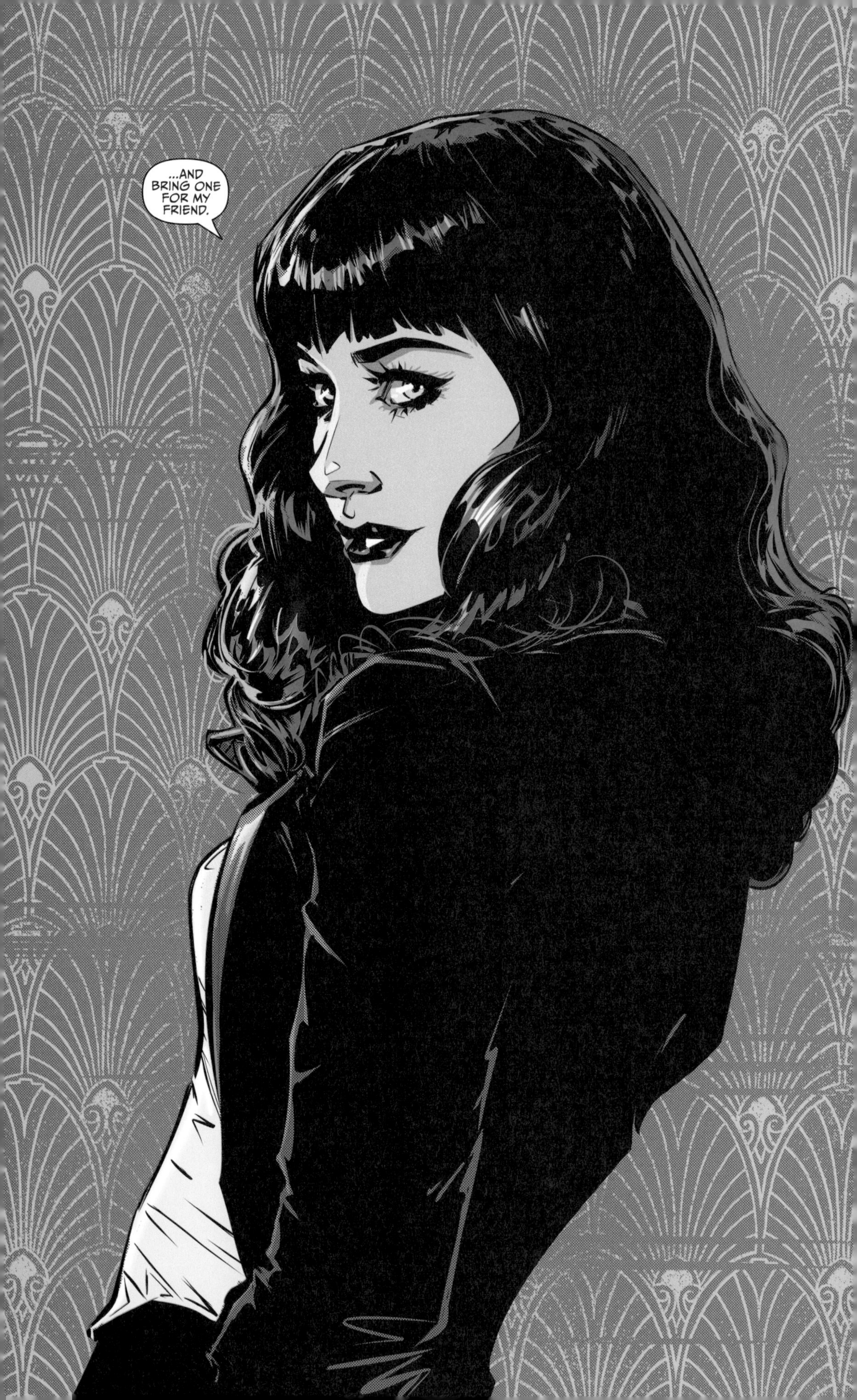
...AND BRING ONE FOR MY FRIEND.

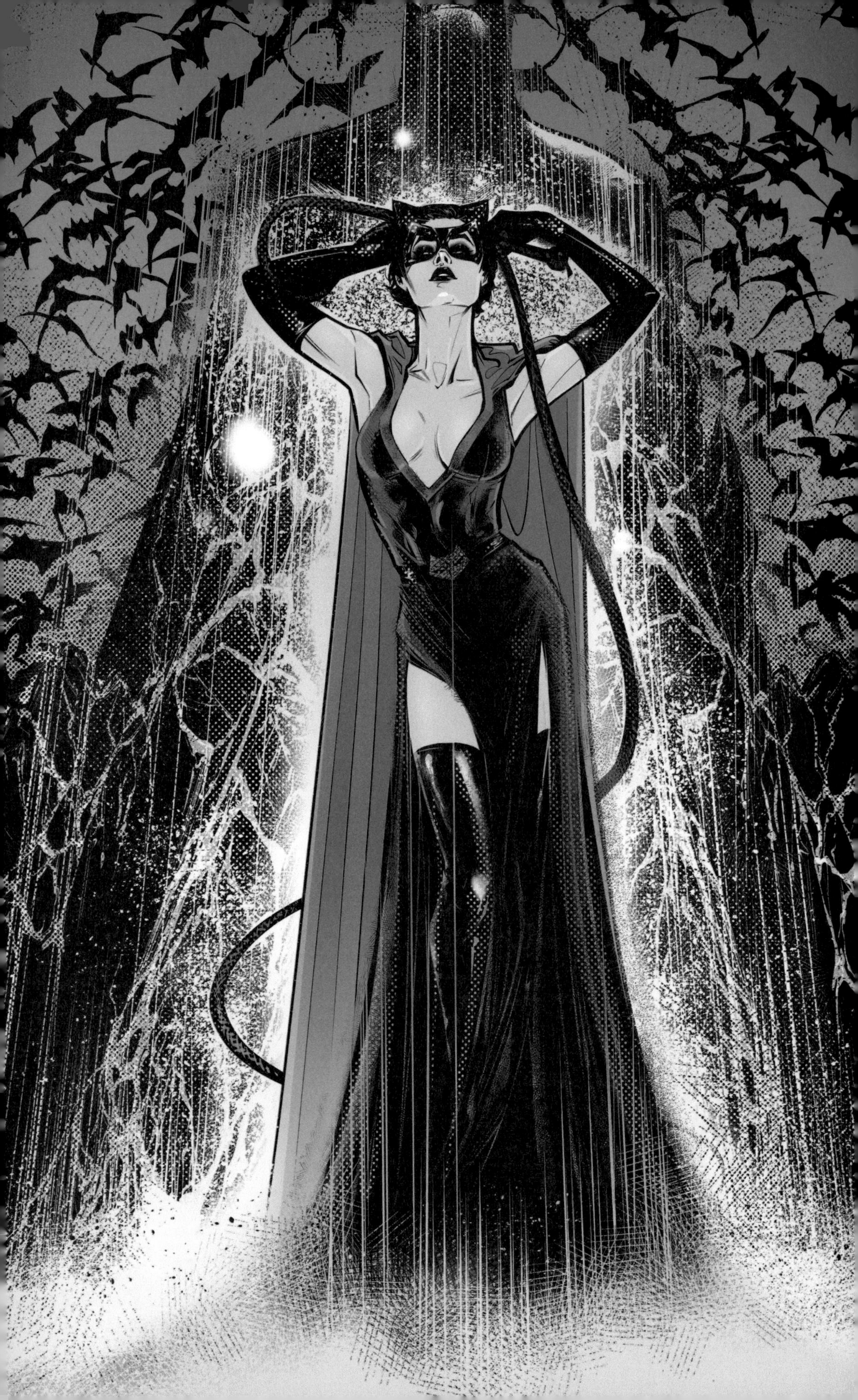

CATWOMAN
#18

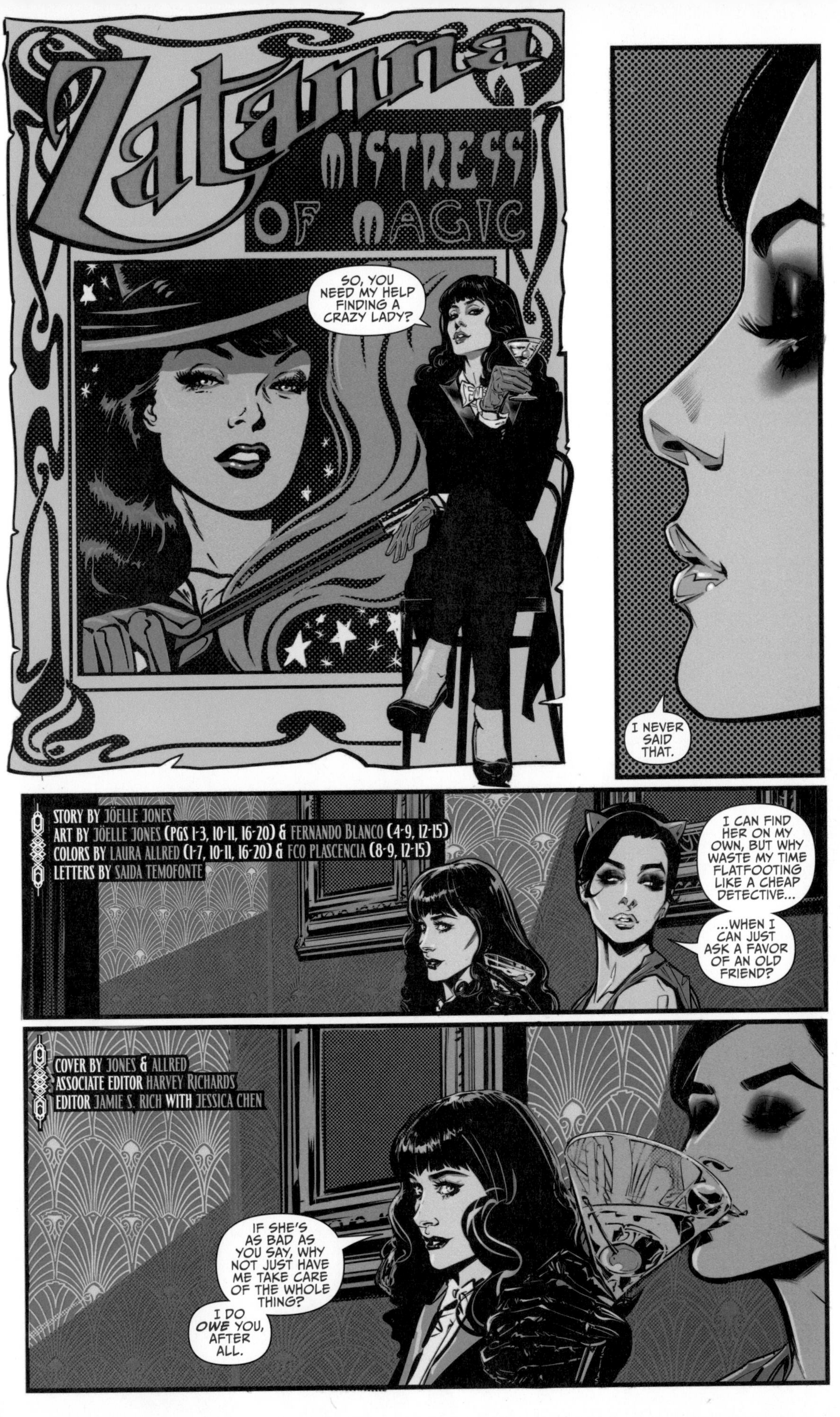

ZATANNA MISTRESS OF MAGIC
SO, YOU NEED MY HELP FINDING A CRAZY LADY?
I NEVER SAID THAT.
STORY BY JÖELLE JONES
ART BY JÖELLE JONES (PGS 1-3, 10-11, 16-20) & FERNANDO BLANCO (4-9, 12-15)
COLORS BY LAURA ALLRED (1-7, 10-11, 16-20) & FCO PLASCENCIA (8-9, 12-15)
LETTERS BY SAIDA TEMOFONTE
I CAN FIND HER ON MY OWN, BUT WHY WASTE MY TIME FLATFOOTING LIKE A CHEAP DETECTIVE...
...WHEN I CAN JUST ASK A FAVOR OF AN OLD FRIEND?
COVER BY JONES & ALLRED
ASSOCIATE EDITOR HARVEY RICHARDS
EDITOR JAMIE S. RICH WITH JESSICA CHEN
IF SHE'S AS BAD AS YOU SAY, WHY NOT JUST HAVE ME TAKE CARE OF THE WHOLE THING?
I DO OWE YOU, AFTER ALL.

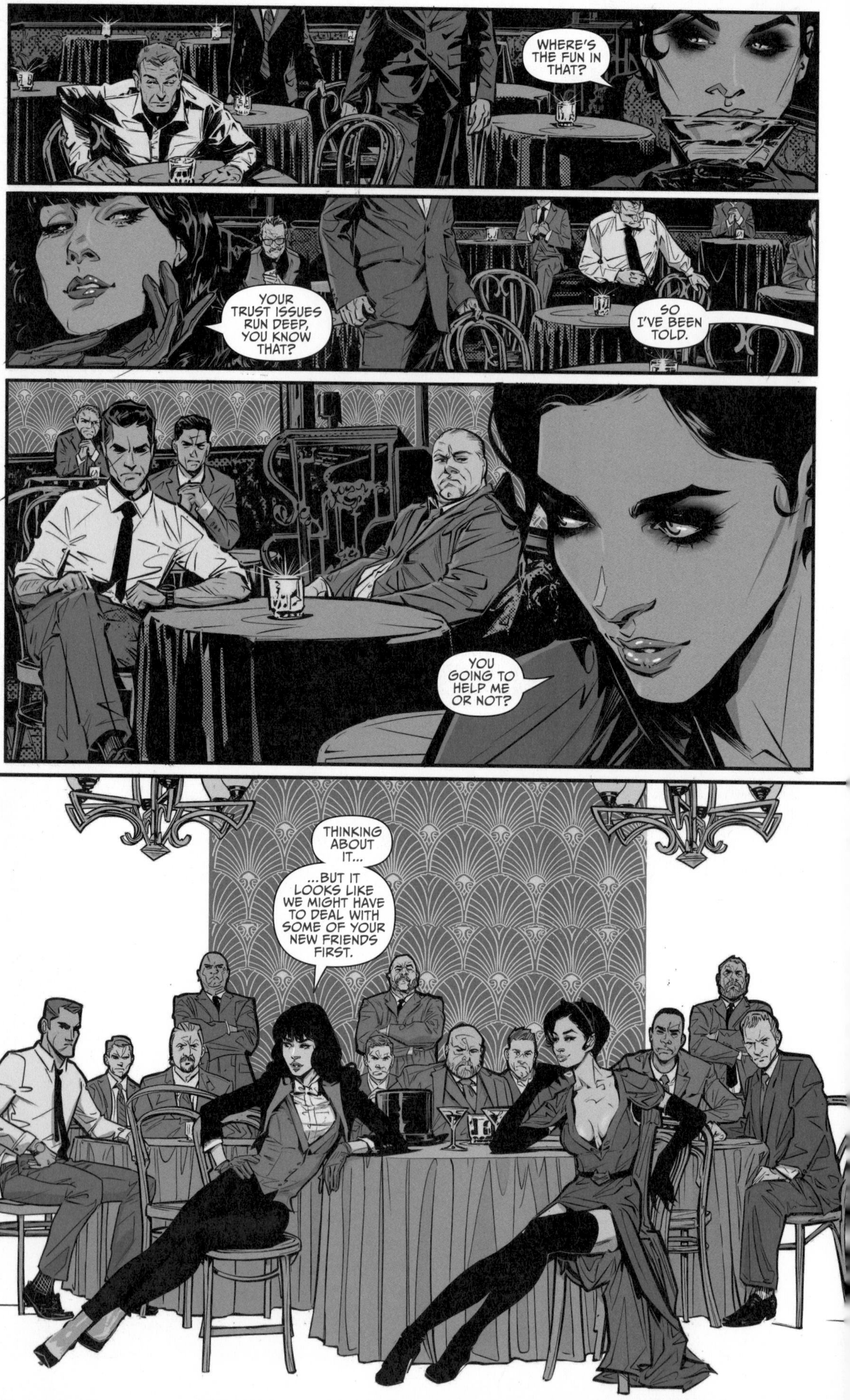
WHERE'S THE FUN IN THAT?
YOUR TRUST ISSUES RUN DEEP, YOU KNOW THAT?
SO I'VE BEEN TOLD.
YOU GOING TO HELP ME OR NOT?
THINKING ABOUT IT...
...BUT IT LOOKS LIKE WE MIGHT HAVE TO DEAL WITH SOME OF YOUR NEW FRIENDS FIRST.

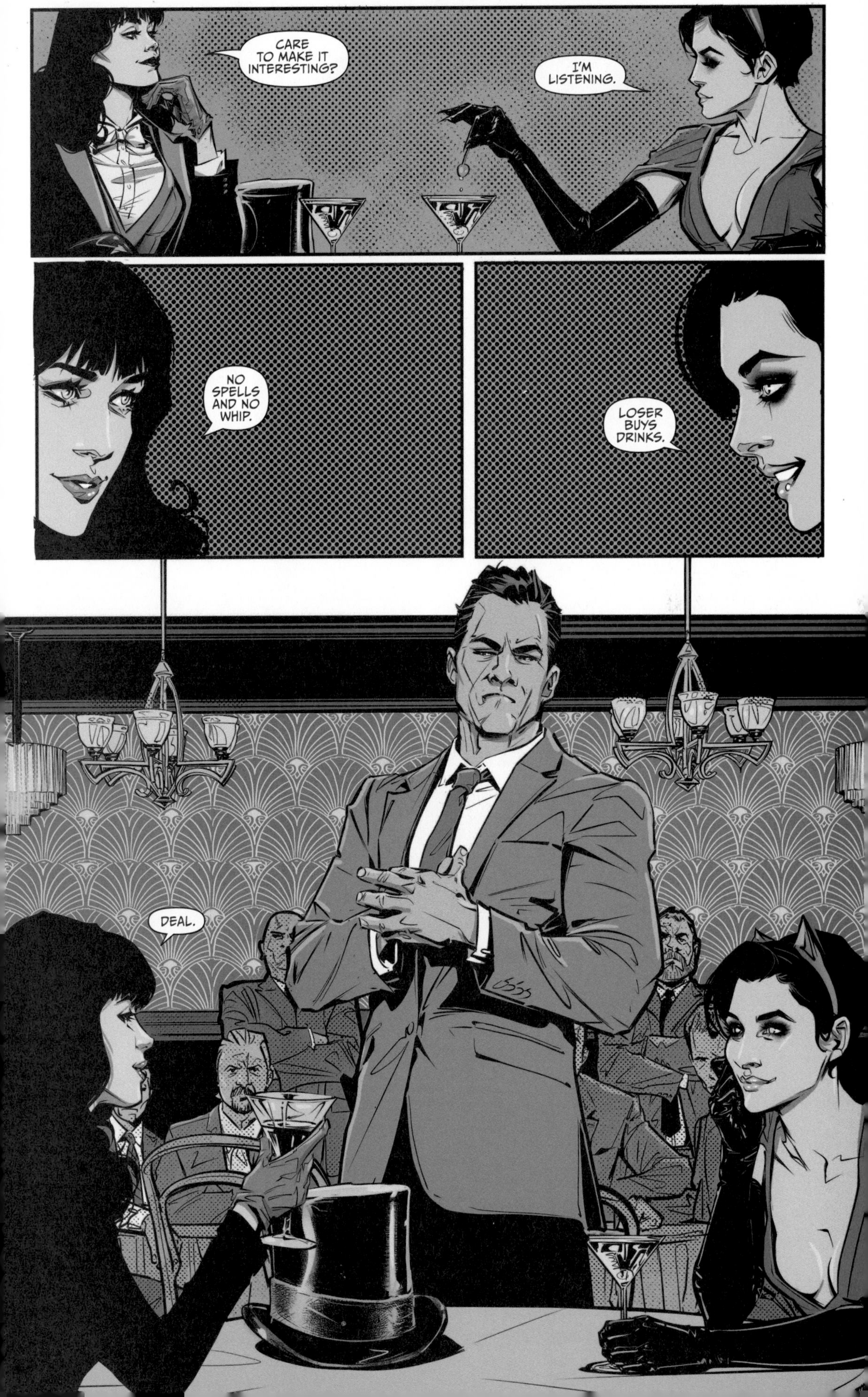
CARE TO MAKE IT INTERESTING?
I'M LISTENING.
NO SPELLS AND NO WHIP.
LOSER BUYS DRINKS.
DEAL.

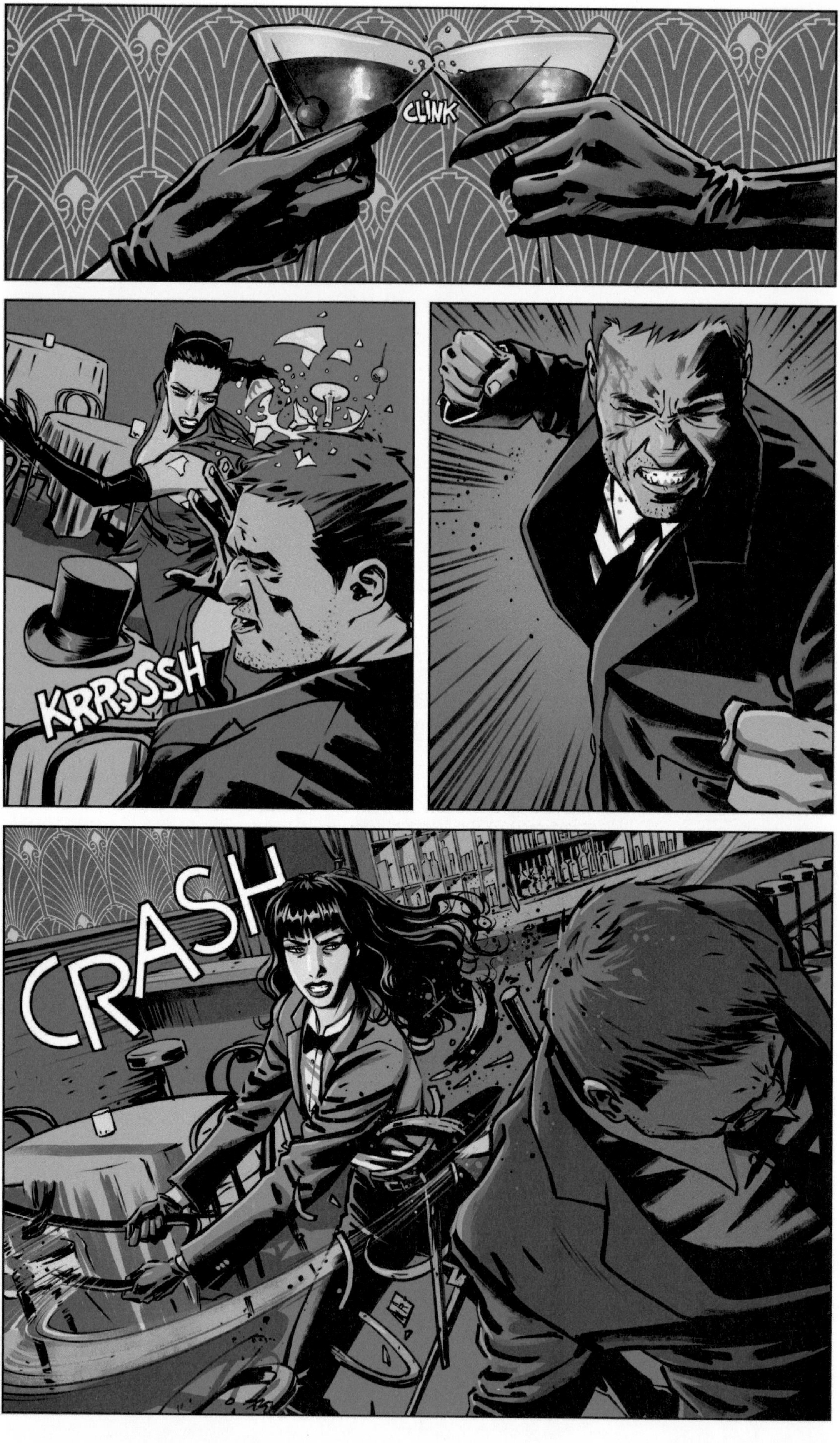
CLINK
KRRSSSH
CRASH

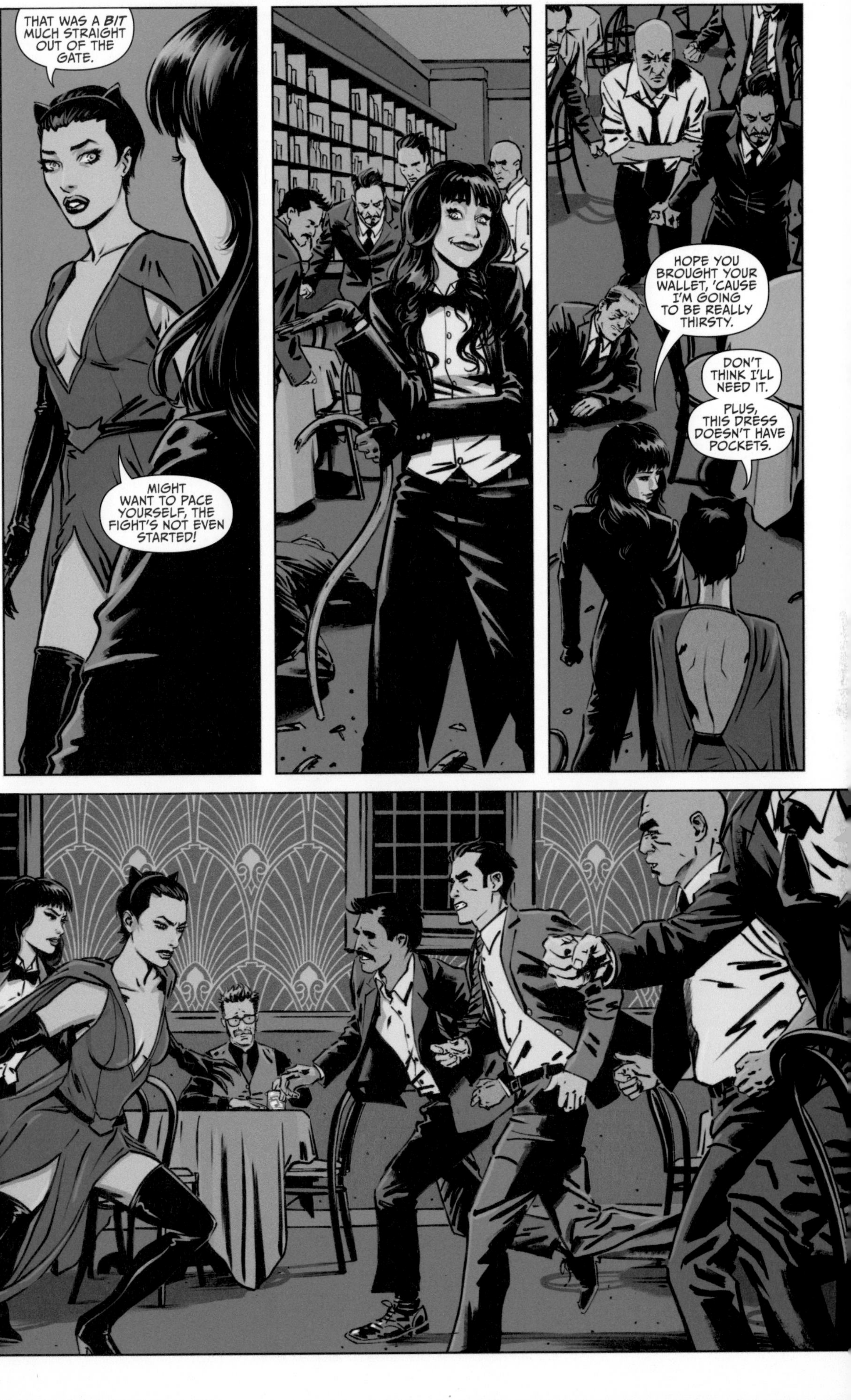
THAT WAS A *BIT* MUCH STRAIGHT OUT OF THE GATE.
MIGHT WANT TO PACE YOURSELF, THE FIGHT'S NOT EVEN STARTED!
HOPE YOU BROUGHT YOUR WALLET, 'CAUSE I'M GOING TO BE REALLY THIRSTY.
DON'T THINK I'LL NEED IT.
PLUS, THIS DRESS DOESN'T HAVE POCKETS.

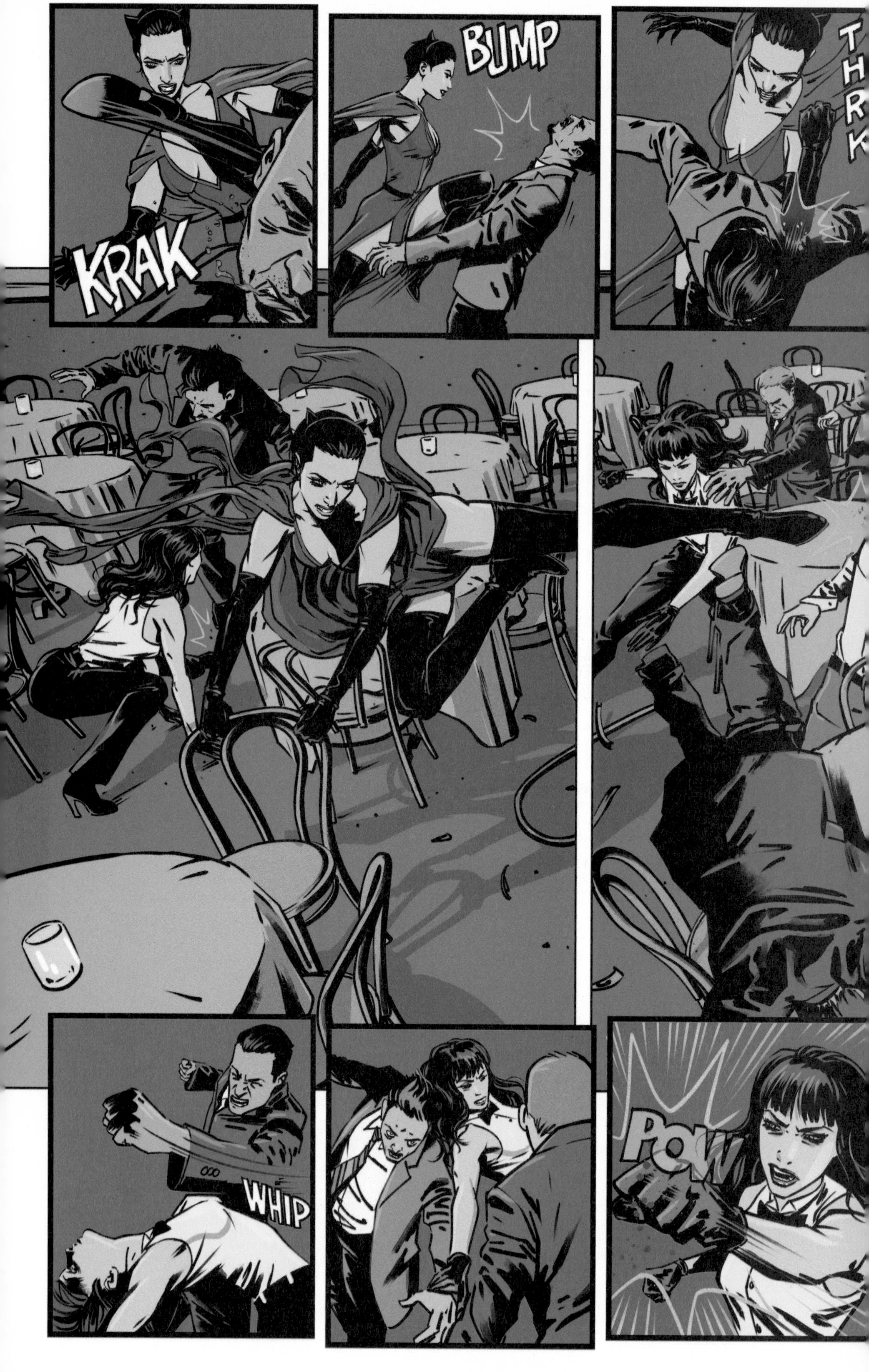
KRAK
BUMP
THRK
WHIP
POW

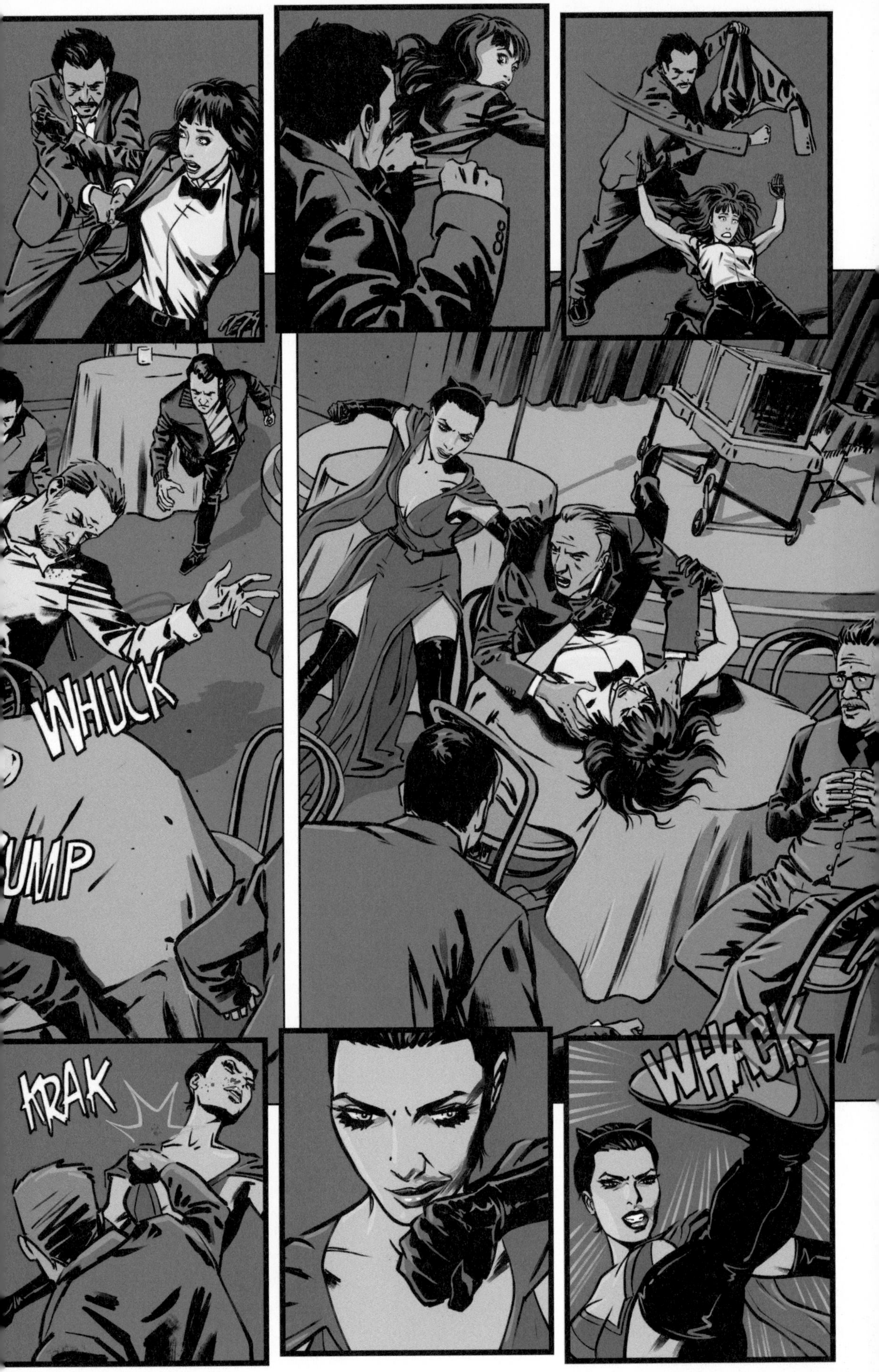
WHUCK
UMP
KRAK
WHACK

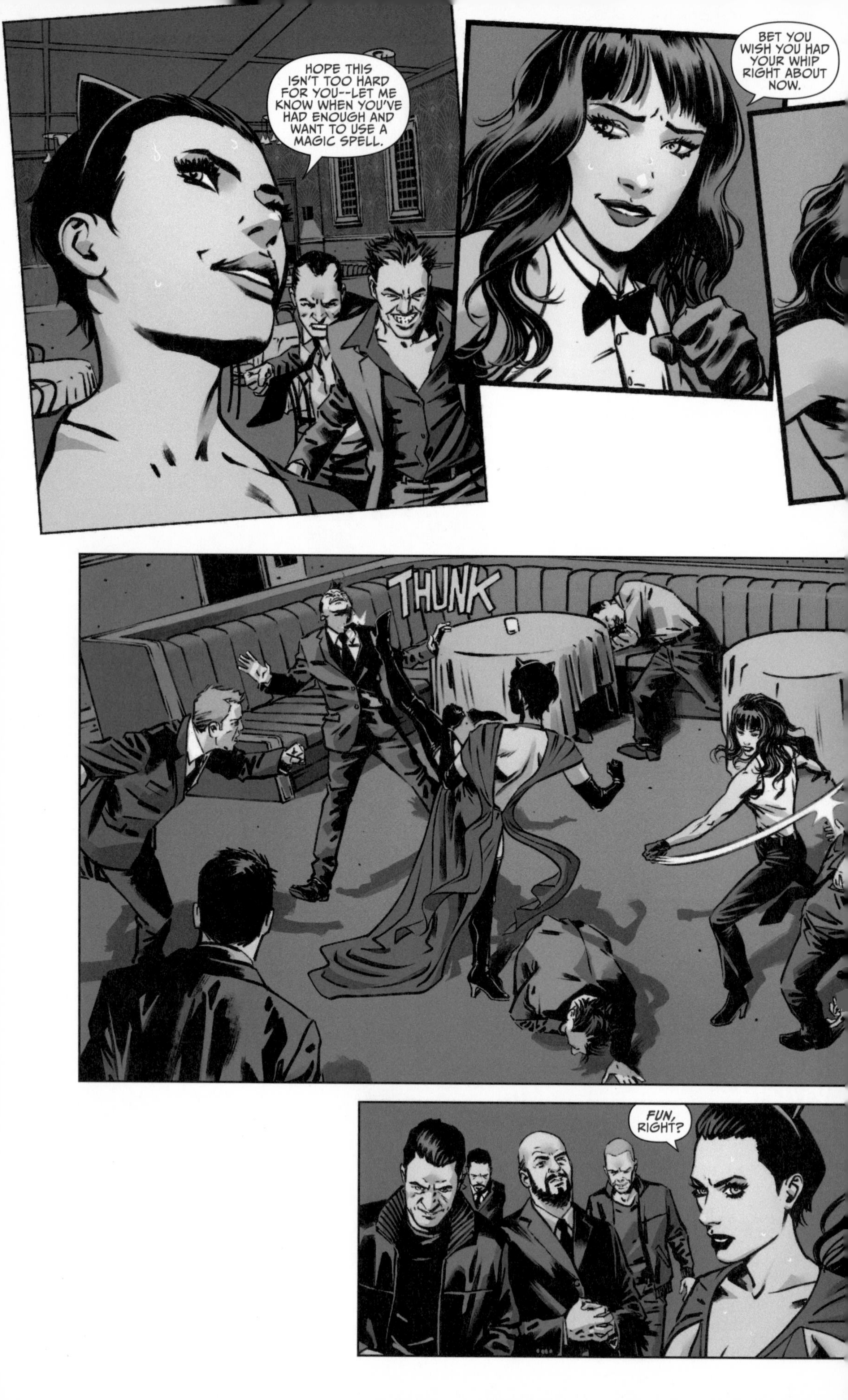
HOPE THIS ISN'T TOO HARD FOR YOU--LET ME KNOW WHEN YOU'VE HAD ENOUGH AND WANT TO USE A MAGIC SPELL.
BET YOU WISH YOU HAD YOUR WHIP RIGHT ABOUT NOW.
THUNK
FUN, RIGHT?

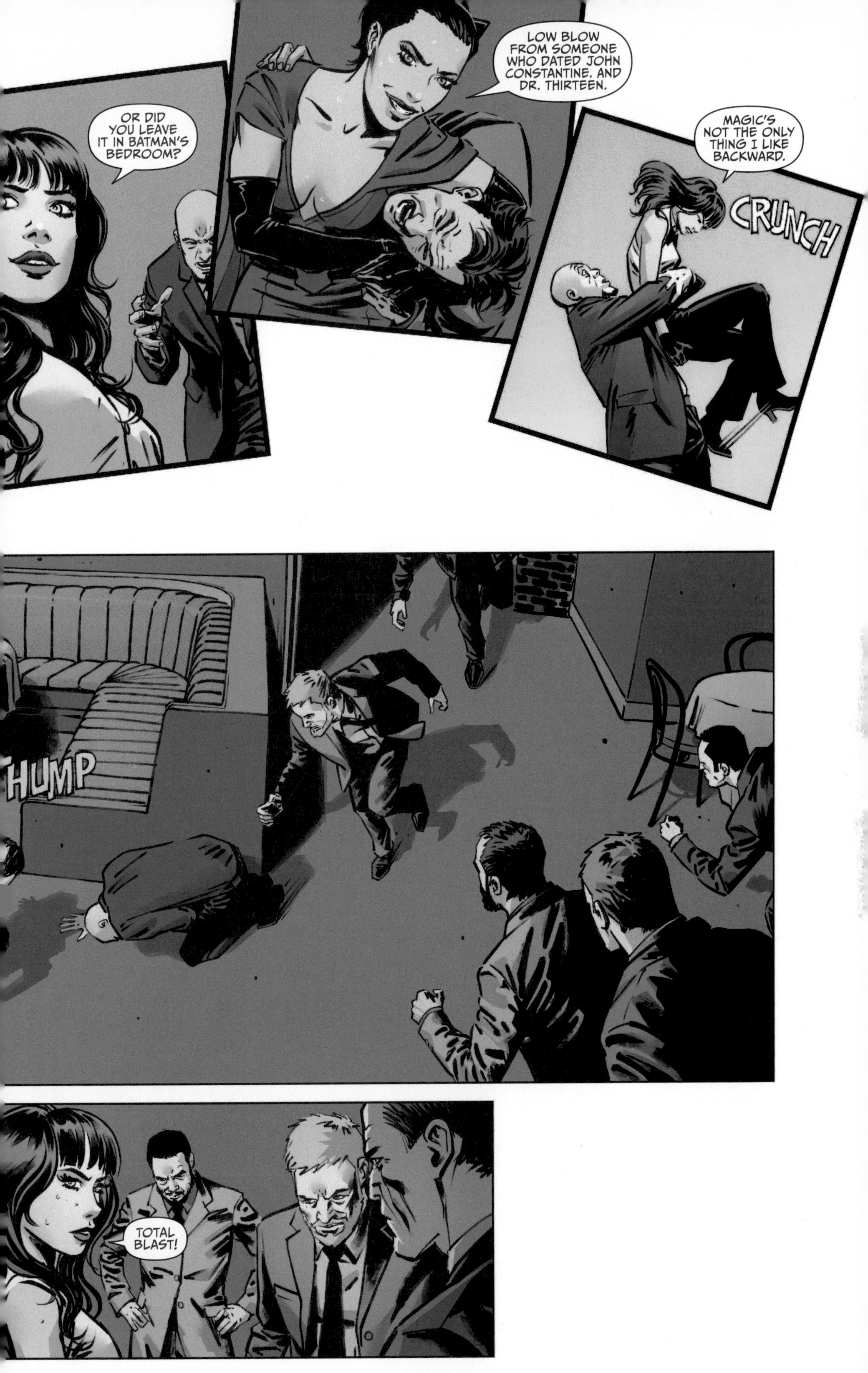
OR DID YOU LEAVE IT IN BATMAN'S BEDROOM?
LOW BLOW FROM SOMEONE WHO DATED JOHN CONSTANTINE. AND DR. THIRTEEN.
MAGIC'S NOT THE ONLY THING I LIKE BACKWARD.
CRUNCH
HUMP
TOTAL BLAST!

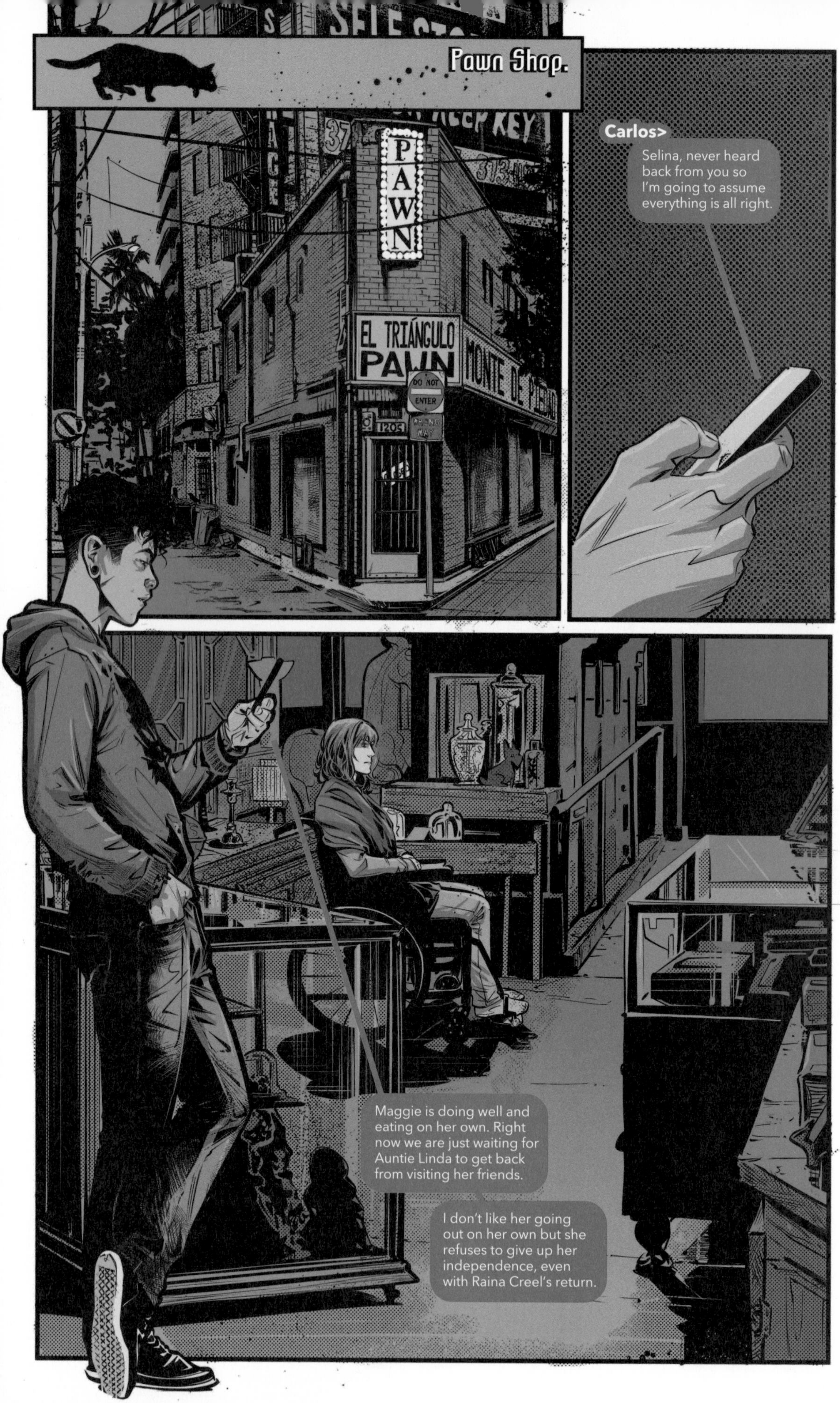
Pawn Shop.
PAWN
EL TRIÁNGULO PAWN
MONTE DE PIEDAD
DO NOT ENTER
1205
Carlos>
Selina, never heard back from you so I'm going to assume everything is all right.
Maggie is doing well and eating on her own. Right now we are just waiting for Auntie Linda to get back from visiting her friends.
I don't like her going out on her own but she refuses to give up her independence, even with Raina Creel's return.

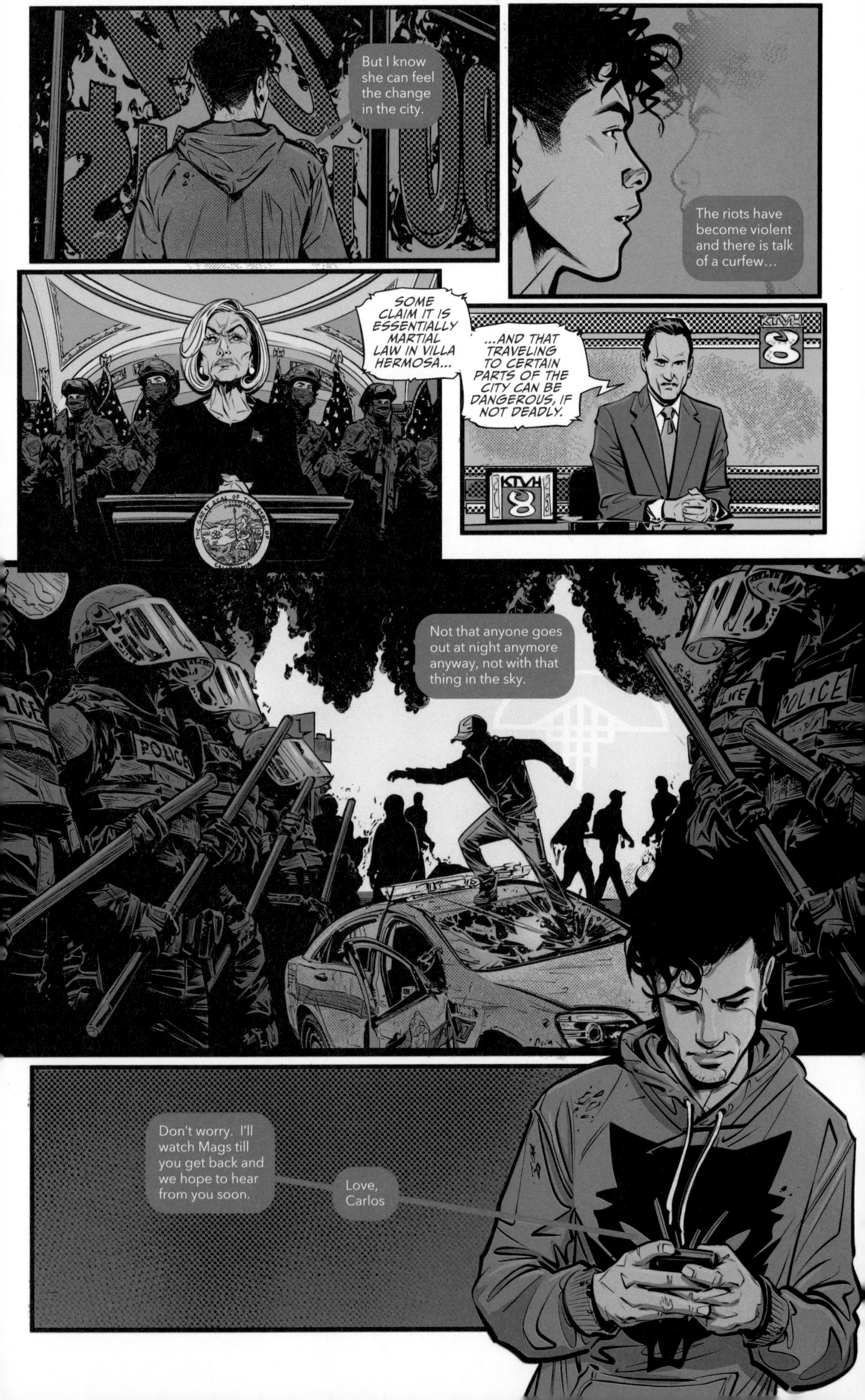
But I know she can feel the change in the city.
The riots have become violent and there is talk of a curfew...
SOME CLAIM IT IS ESSENTIALLY MARTIAL LAW IN VILLA HERMOSA...
...AND THAT TRAVELING TO CERTAIN PARTS OF THE CITY CAN BE DANGEROUS, IF NOT DEADLY.
KTVH 8
POLICE
Not that anyone goes out at night anymore anyway, not with that thing in the sky.
Don't worry. I'll watch Mags till you get back and we hope to hear from you soon.
Love, Carlos

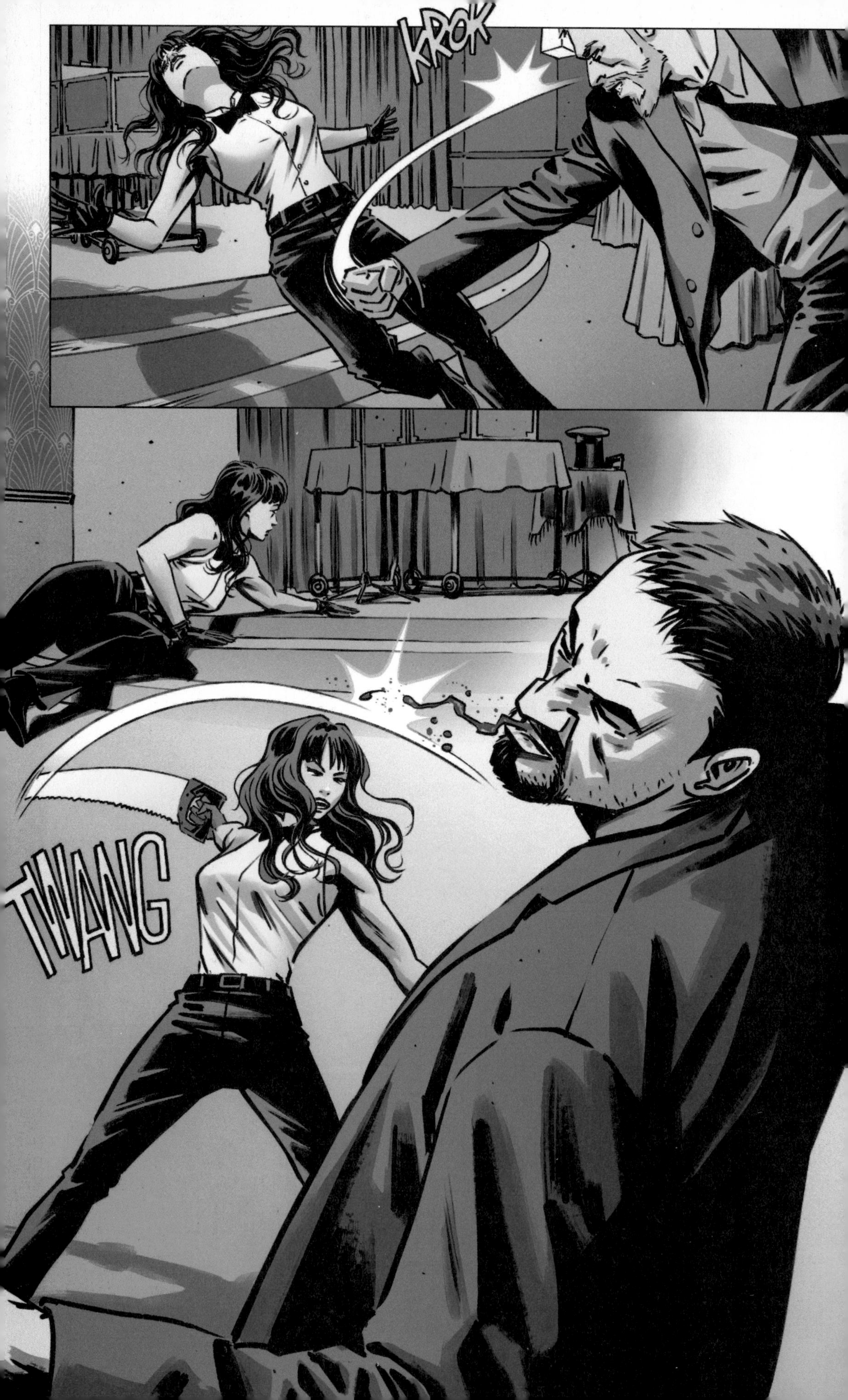
KROK
TWANG

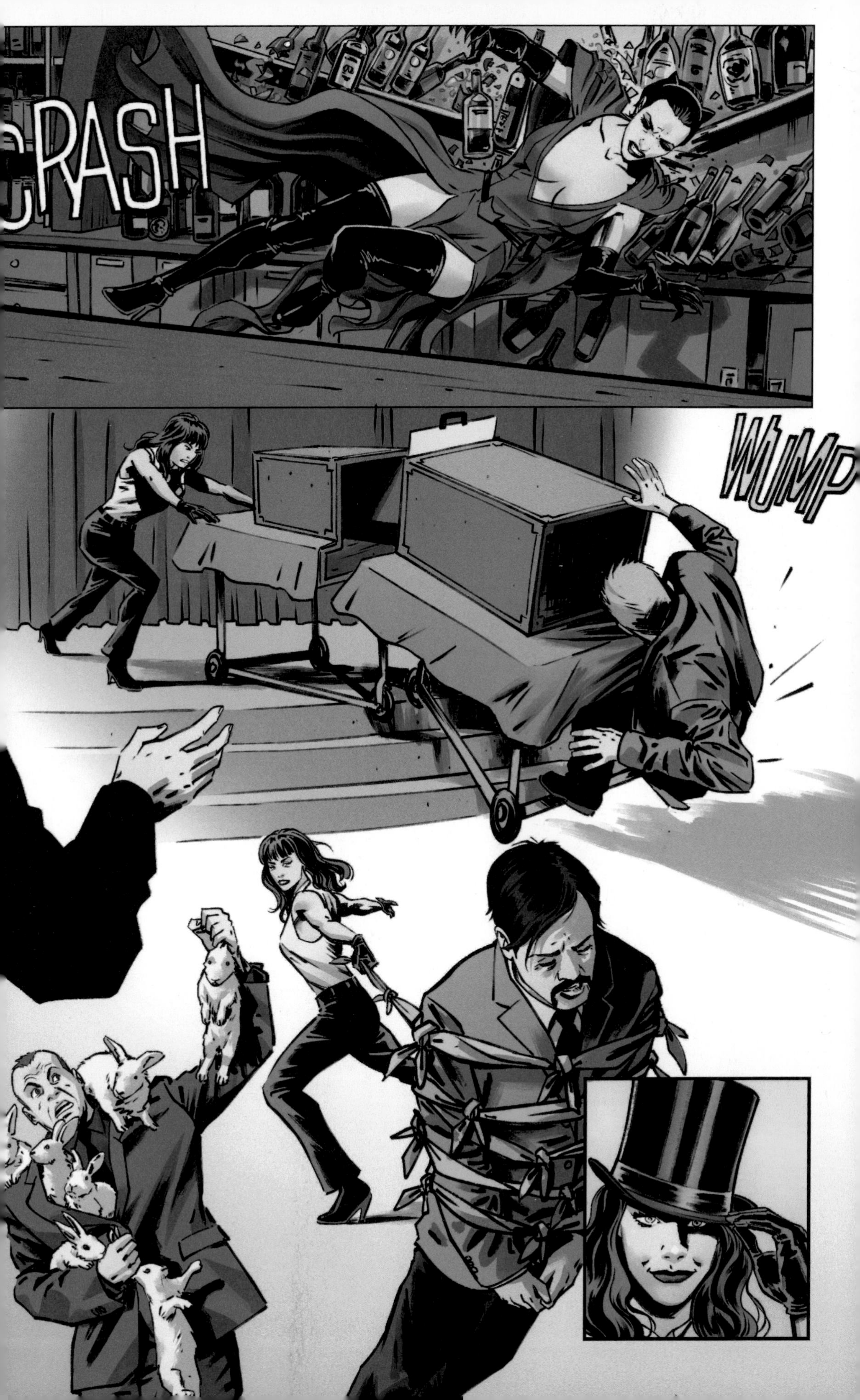
CRASH
WUMP

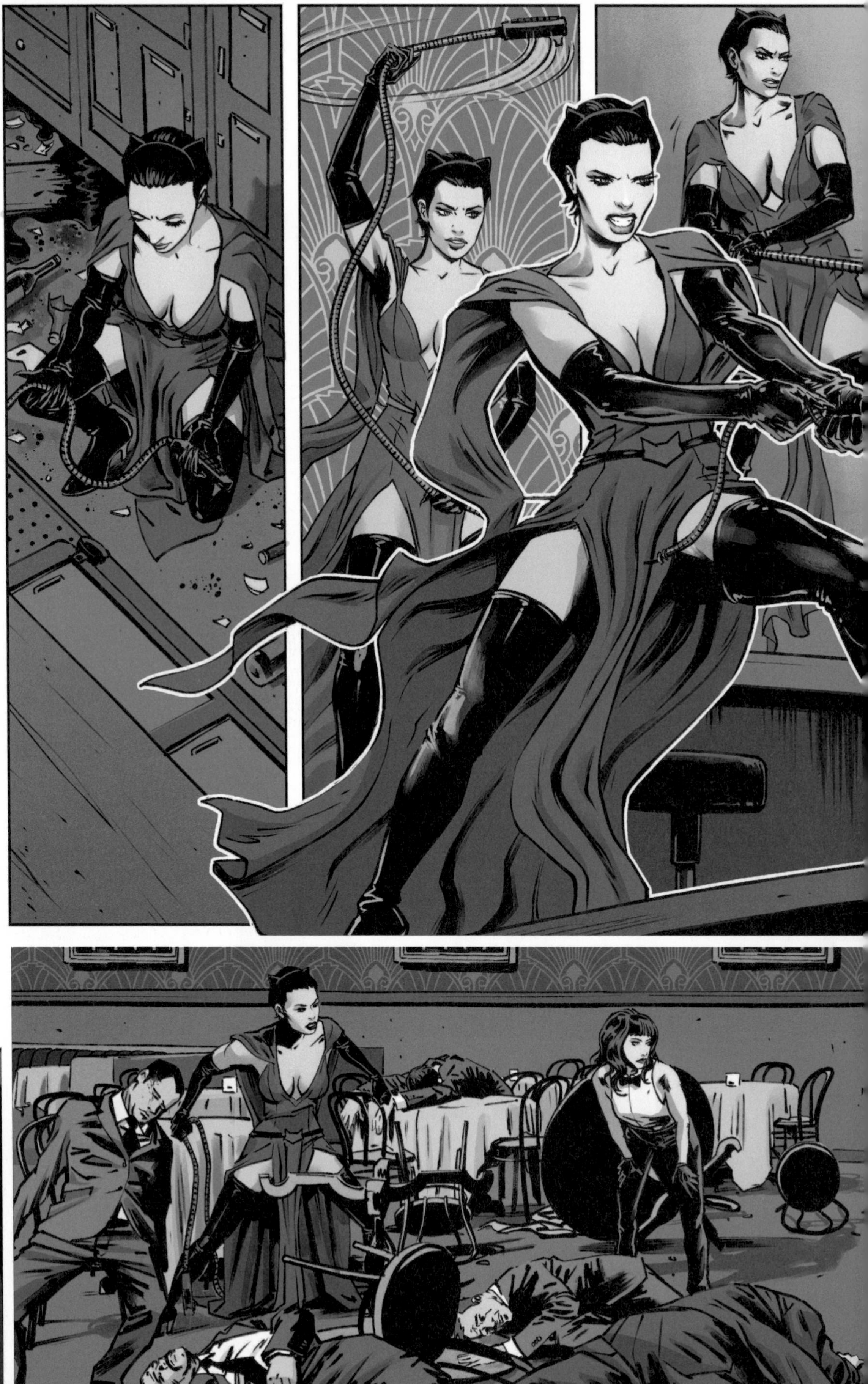

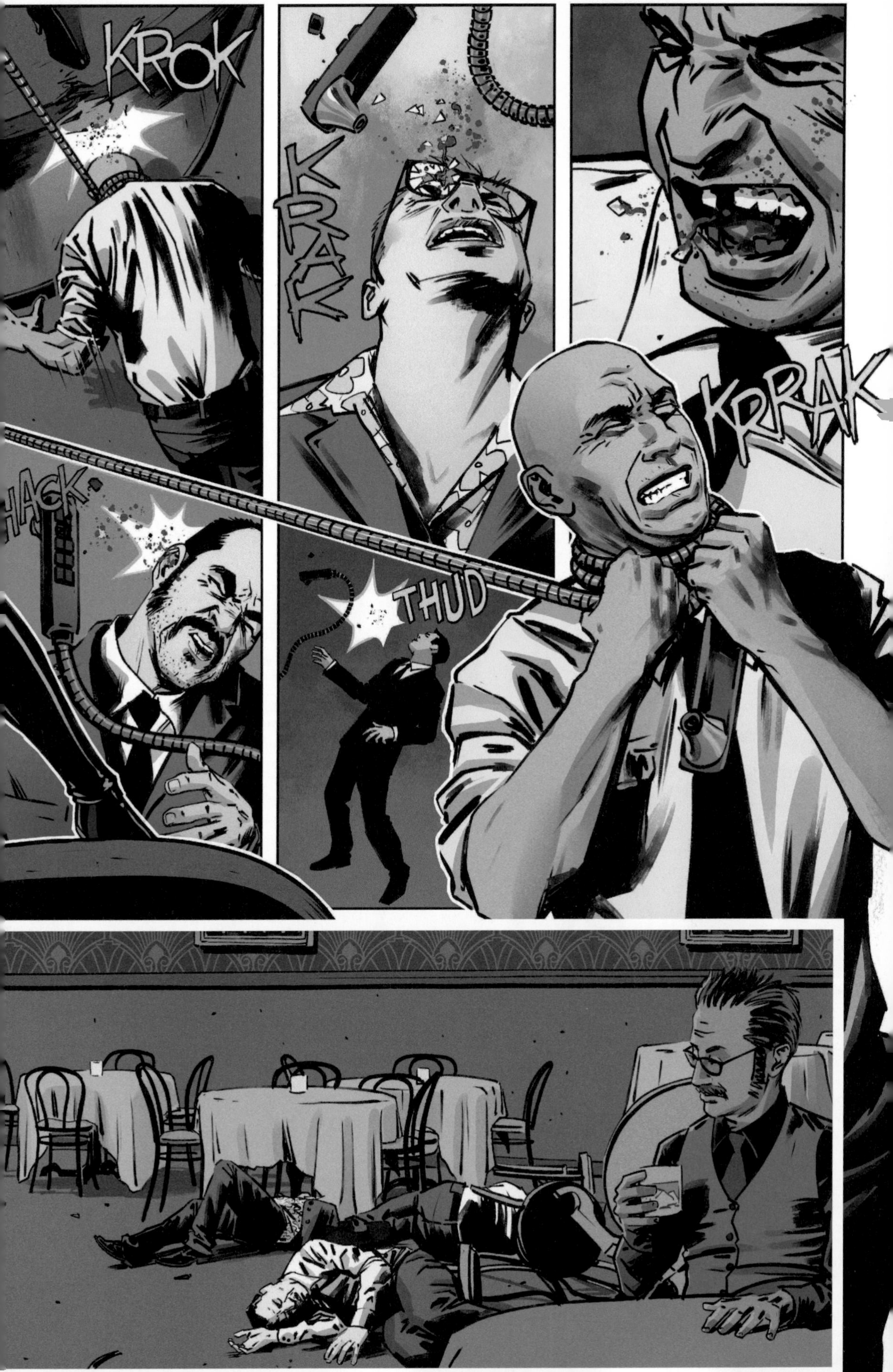
KROK
KRAK
KRRAK
HACK
THUD

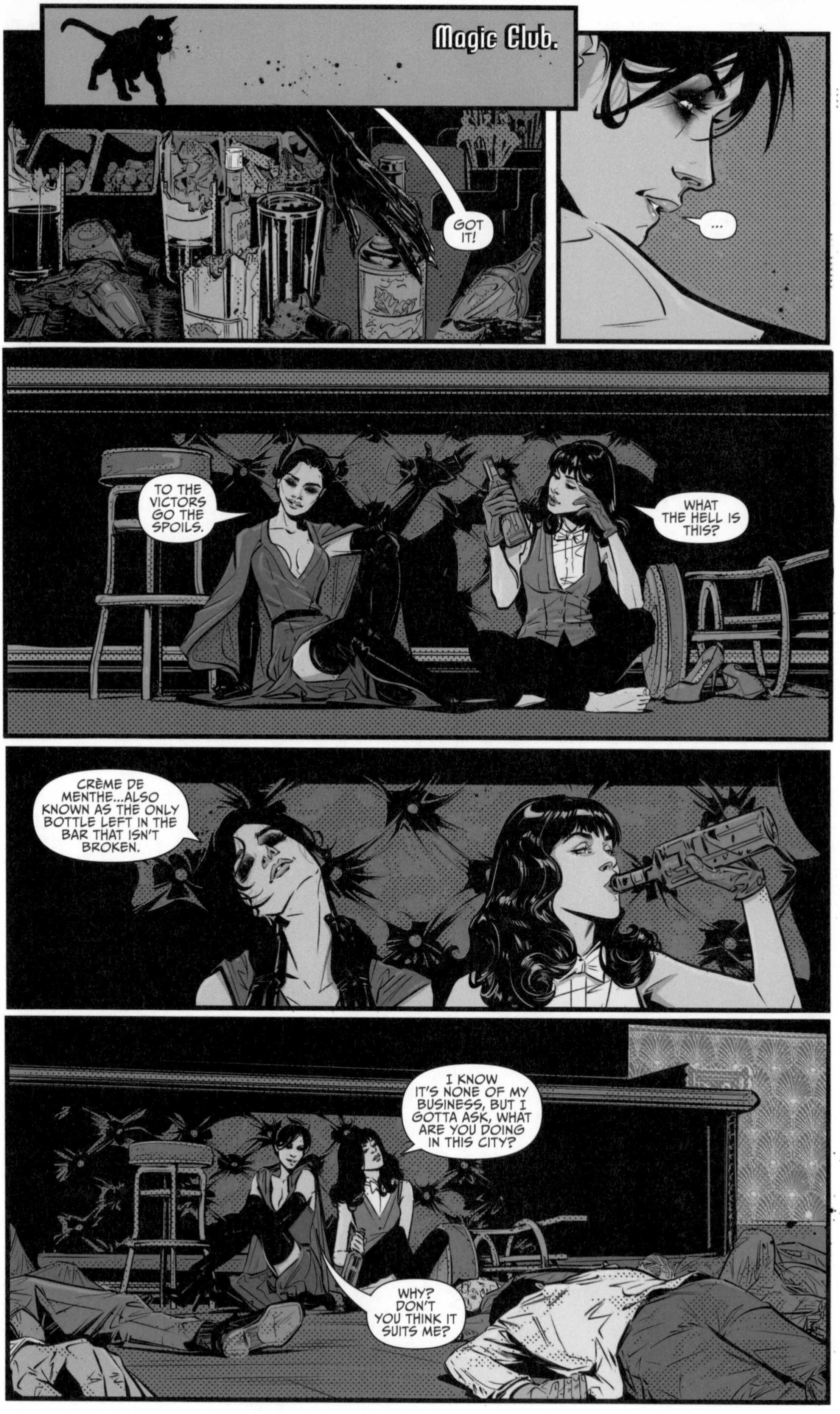
Magic Club.
GOT IT!
...
TO THE VICTORS GO THE SPOILS.
WHAT THE HELL IS THIS?
CRÈME DE MENTHE...ALSO KNOWN AS THE ONLY BOTTLE LEFT IN THE BAR THAT ISN'T BROKEN.
I KNOW IT'S NONE OF MY BUSINESS, BUT I GOTTA ASK, WHAT ARE YOU DOING IN THIS CITY?
WHY? DON'T YOU THINK IT SUITS ME?

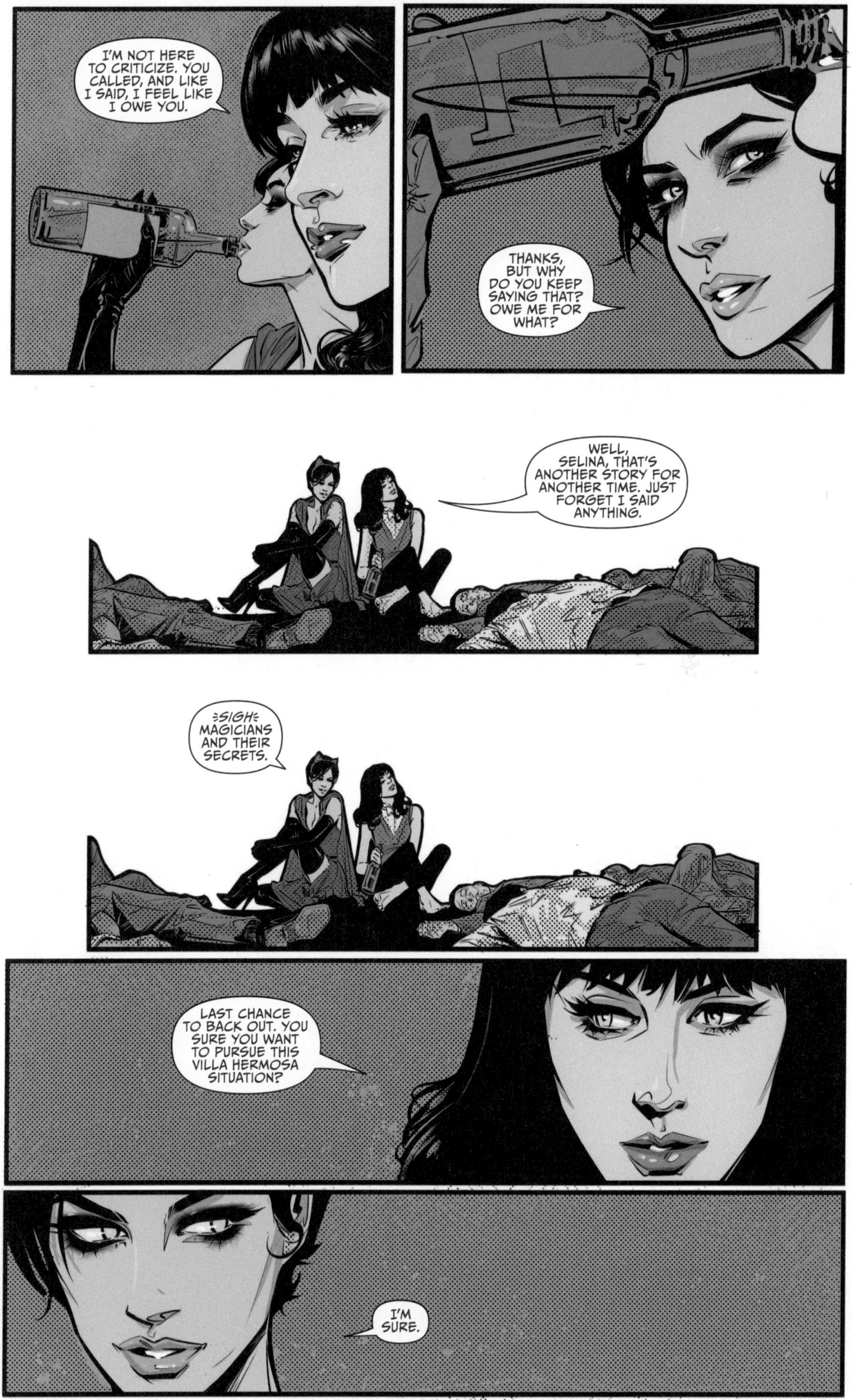
I'M NOT HERE TO CRITICIZE. YOU CALLED, AND LIKE I SAID, I FEEL LIKE I OWE YOU.
THANKS, BUT WHY DO YOU KEEP SAYING THAT? OWE ME FOR WHAT?
WELL, SELINA, THAT'S ANOTHER STORY FOR ANOTHER TIME. JUST FORGET I SAID ANYTHING.
SIGH
MAGICIANS AND THEIR SECRETS.
LAST CHANCE TO BACK OUT. YOU SURE YOU WANT TO PURSUE THIS VILLA HERMOSA SITUATION?
I'M SURE.

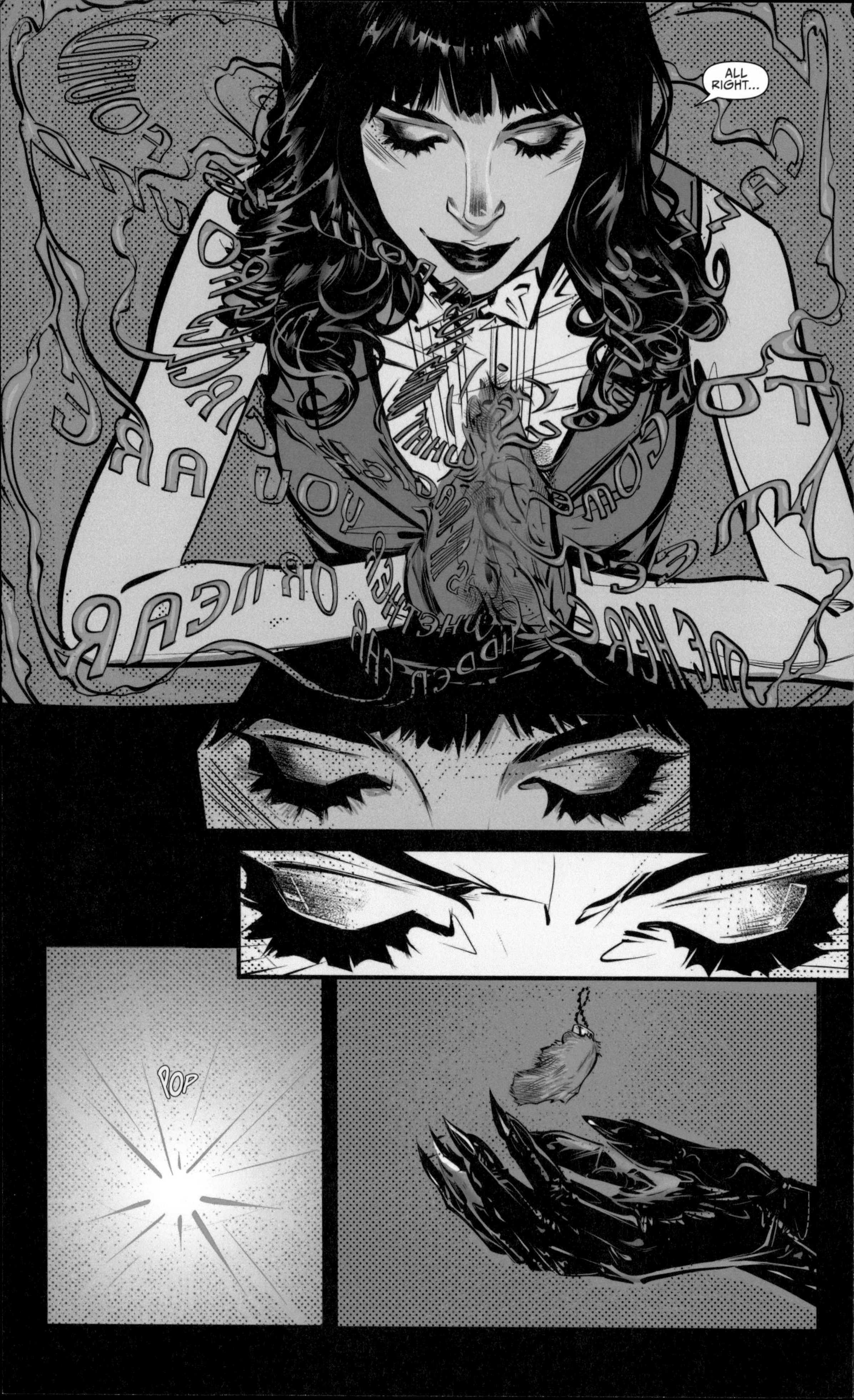
ALL RIGHT...
POP

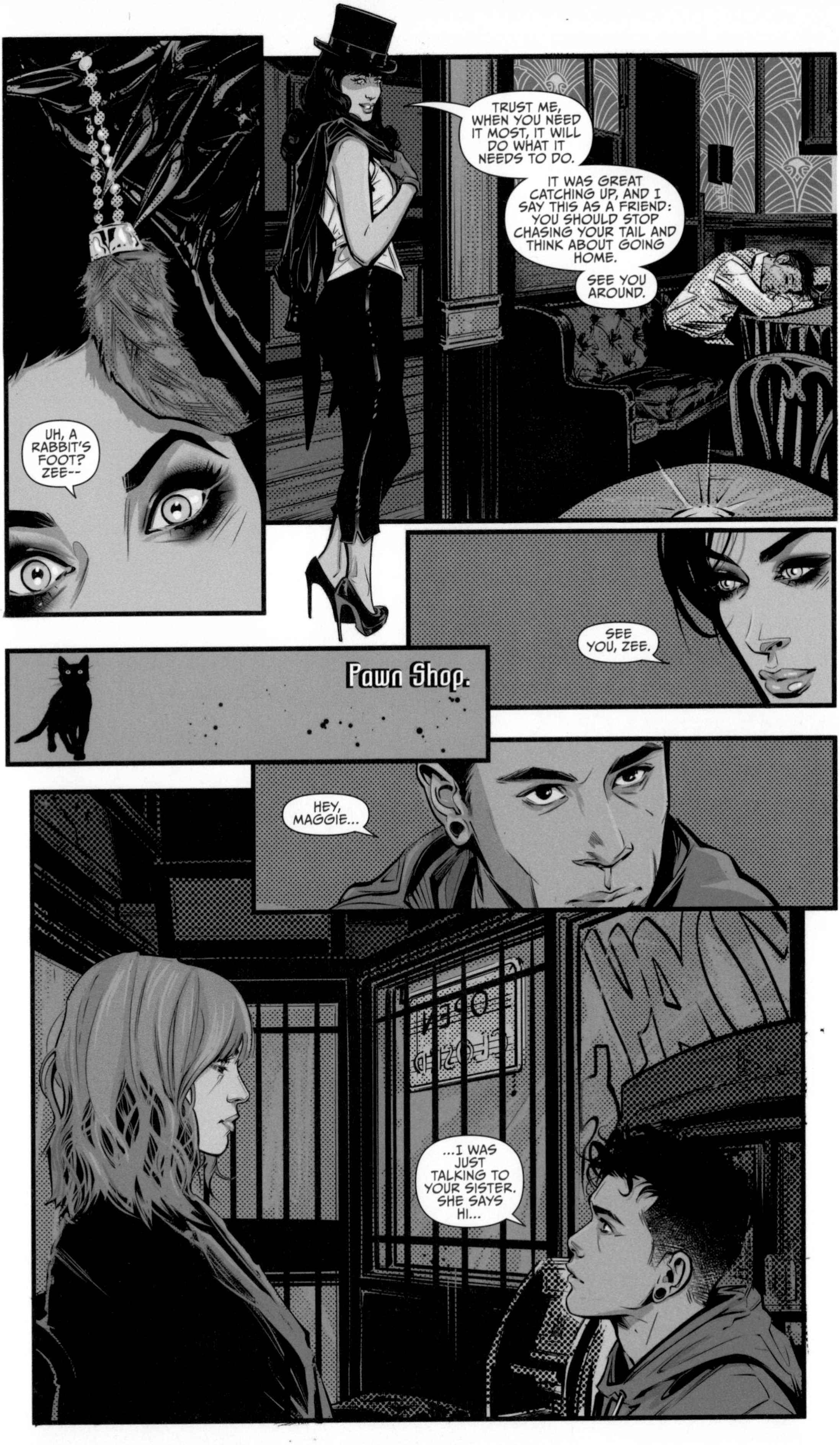
UH, A RABBIT'S FOOT? ZEE--
TRUST ME, WHEN YOU NEED IT MOST, IT WILL DO WHAT IT NEEDS TO DO.
IT WAS GREAT CATCHING UP, AND I SAY THIS AS A FRIEND: YOU SHOULD STOP CHASING YOUR TAIL AND THINK ABOUT GOING HOME.
SEE YOU AROUND.
SEE YOU, ZEE.
Pawn Shop.
HEY, MAGGIE...
...I WAS JUST TALKING TO YOUR SISTER. SHE SAYS HI...

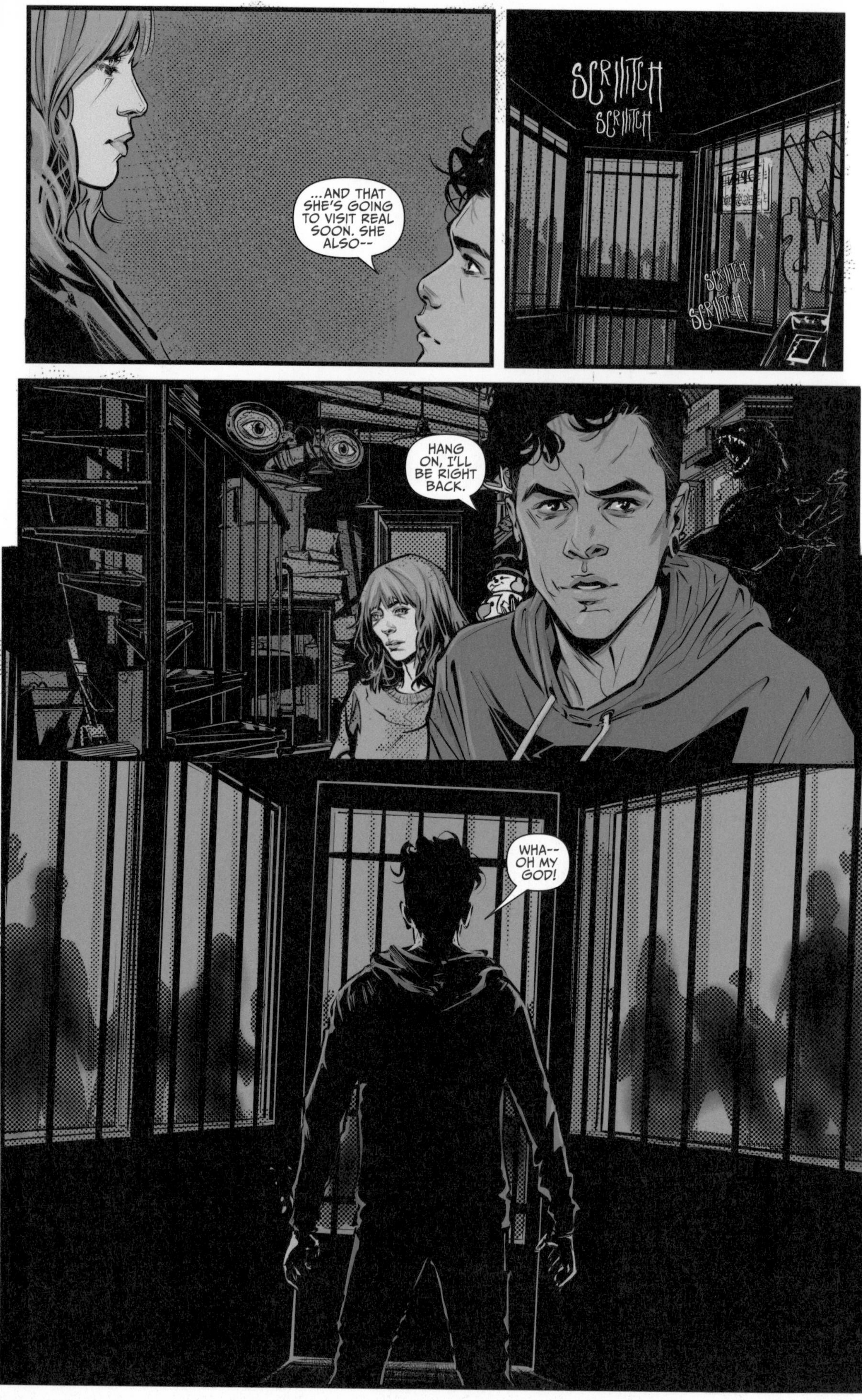
...AND THAT SHE'S GOING TO VISIT REAL SOON. SHE ALSO--
SCRIITCH
SCRIITCH
SCRIITCH
SCRIITCH
HANG ON, I'LL BE RIGHT BACK.
WHA--
OH MY GOD!

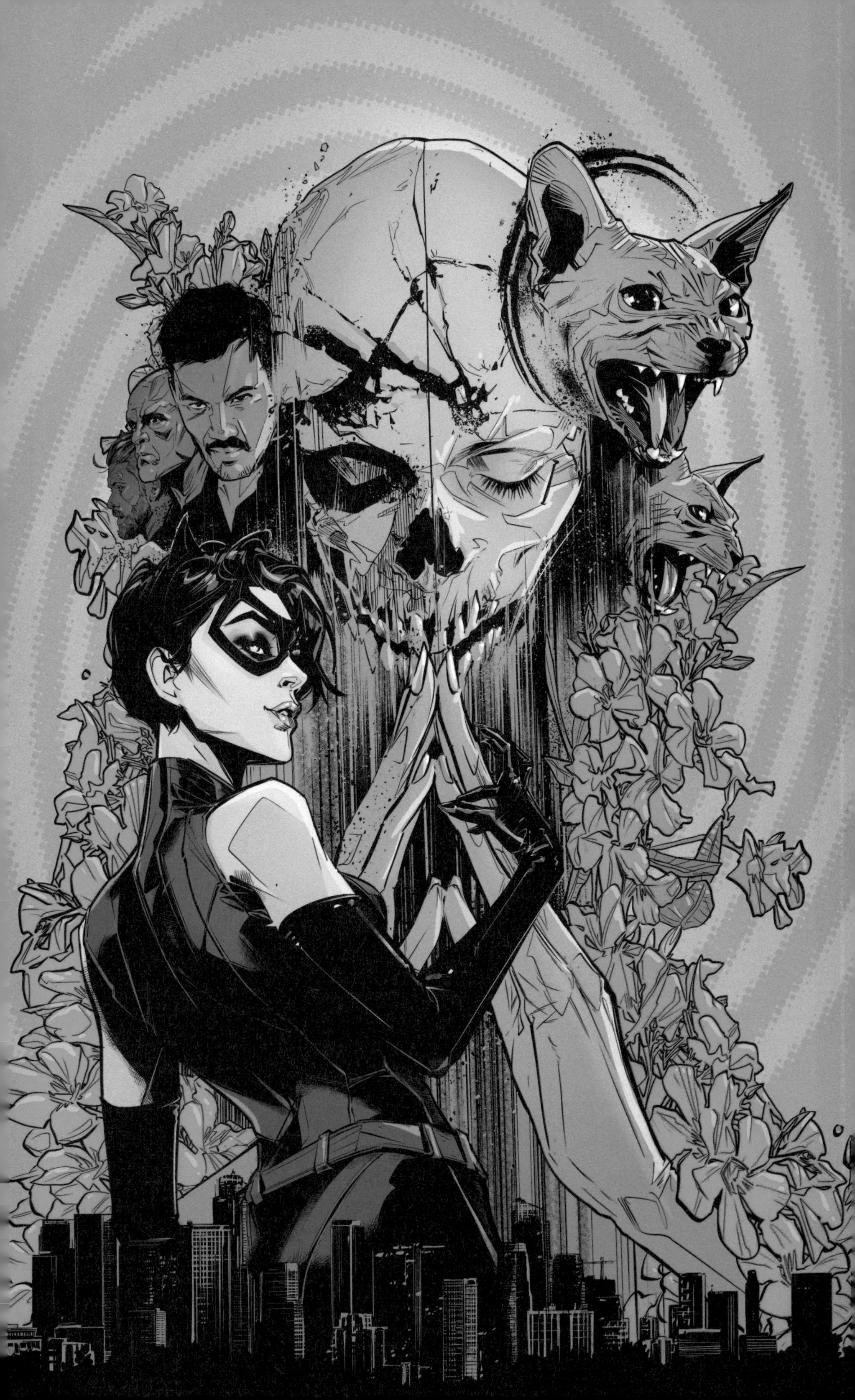

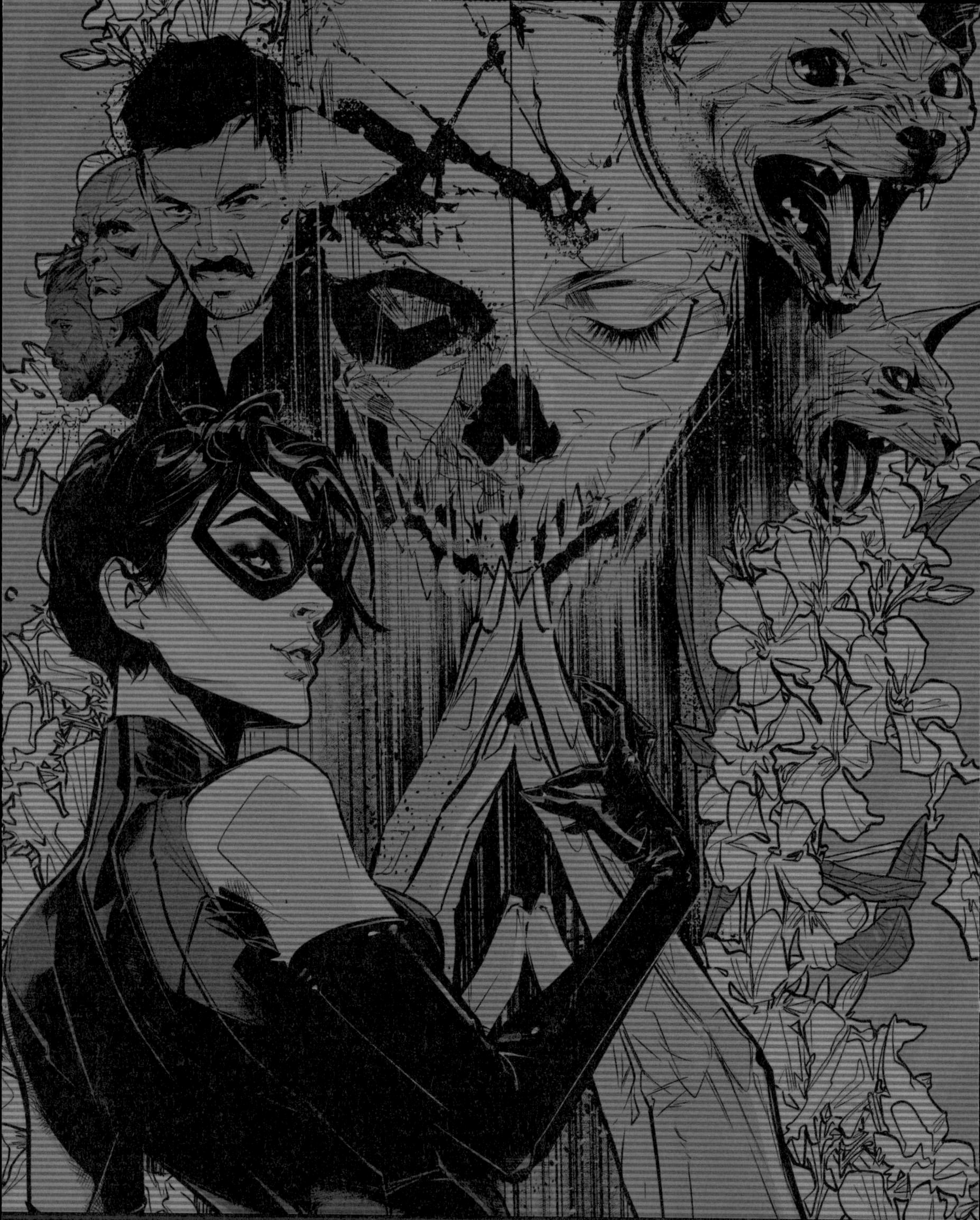

CATWOMAN

#19

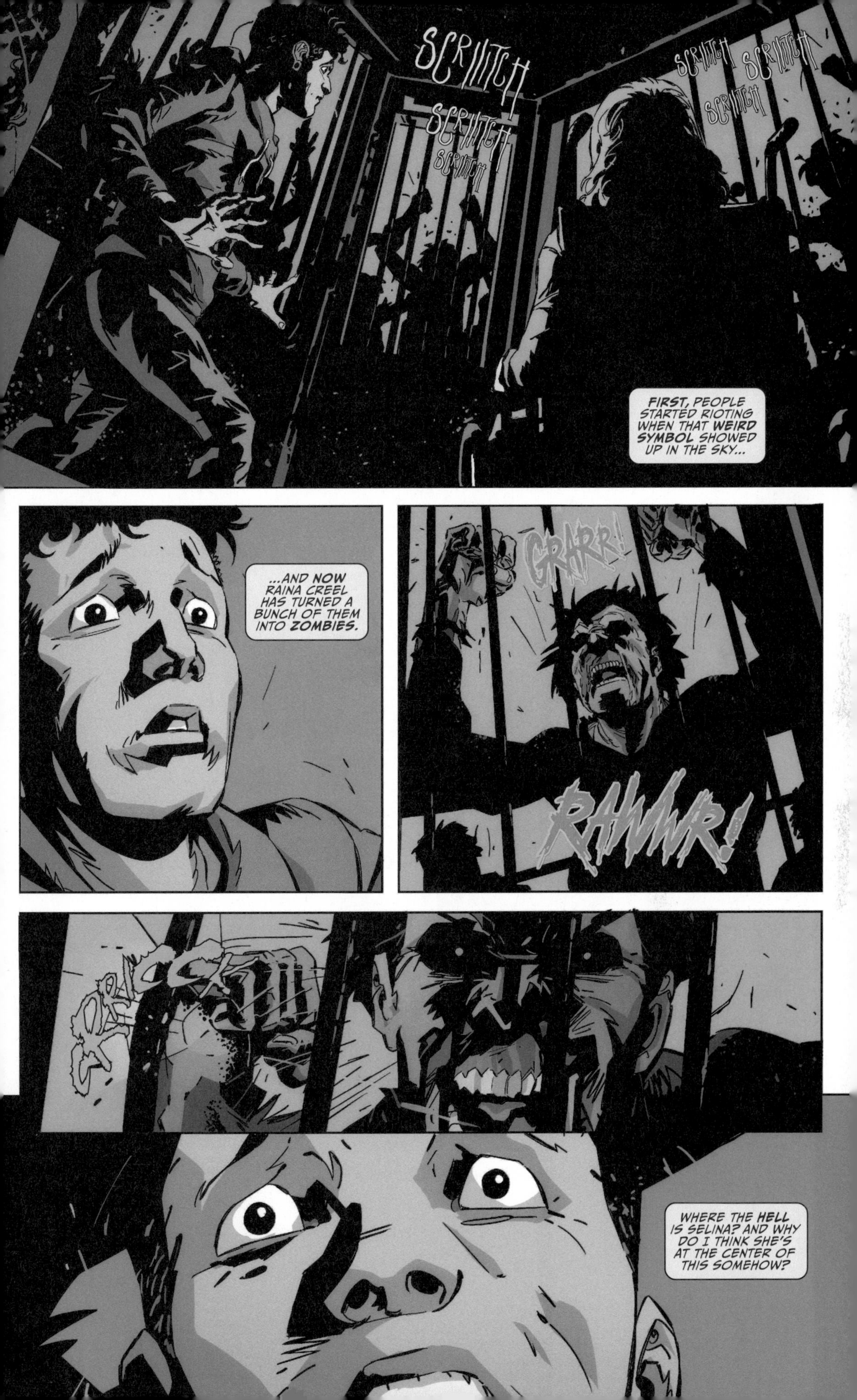
SCRITCH
SCRITCH
SCRITCH
SCRITCH
SCRITCH
SCRITCH
FIRST, PEOPLE STARTED RIOTING WHEN THAT WEIRD SYMBOL SHOWED UP IN THE SKY...
...AND NOW RAINA CREEL HAS TURNED A BUNCH OF THEM INTO ZOMBIES.
GRARR!
RAWWR!
WHERE THE HELL IS SELINA? AND WHY DO I THINK SHE'S AT THE CENTER OF THIS SOMEHOW?

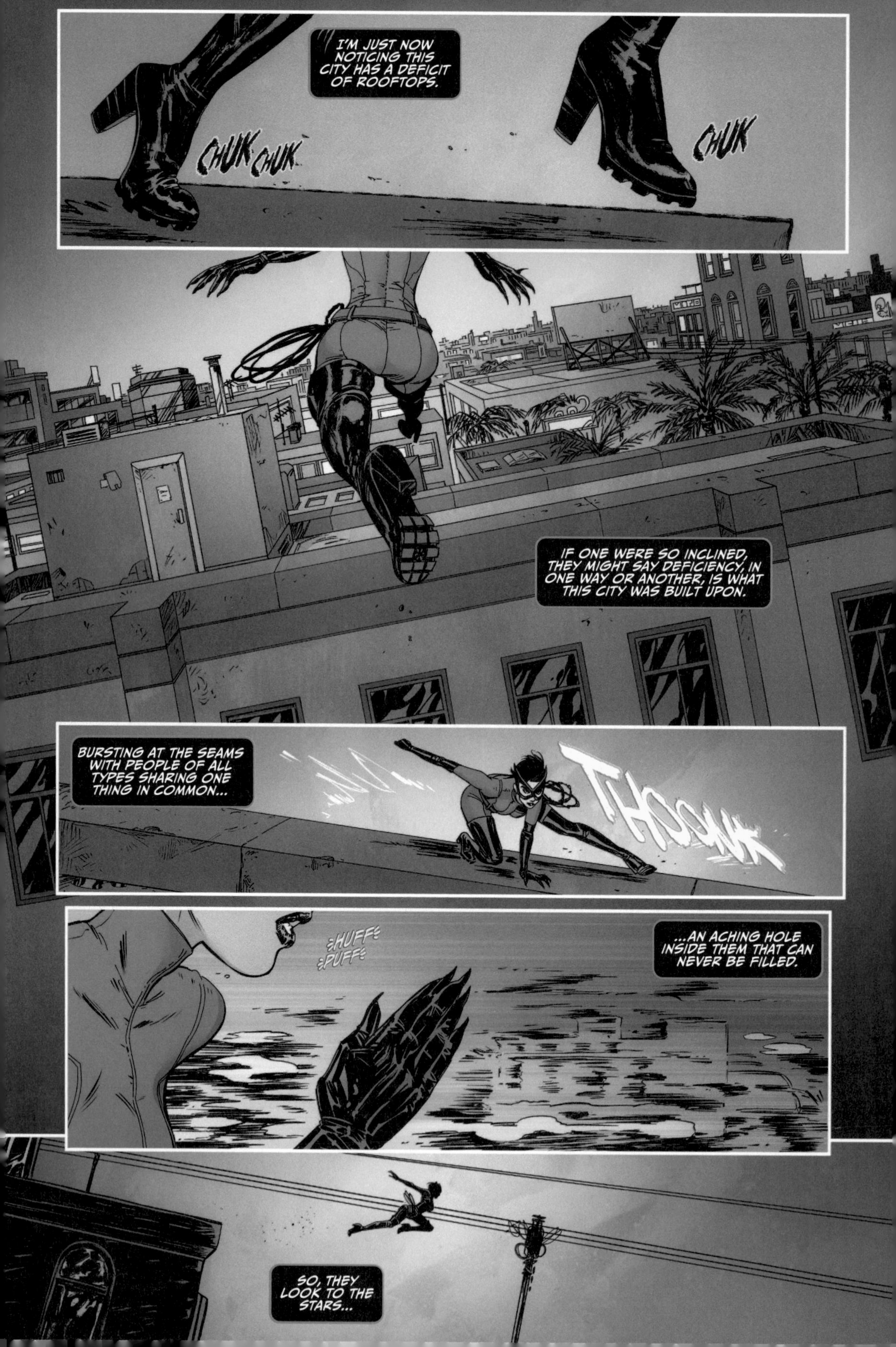
I'M JUST NOW NOTICING THIS CITY HAS A DEFICIT OF ROOFTOPS.
CHUK CHUK
CHUK
IF ONE WERE SO INCLINED, THEY MIGHT SAY DEFICIENCY, IN ONE WAY OR ANOTHER, IS WHAT THIS CITY WAS BUILT UPON.
BURSTING AT THE SEAMS WITH PEOPLE OF ALL TYPES SHARING ONE THING IN COMMON...
THOOMK
HUFF
PUFF
...AN ACHING HOLE INSIDE THEM THAT CAN NEVER BE FILLED.
SO, THEY LOOK TO THE STARS...

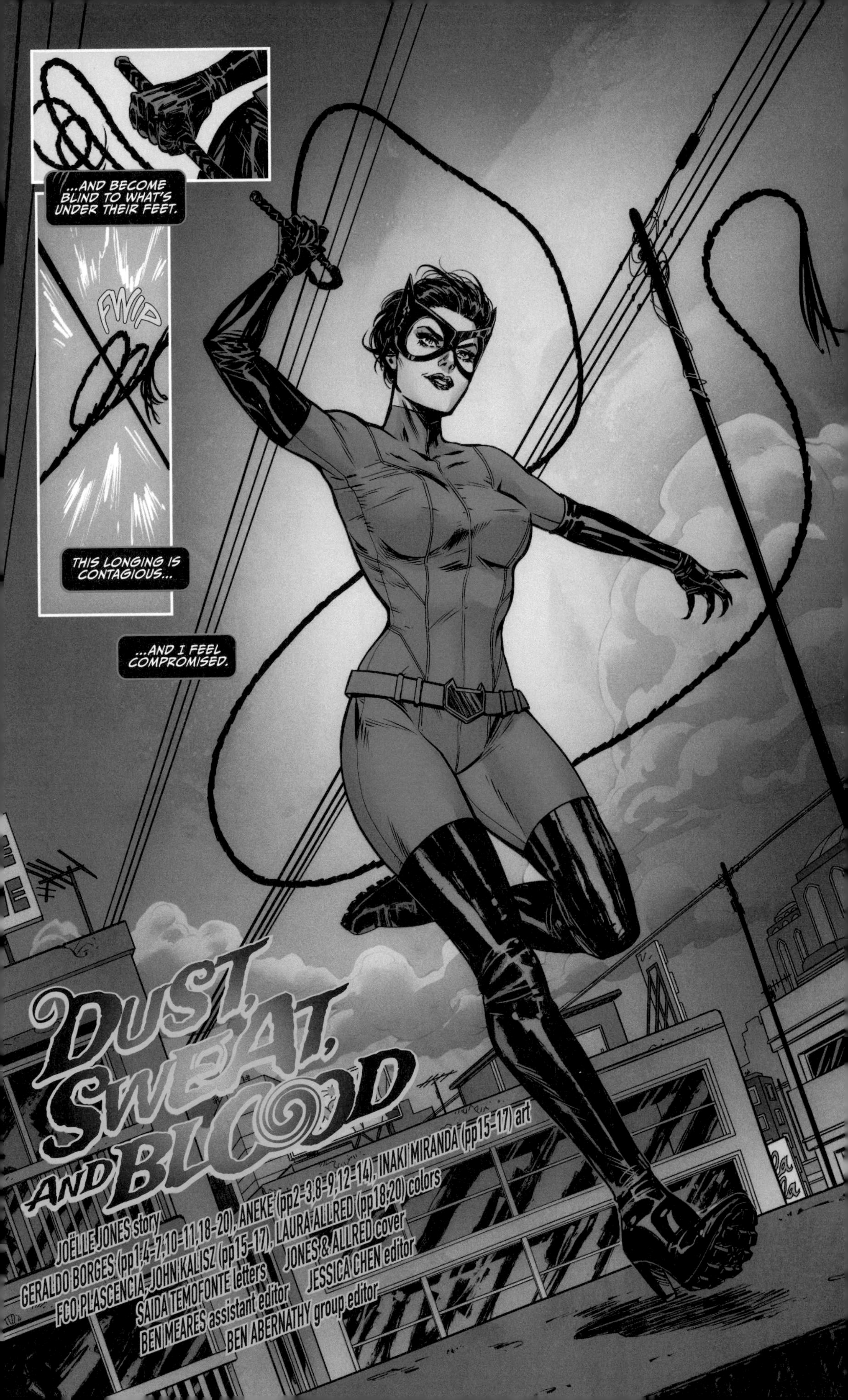
...AND BECOME BLIND TO WHAT'S UNDER THEIR FEET.
FWIP
THIS LONGING IS CONTAGIOUS...
...AND I FEEL COMPROMISED.
DUST, SWEAT, AND BLOOD
JOËLLE JONES story
GERALDO BORGES (pp1,4-7,10-11,18-20), ANEKE (pp2-3,8-9,12-14), INAKI MIRANDA (pp15-17) art
FCO PLASCENCIA, JOHN KALISZ (pp15-17), LAURA ALLRED (pp18,20) colors
SAIDA TEMOFONTE letters
JONES & ALLRED cover
BEN MEARES assistant editor
JESSICA CHEN editor
BEN ABERNATHY group editor

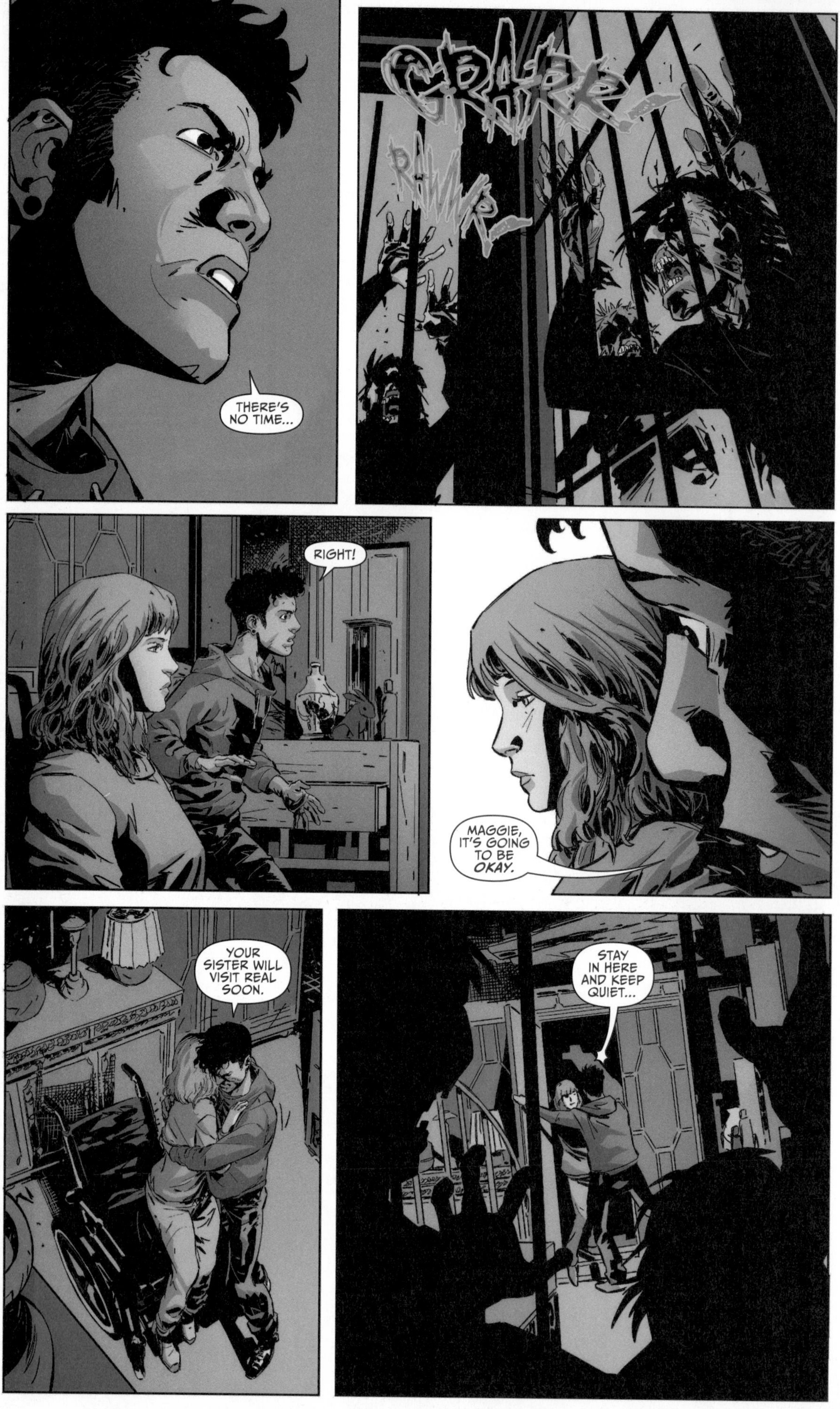
THERE'S NO TIME...
GRAAA
RAWWR
RIGHT!
MAGGIE, IT'S GOING TO BE *OKAY.*
YOUR SISTER WILL VISIT REAL SOON.
STAY IN HERE AND KEEP QUIET...

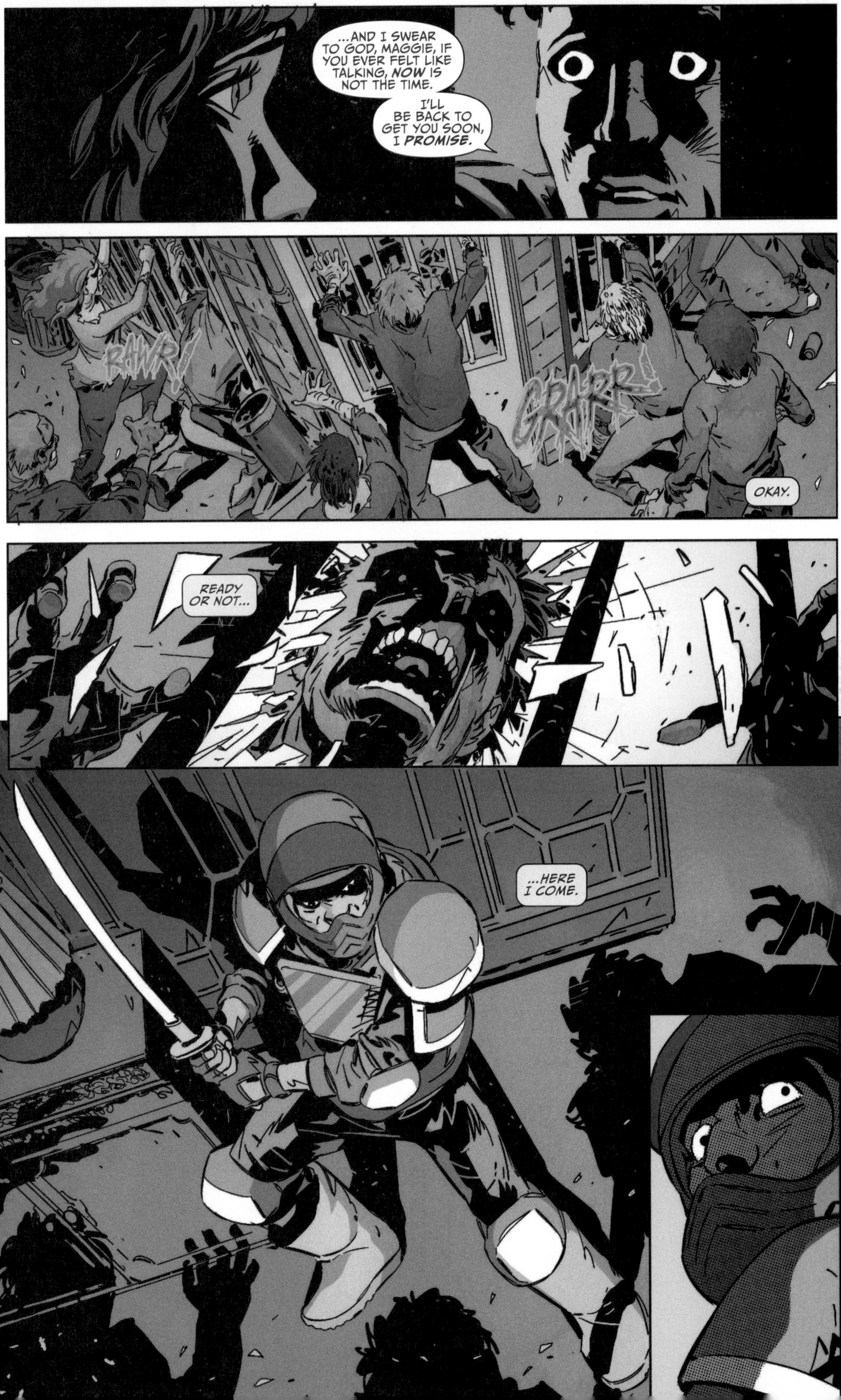
...AND I SWEAR TO GOD, MAGGIE, IF YOU EVER FELT LIKE TALKING, NOW IS NOT THE TIME.
I'LL BE BACK TO GET YOU SOON, I PROMISE.
RAWR!
GRAARR!
OKAY.
READY OR NOT...
...HERE I COME.

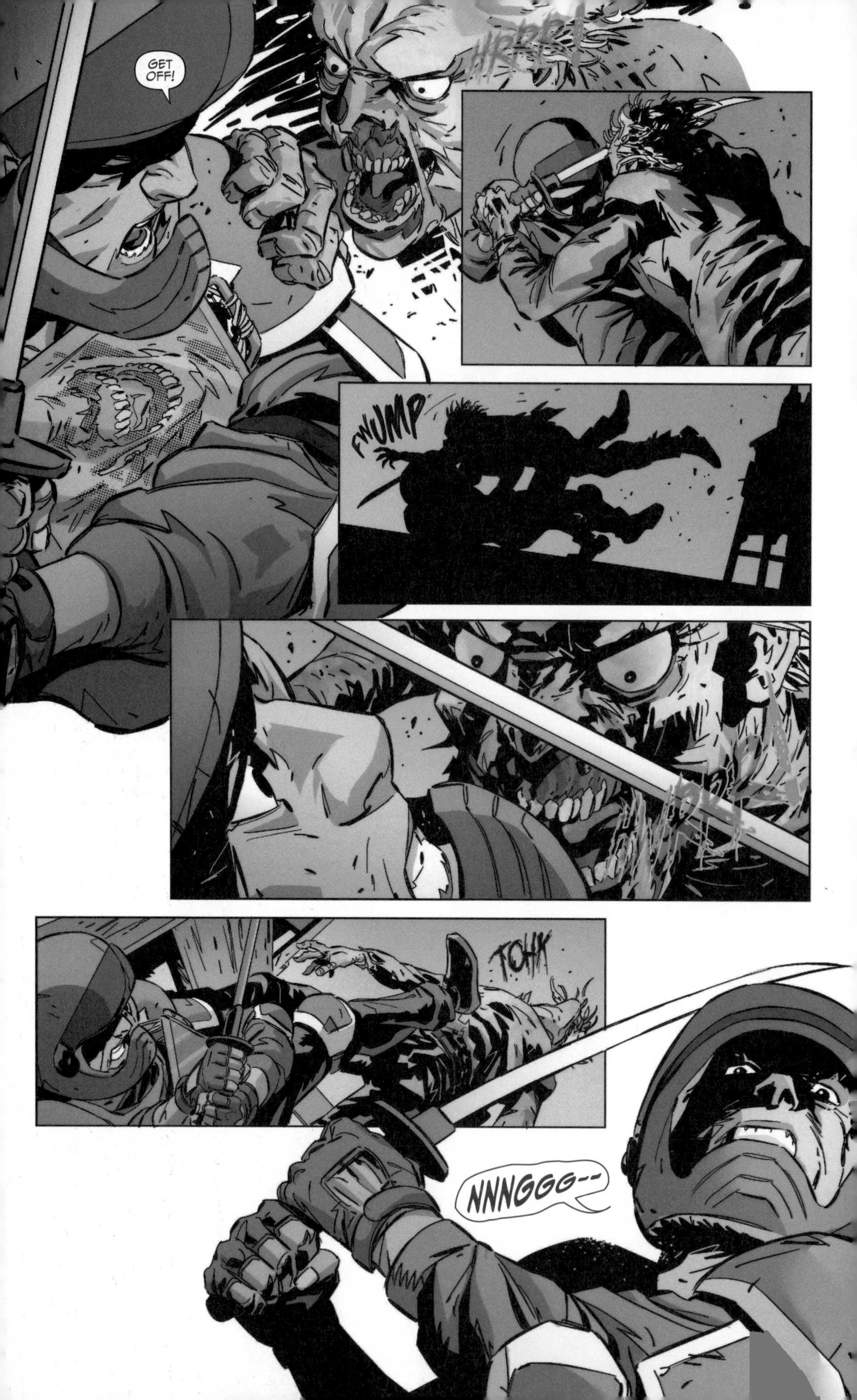
GET OFF!
HRRR!
FWUMP
TCHK
NNNGGG--

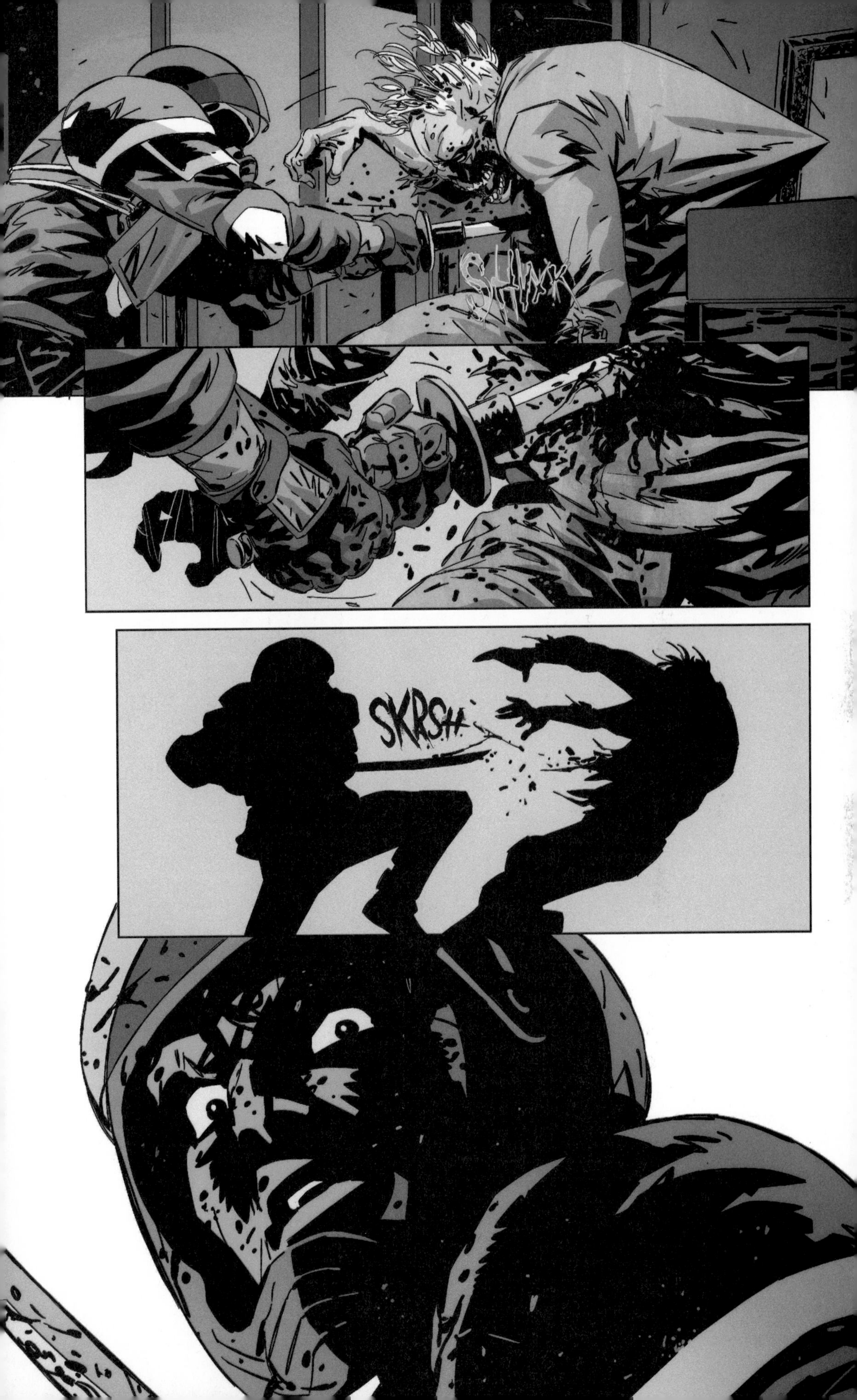
SHINK
SKRSH

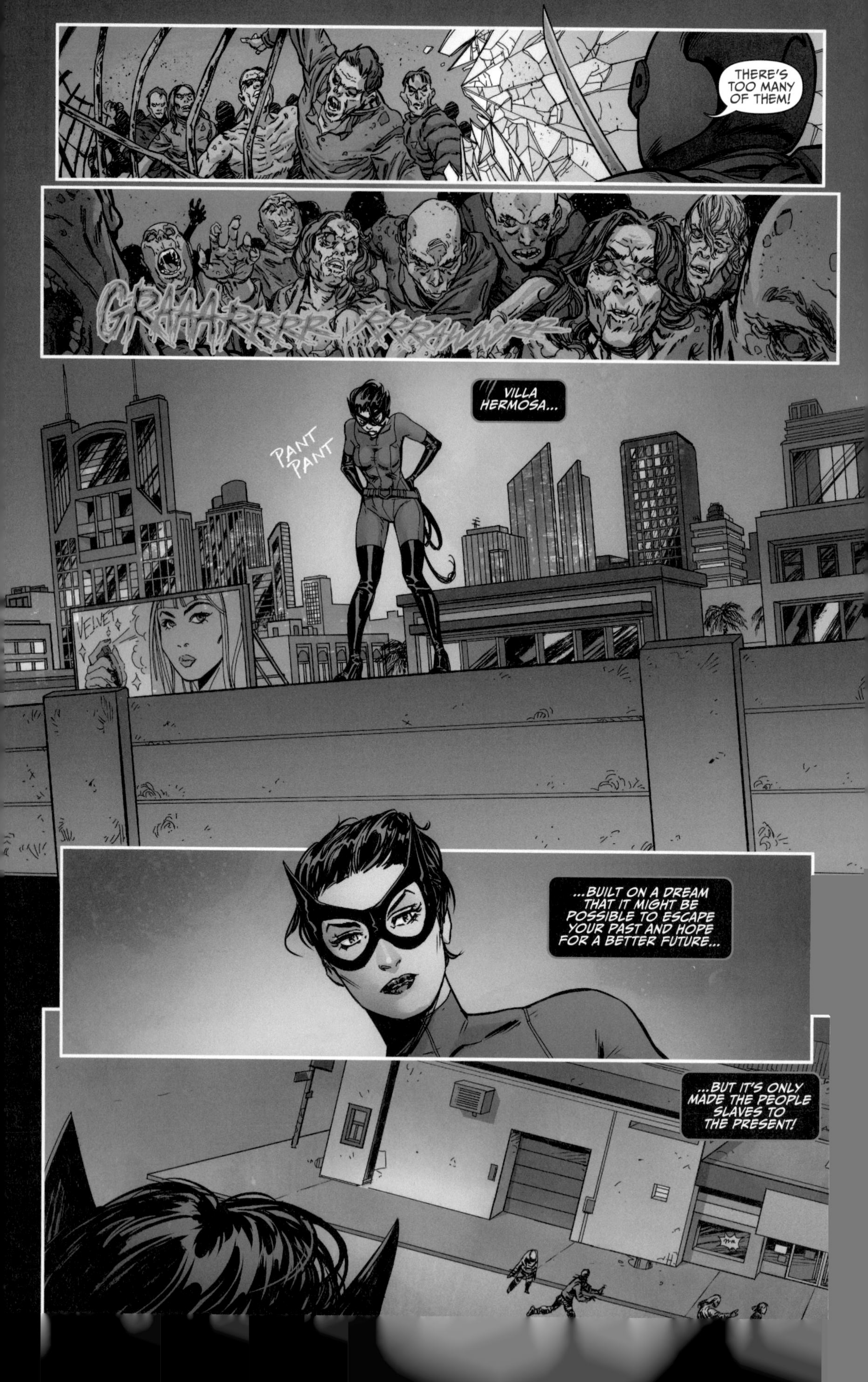
THERE'S TOO MANY OF THEM!
GRAAARRRR
RRRAWWRR
VILLA HERMOSA...
PANT PANT
VELVET
...BUILT ON A DREAM THAT IT MIGHT BE POSSIBLE TO ESCAPE YOUR PAST AND HOPE FOR A BETTER FUTURE...
...BUT IT'S ONLY MADE THE PEOPLE SLAVES TO THE PRESENT!

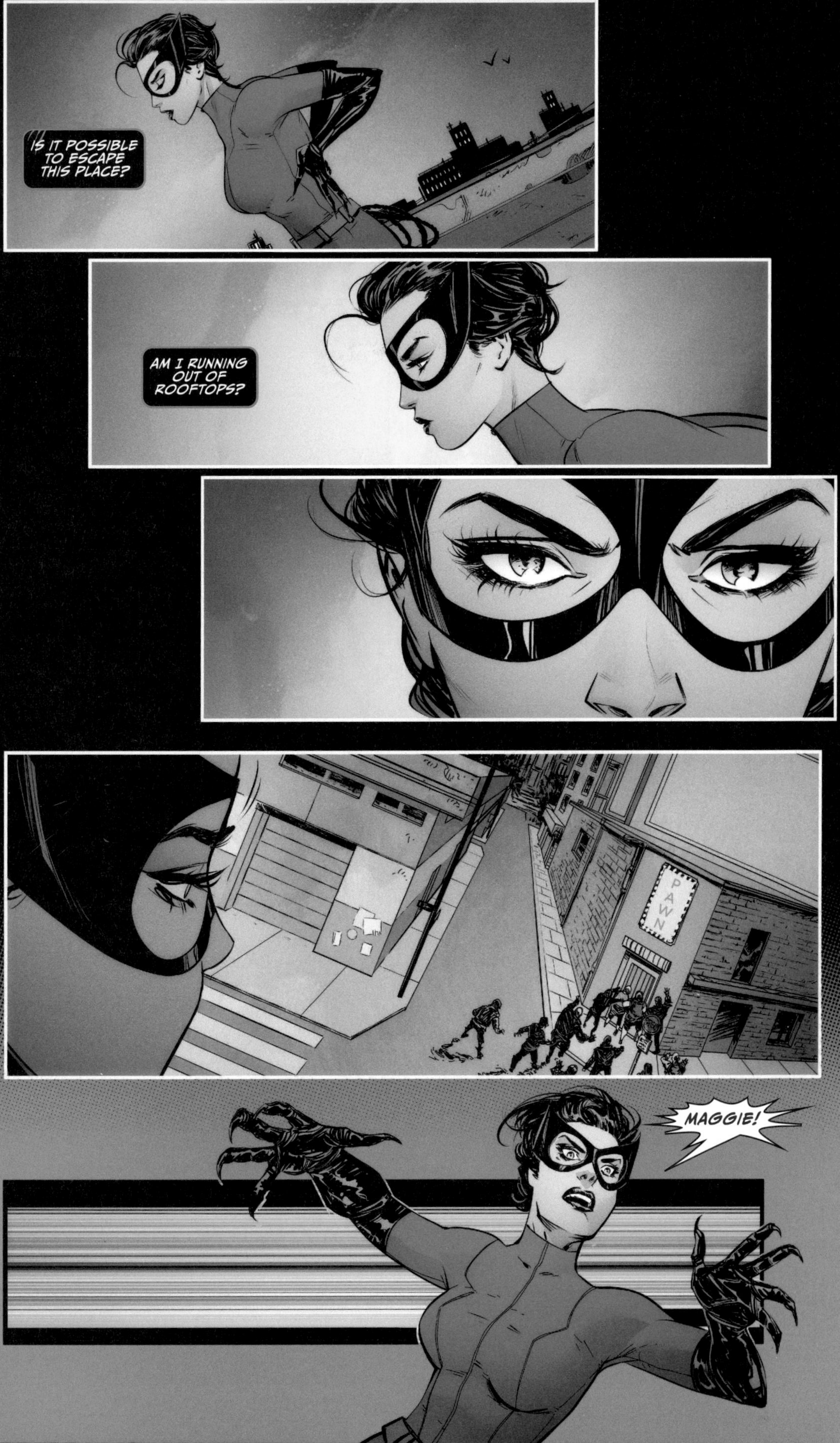
IS IT POSSIBLE TO ESCAPE THIS PLACE?
AM I RUNNING OUT OF ROOFTOPS?
PAWN
MAGGIE!

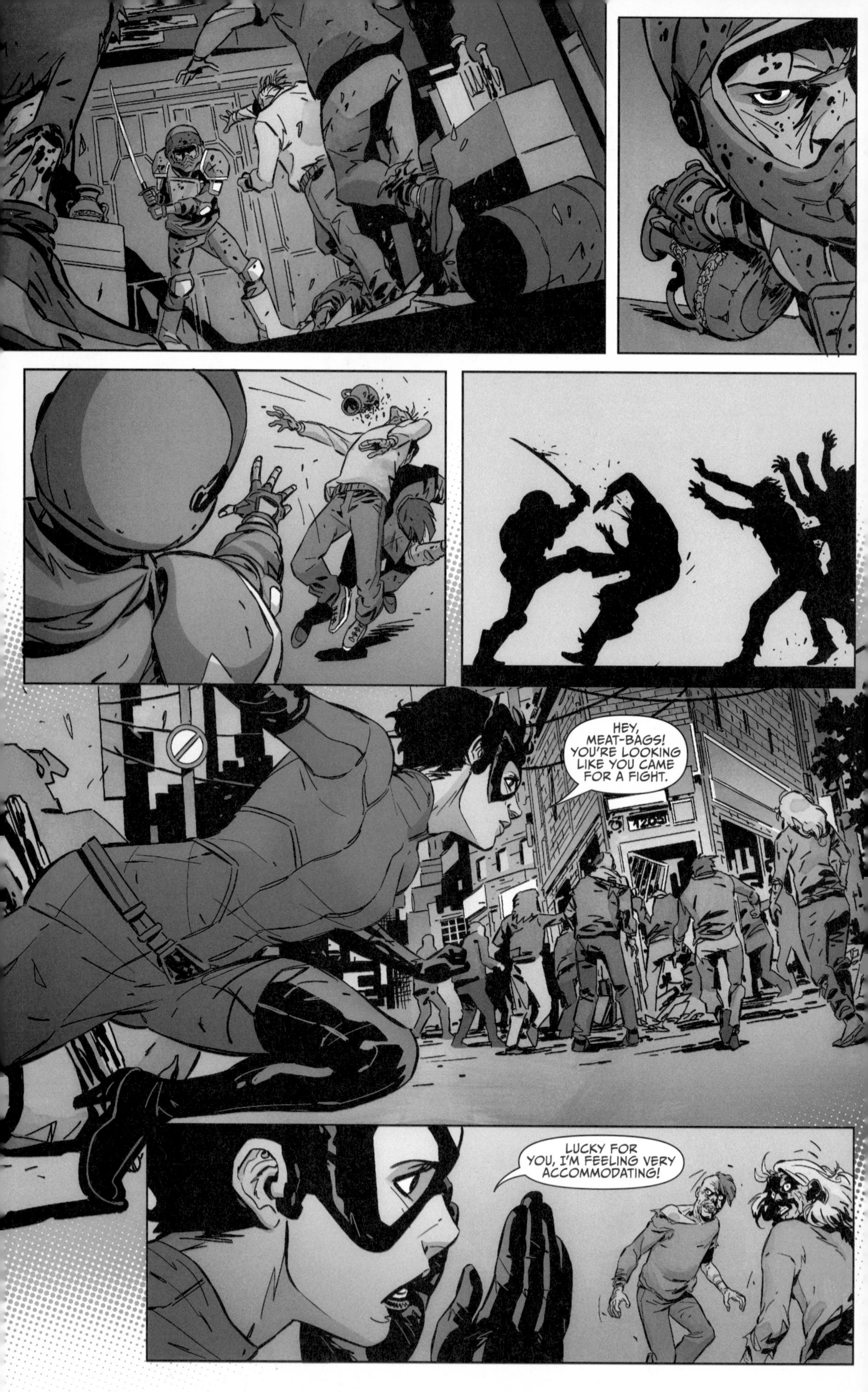
HEY, MEAT-BAGS! YOU'RE LOOKING LIKE YOU CAME FOR A FIGHT.
1205
LUCKY FOR YOU, I'M FEELING VERY ACCOMMODATING!

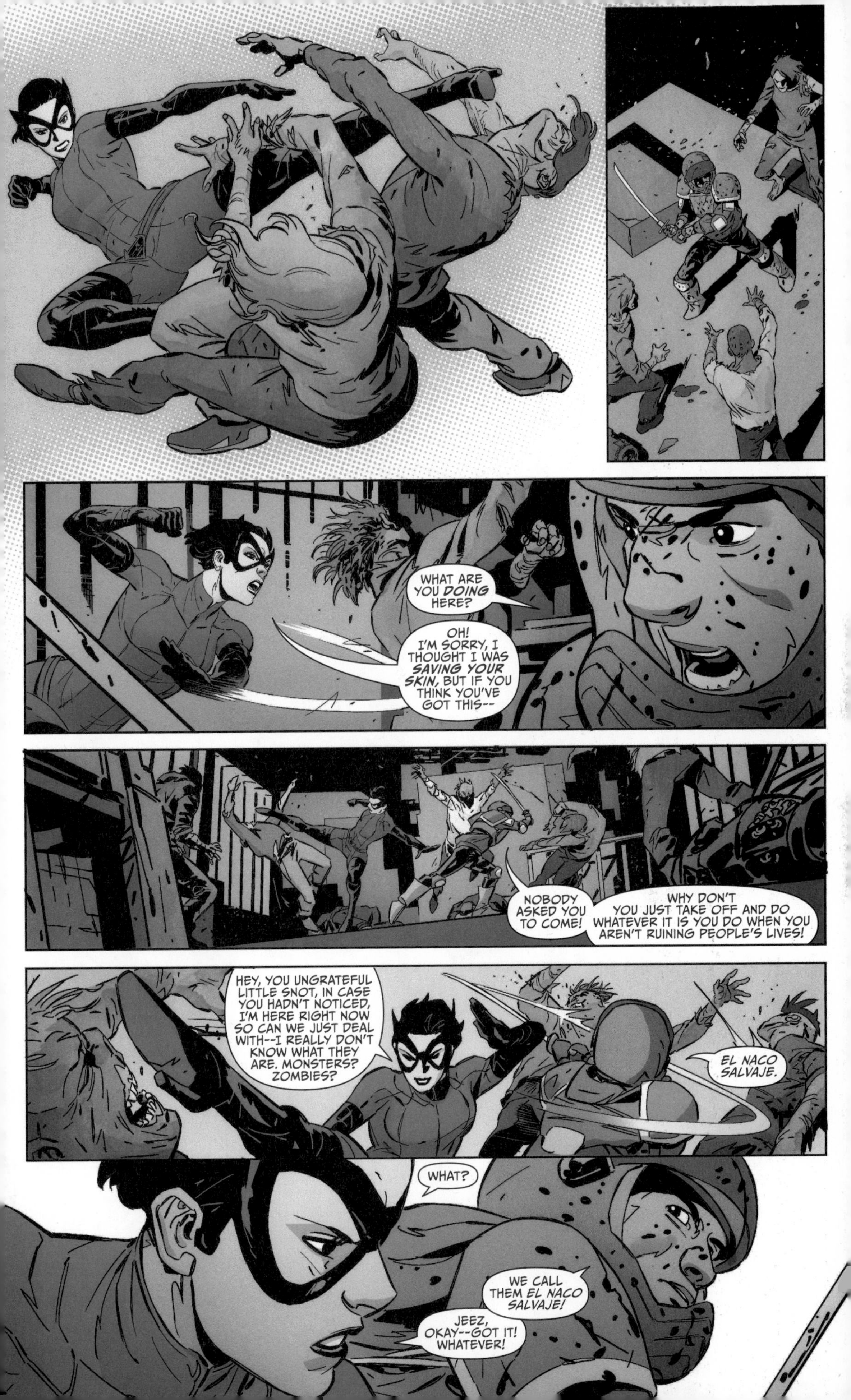
WHAT ARE YOU DOING HERE?
OH! I'M SORRY, I THOUGHT I WAS SAVING YOUR SKIN, BUT IF YOU THINK YOU'VE GOT THIS--
NOBODY ASKED YOU TO COME!
WHY DON'T YOU JUST TAKE OFF AND DO WHATEVER IT IS YOU DO WHEN YOU AREN'T RUINING PEOPLE'S LIVES!
HEY, YOU UNGRATEFUL LITTLE SNOT, IN CASE YOU HADN'T NOTICED, I'M HERE RIGHT NOW SO CAN WE JUST DEAL WITH--I REALLY DON'T KNOW WHAT THEY ARE. MONSTERS? ZOMBIES?
EL NACO SALVAJE.
WHAT?
WE CALL THEM EL NACO SALVAJE!
JEEZ, OKAY--GOT IT! WHATEVER!

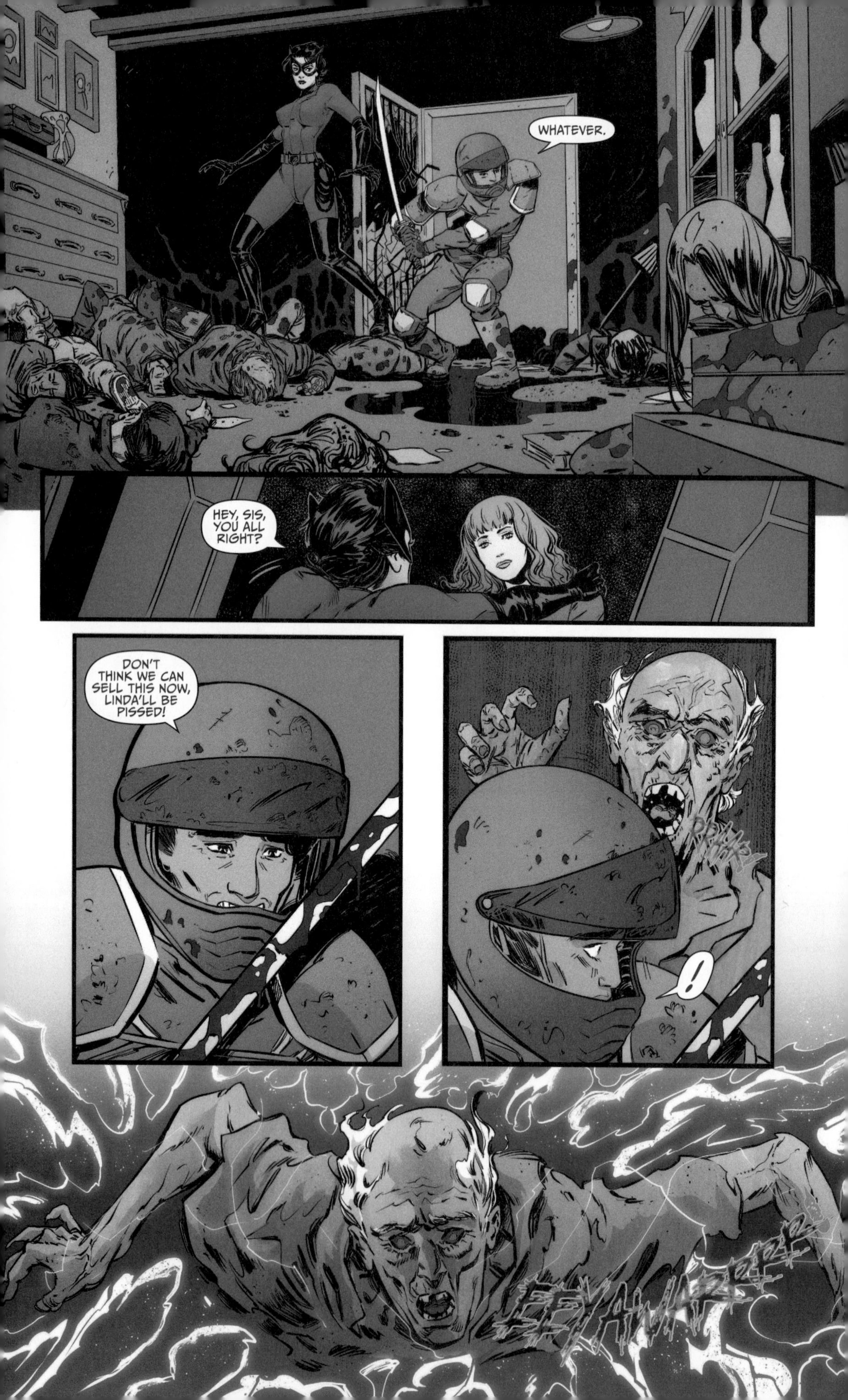
WHATEVER.
HEY, SIS, YOU ALL RIGHT?
DON'T THINK WE CAN SELL THIS NOW, LINDA'LL BE PISSED!
!

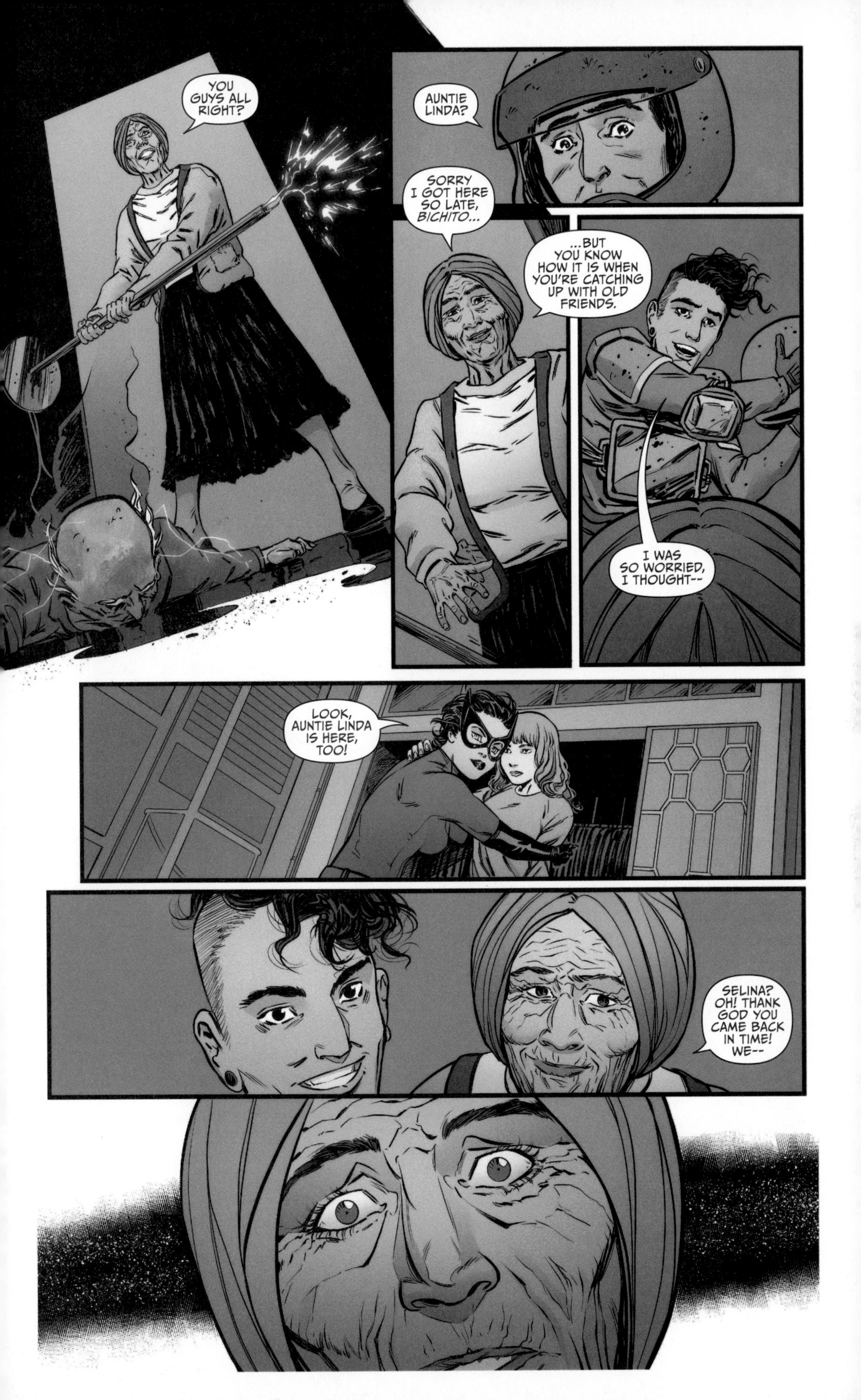
YOU GUYS ALL RIGHT?
AUNTIE LINDA?
SORRY I GOT HERE SO LATE, BICHITO...
...BUT YOU KNOW HOW IT IS WHEN YOU'RE CATCHING UP WITH OLD FRIENDS.
I WAS SO WORRIED, I THOUGHT--
LOOK, AUNTIE LINDA IS HERE, TOO!
SELINA? OH! THANK GOD YOU CAME BACK IN TIME! WE--

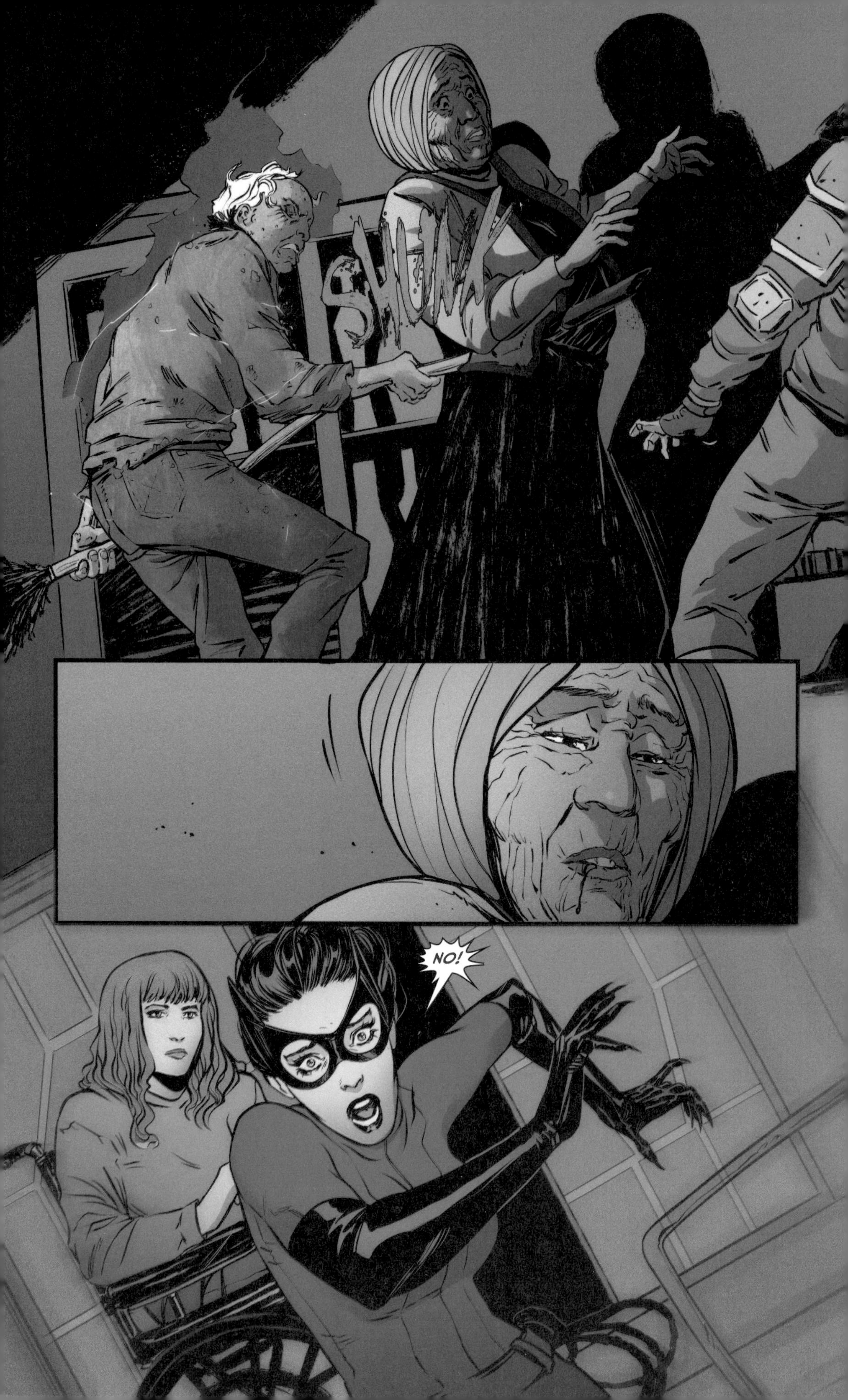
SHUNK
NO!

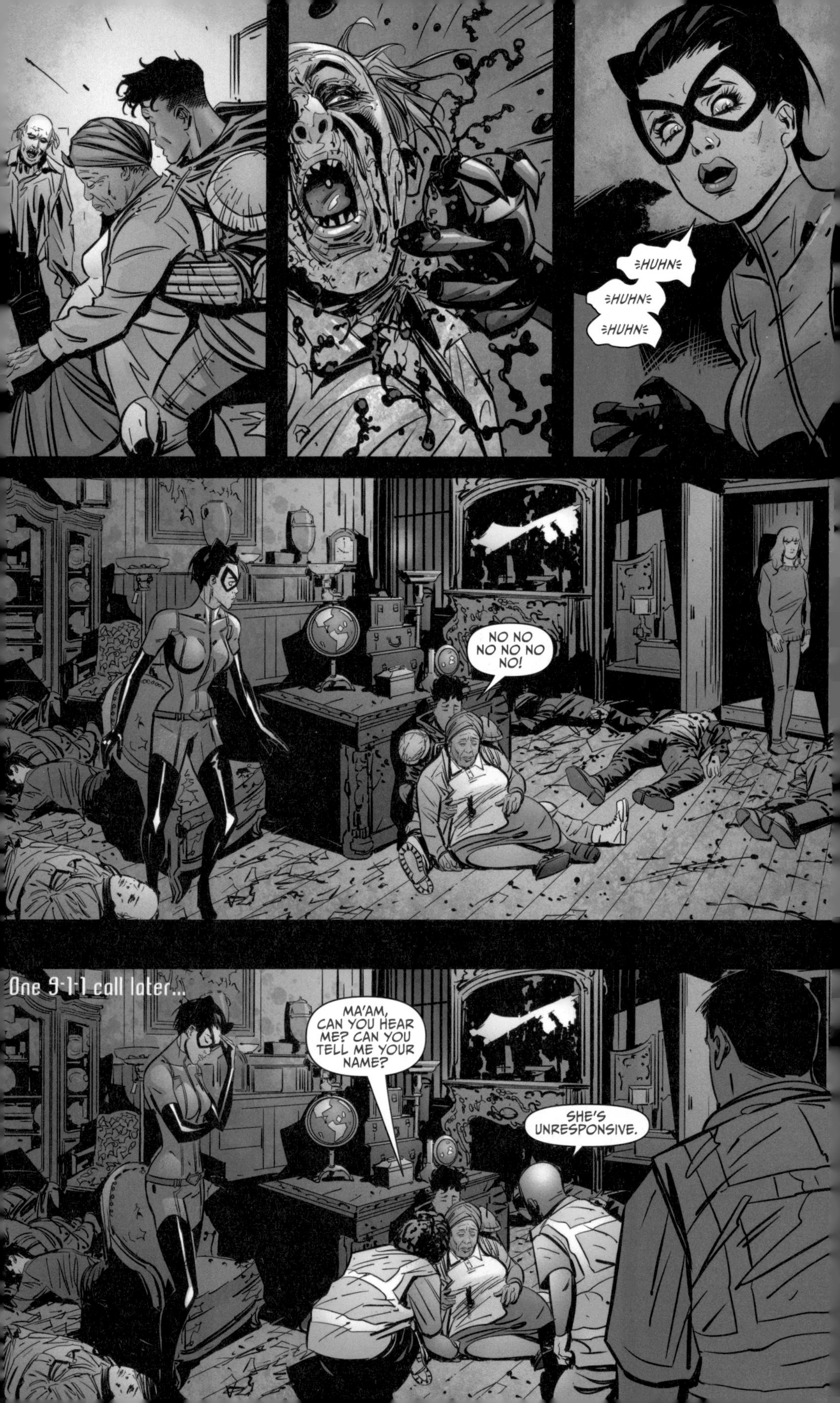

HUHN
HUHN
HUHN
NO NO NO NO NO NO!
One 9-1-1 call later...
MA'AM, CAN YOU HEAR ME? CAN YOU TELL ME YOUR NAME?
SHE'S UNRESPONSIVE.

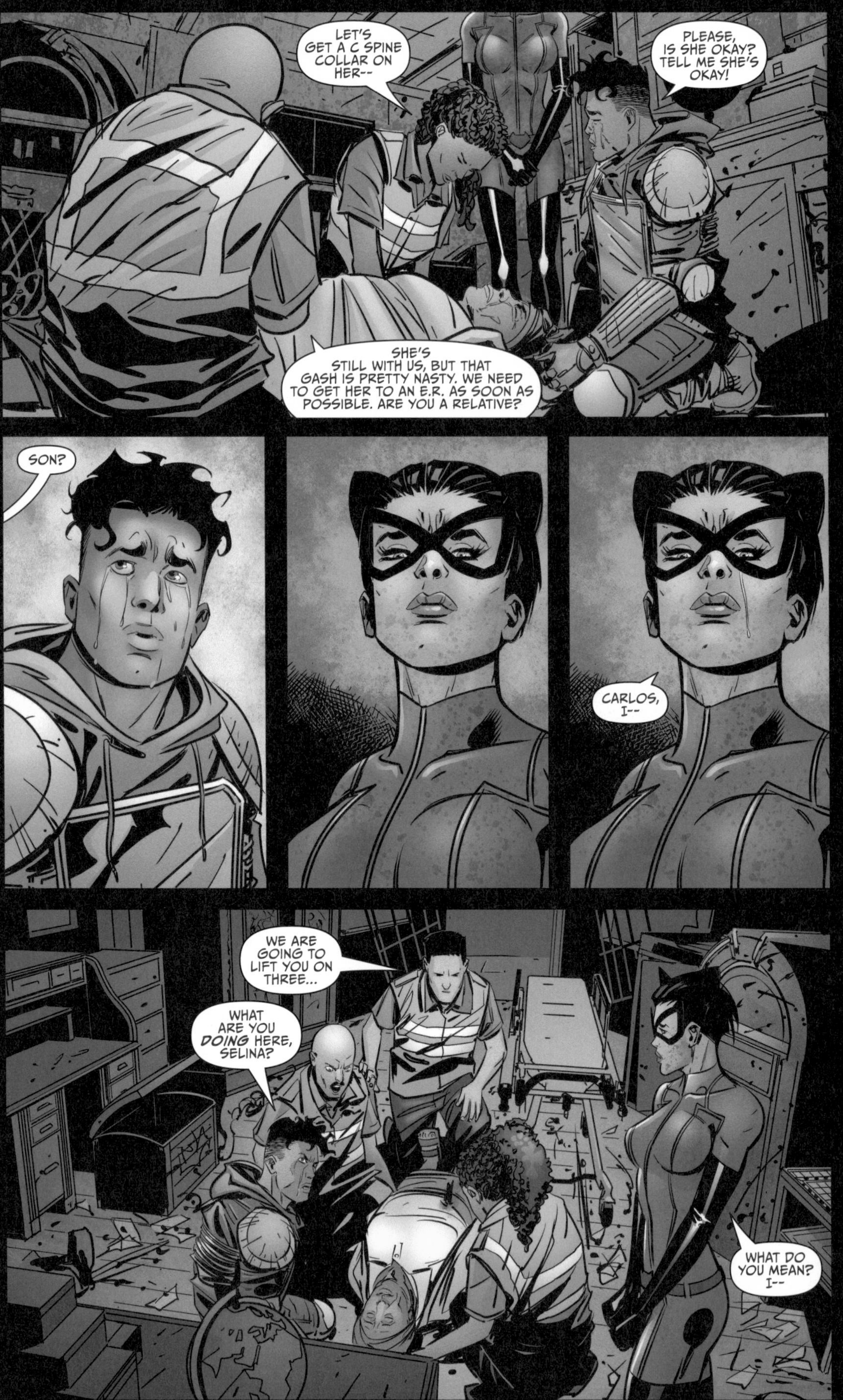
LET'S GET A C SPINE COLLAR ON HER--
PLEASE, IS SHE OKAY? TELL ME SHE'S OKAY!
SHE'S STILL WITH US, BUT THAT GASH IS PRETTY NASTY. WE NEED TO GET HER TO AN E.R. AS SOON AS POSSIBLE. ARE YOU A RELATIVE?
SON?
CARLOS, I--
WE ARE GOING TO LIFT YOU ON THREE...
WHAT ARE YOU *DOING* HERE, SELINA?
WHAT DO YOU MEAN? I--

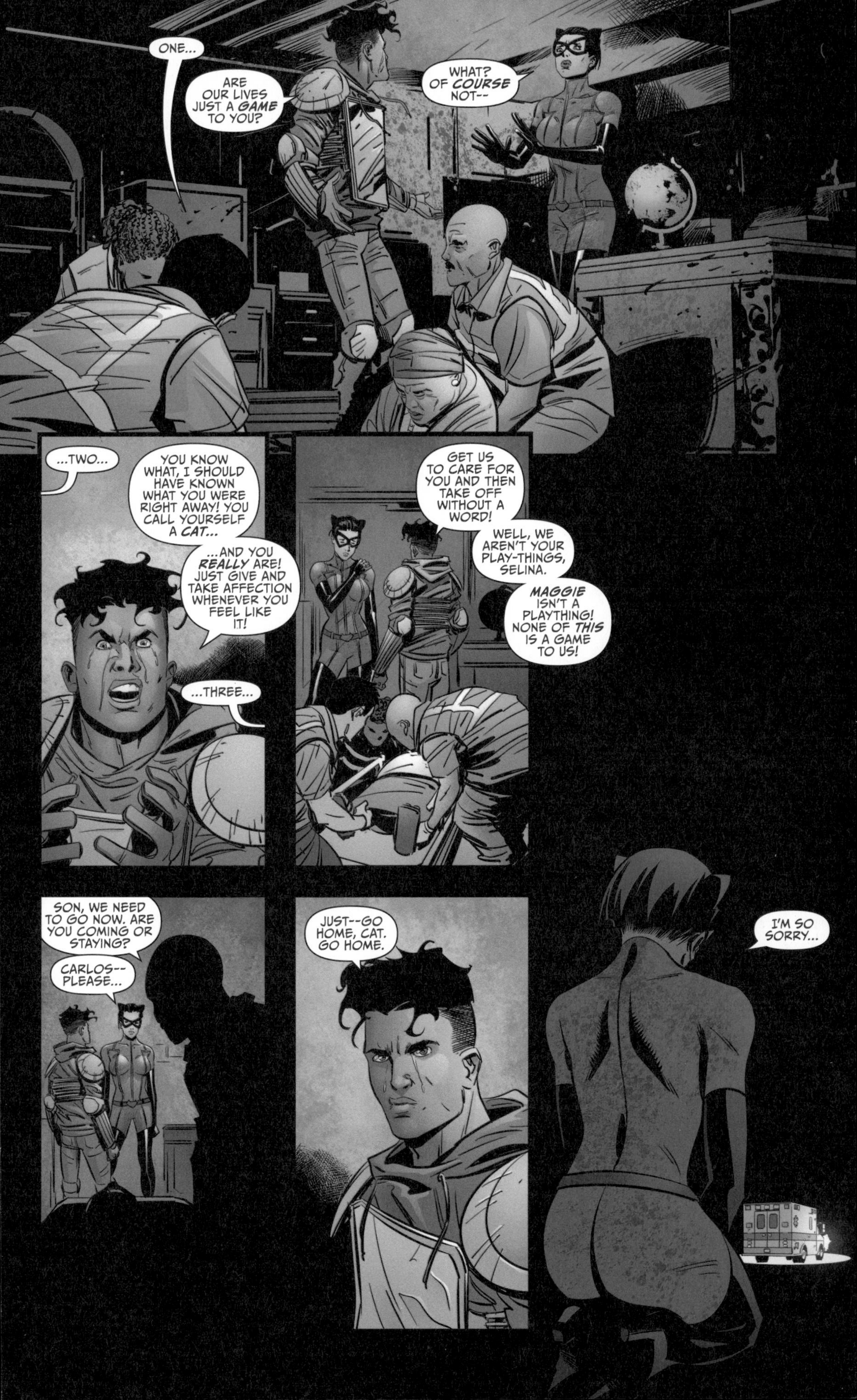
ONE...
ARE OUR LIVES JUST A *GAME* TO YOU?
WHAT? OF *COURSE* NOT--
...TWO...
YOU KNOW WHAT, I SHOULD HAVE KNOWN WHAT YOU WERE RIGHT AWAY! YOU CALL YOURSELF A *CAT*...
...AND YOU *REALLY* ARE! JUST GIVE AND TAKE AFFECTION WHENEVER YOU FEEL LIKE IT!
...THREE...
GET US TO CARE FOR YOU AND THEN TAKE OFF WITHOUT A WORD!
WELL, WE AREN'T YOUR PLAY-THINGS, SELINA.
MAGGIE ISN'T A PLAYTHING! NONE OF *THIS* IS A GAME TO US!
SON, WE NEED TO GO NOW. ARE YOU COMING OR STAYING?
CARLOS-- PLEASE...
JUST--GO HOME, CAT. GO HOME.
I'M SO SORRY...

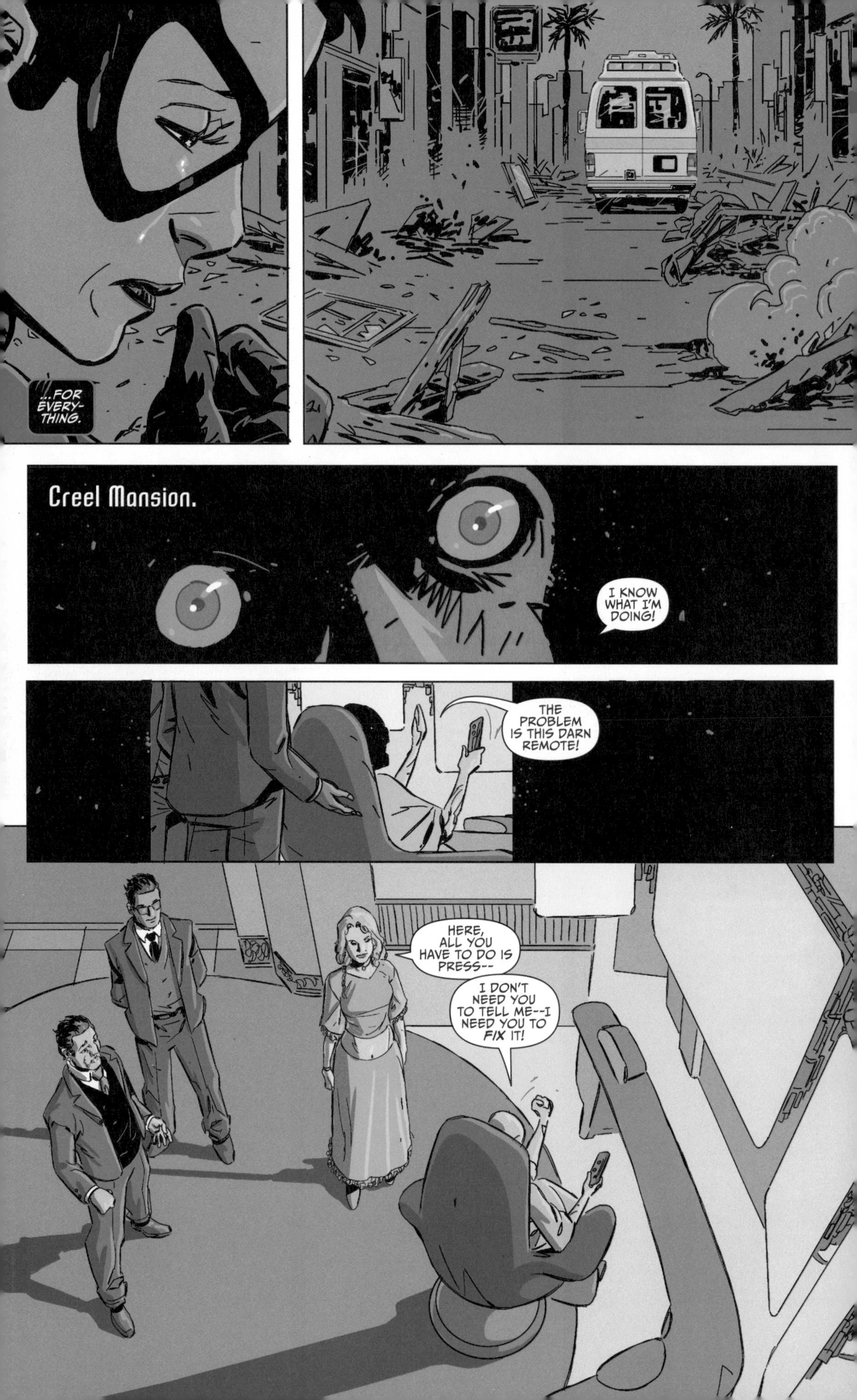
...FOR EVERY-THING.
Creel Mansion.
I KNOW WHAT I'M DOING!
THE PROBLEM IS THIS DARN REMOTE!
HERE, ALL YOU HAVE TO DO IS PRESS--
I DON'T NEED YOU TO TELL ME--I NEED YOU TO *FIX* IT!

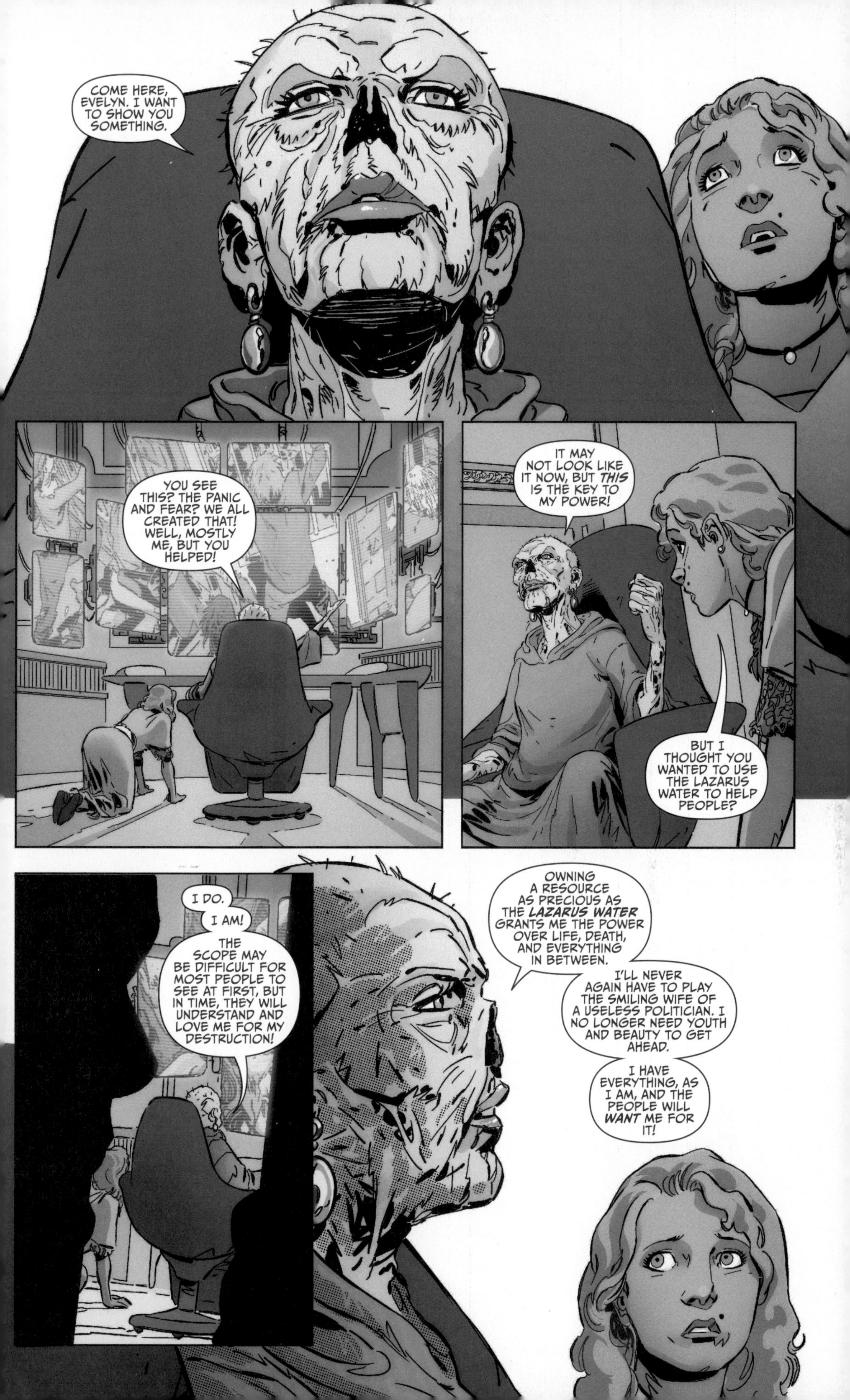
COME HERE, EVELYN. I WANT TO SHOW YOU SOMETHING.
YOU SEE THIS? THE PANIC AND FEAR? WE ALL CREATED THAT! WELL, MOSTLY ME, BUT YOU HELPED!
IT MAY NOT LOOK LIKE IT NOW, BUT THIS IS THE KEY TO MY POWER!
BUT I THOUGHT YOU WANTED TO USE THE LAZARUS WATER TO HELP PEOPLE?
I DO.
I AM!
THE SCOPE MAY BE DIFFICULT FOR MOST PEOPLE TO SEE AT FIRST, BUT IN TIME, THEY WILL UNDERSTAND AND LOVE ME FOR MY DESTRUCTION!
OWNING A RESOURCE AS PRECIOUS AS THE LAZARUS WATER GRANTS ME THE POWER OVER LIFE, DEATH, AND EVERYTHING IN BETWEEN.
I'LL NEVER AGAIN HAVE TO PLAY THE SMILING WIFE OF A USELESS POLITICIAN. I NO LONGER NEED YOUTH AND BEAUTY TO GET AHEAD.
I HAVE EVERYTHING, AS I AM, AND THE PEOPLE WILL WANT ME FOR IT!

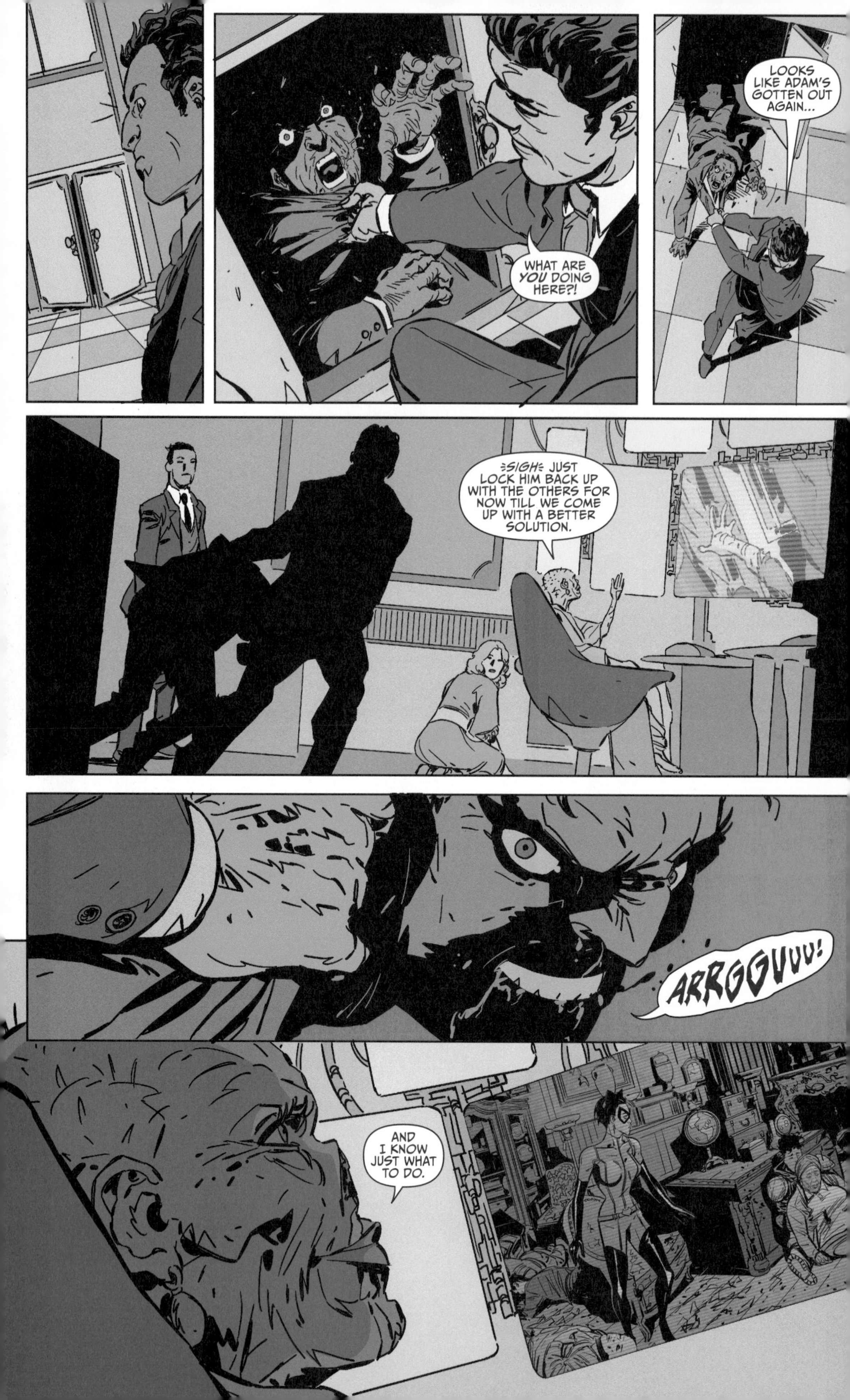
WHAT ARE YOU DOING HERE?!
LOOKS LIKE ADAM'S GOTTEN OUT AGAIN...
=SIGH= JUST LOCK HIM BACK UP WITH THE OTHERS FOR NOW TILL WE COME UP WITH A BETTER SOLUTION.
ARRGGUUU!
AND I KNOW JUST WHAT TO DO.

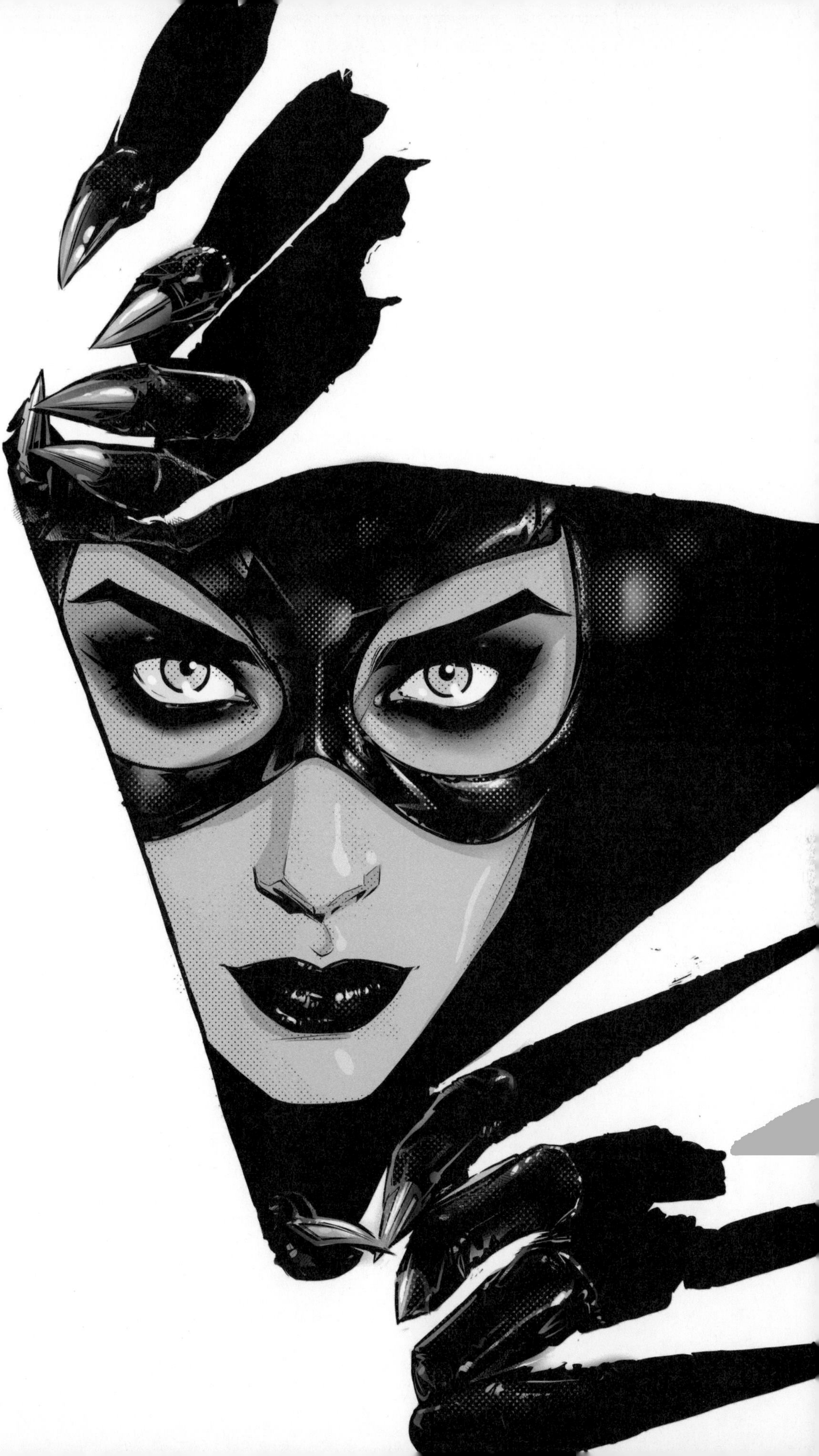

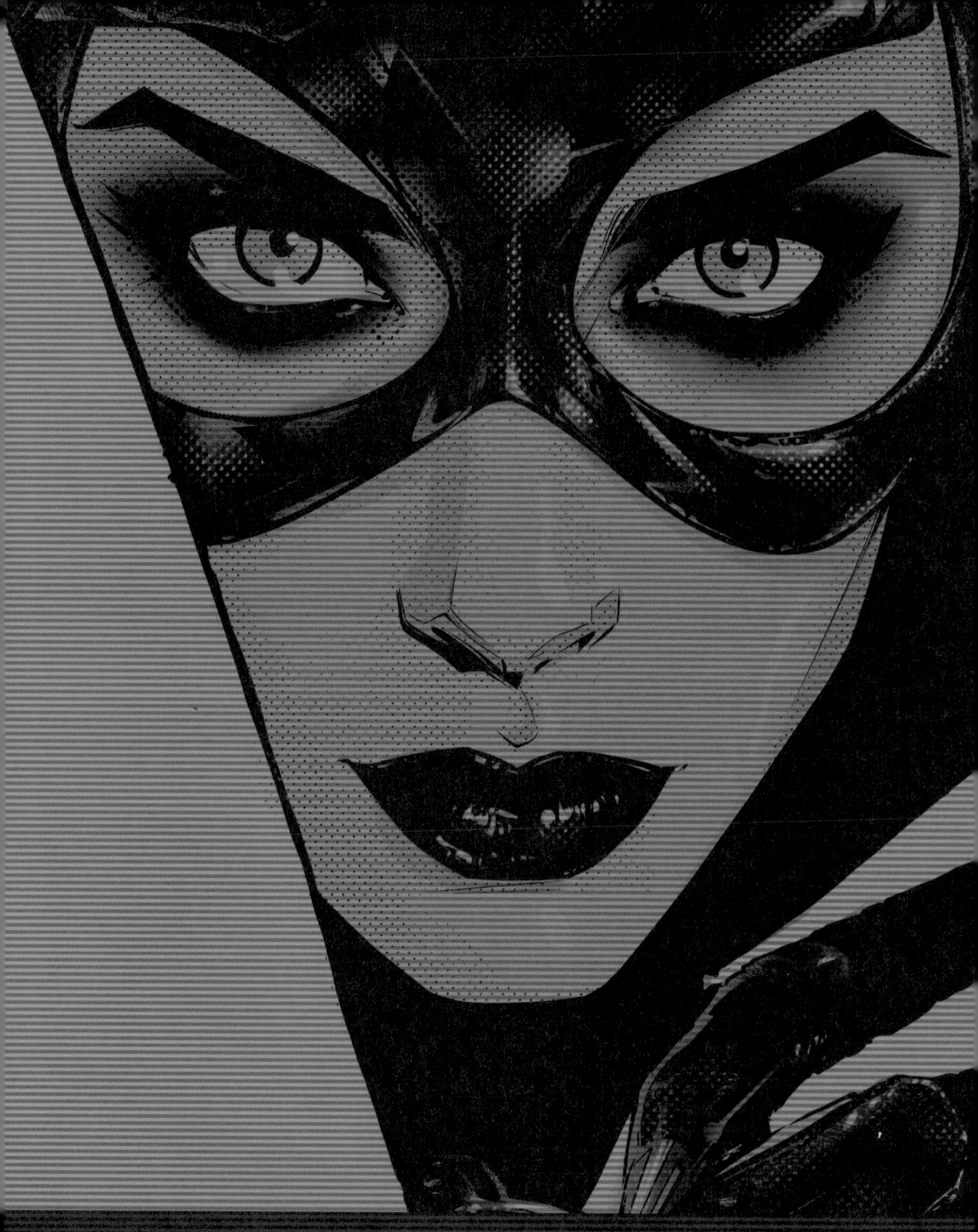

CATWOMAN
#20

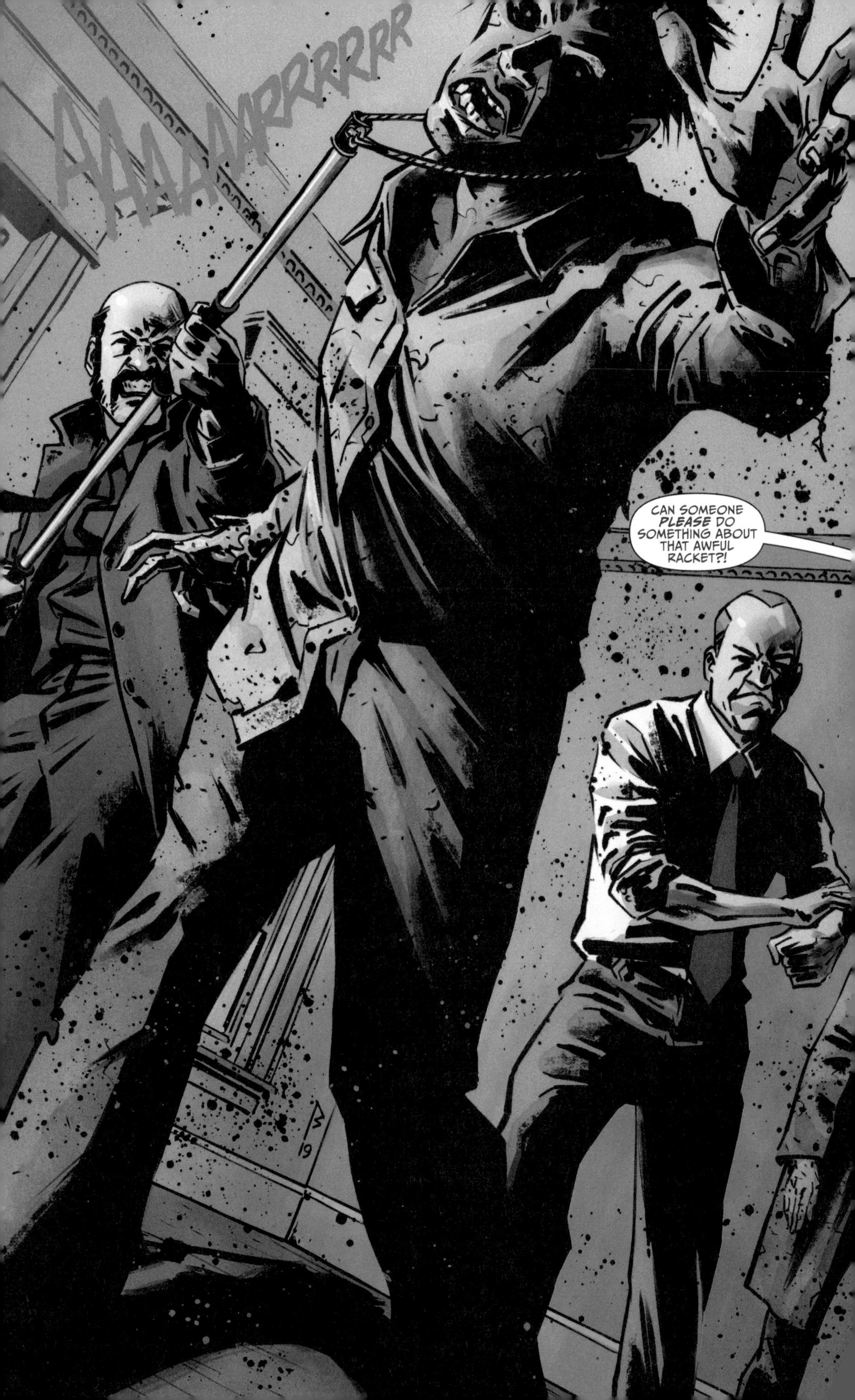
AAAAARRRRRR
CAN SOMEONE *PLEASE* DO SOMETHING ABOUT THAT AWFUL RACKET?!

GRRRRRRRRRR

IT'S QUITE *DISRUPTIVE.*

THROW ADAM IN WITH THE REST OF THEM.

CAMERA 13

SORRY, MRS. CREEL...

AAAAIRRRRRRRRRRRR

...WE'LL GET IT SORTED...

WHACK

...SHORTLY!

HELP ME WITH THIS THING, WILL YA?

UUHRRRRR

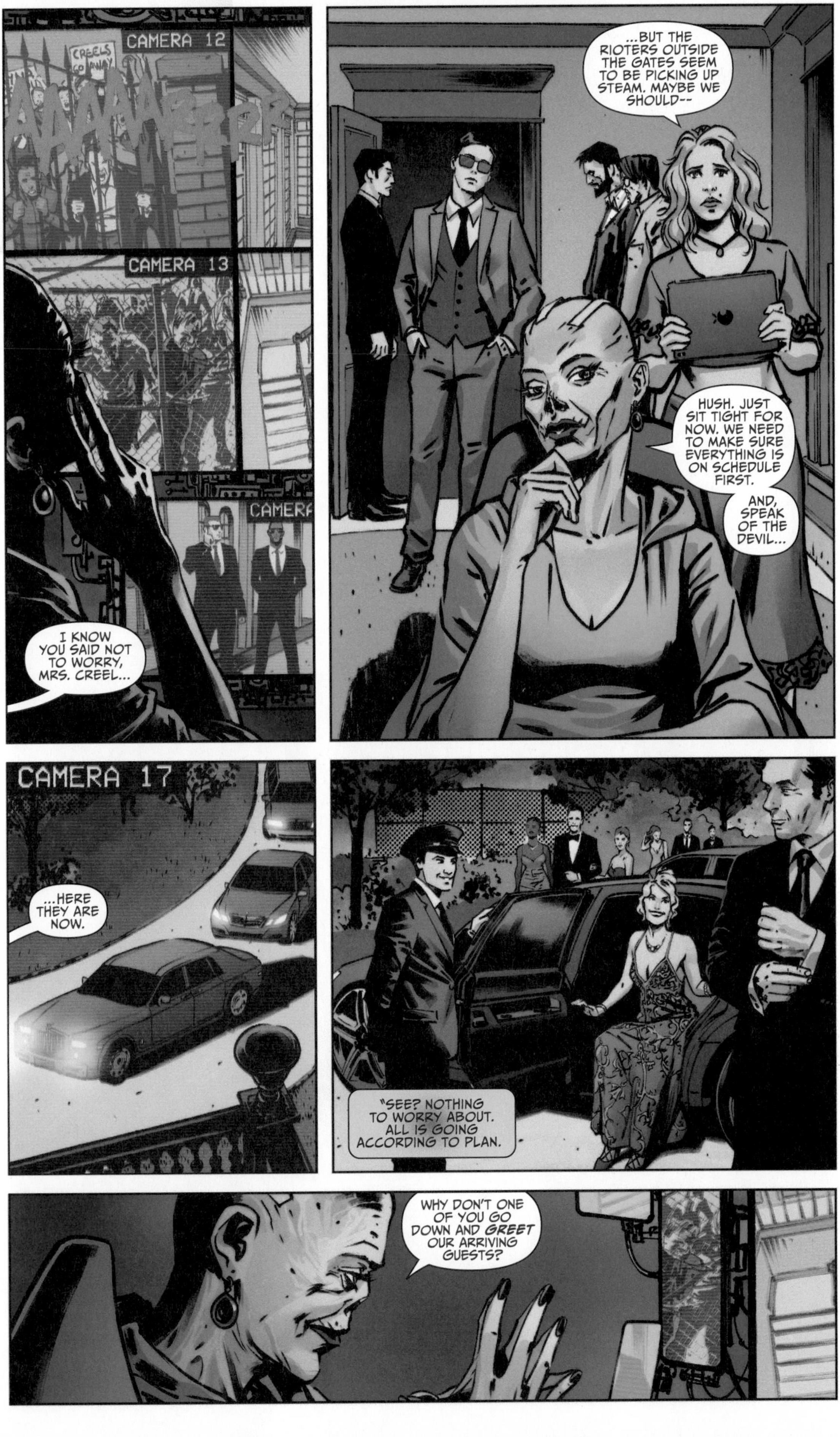
CAMERA 12
CREELS GO AWAY
AAAAARRR
CAMERA 13
CAMERA
I KNOW YOU SAID NOT TO WORRY, MRS. CREEL...
...BUT THE RIOTERS OUTSIDE THE GATES SEEM TO BE PICKING UP STEAM. MAYBE WE SHOULD--
HUSH. JUST SIT TIGHT FOR NOW. WE NEED TO MAKE SURE EVERYTHING IS ON SCHEDULE FIRST.
AND, SPEAK OF THE DEVIL...
CAMERA 17
...HERE THEY ARE NOW.
"SEE? NOTHING TO WORRY ABOUT. ALL IS GOING ACCORDING TO PLAN.
WHY DON'T ONE OF YOU GO DOWN AND GREET OUR ARRIVING GUESTS?

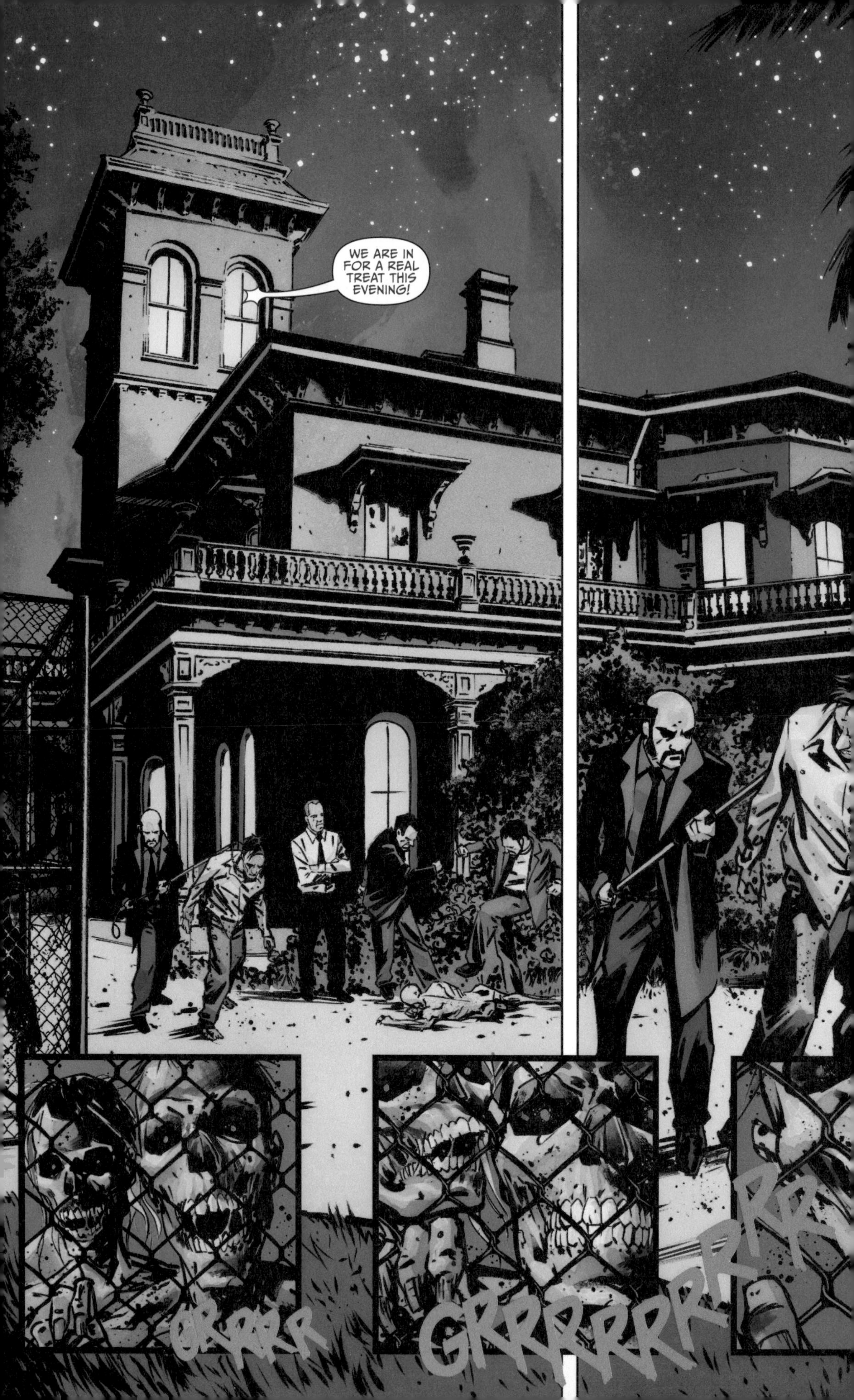
WE ARE IN FOR A REAL TREAT THIS EVENING!
GRRRR
GRRRRRRRRRRR

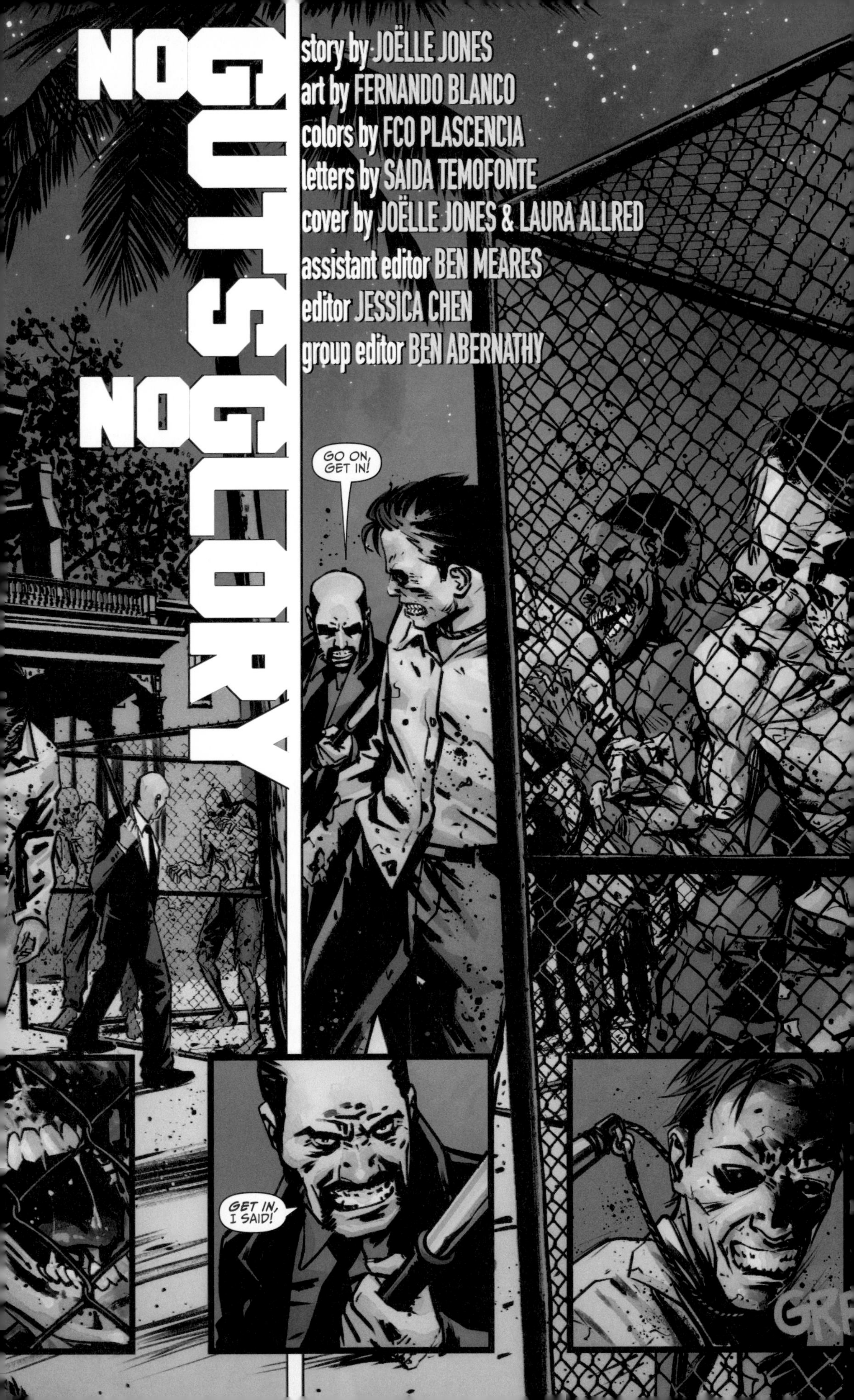
NO GUTS NO GLORY
story by JOËLLE JONES
art by FERNANDO BLANCO
colors by FCO PLASCENCIA
letters by SAIDA TEMOFONTE
cover by JOËLLE JONES & LAURA ALLRED
assistant editor BEN MEARES
editor JESSICA CHEN
group editor BEN ABERNATHY
GO ON, GET IN!
GET IN, I SAID!

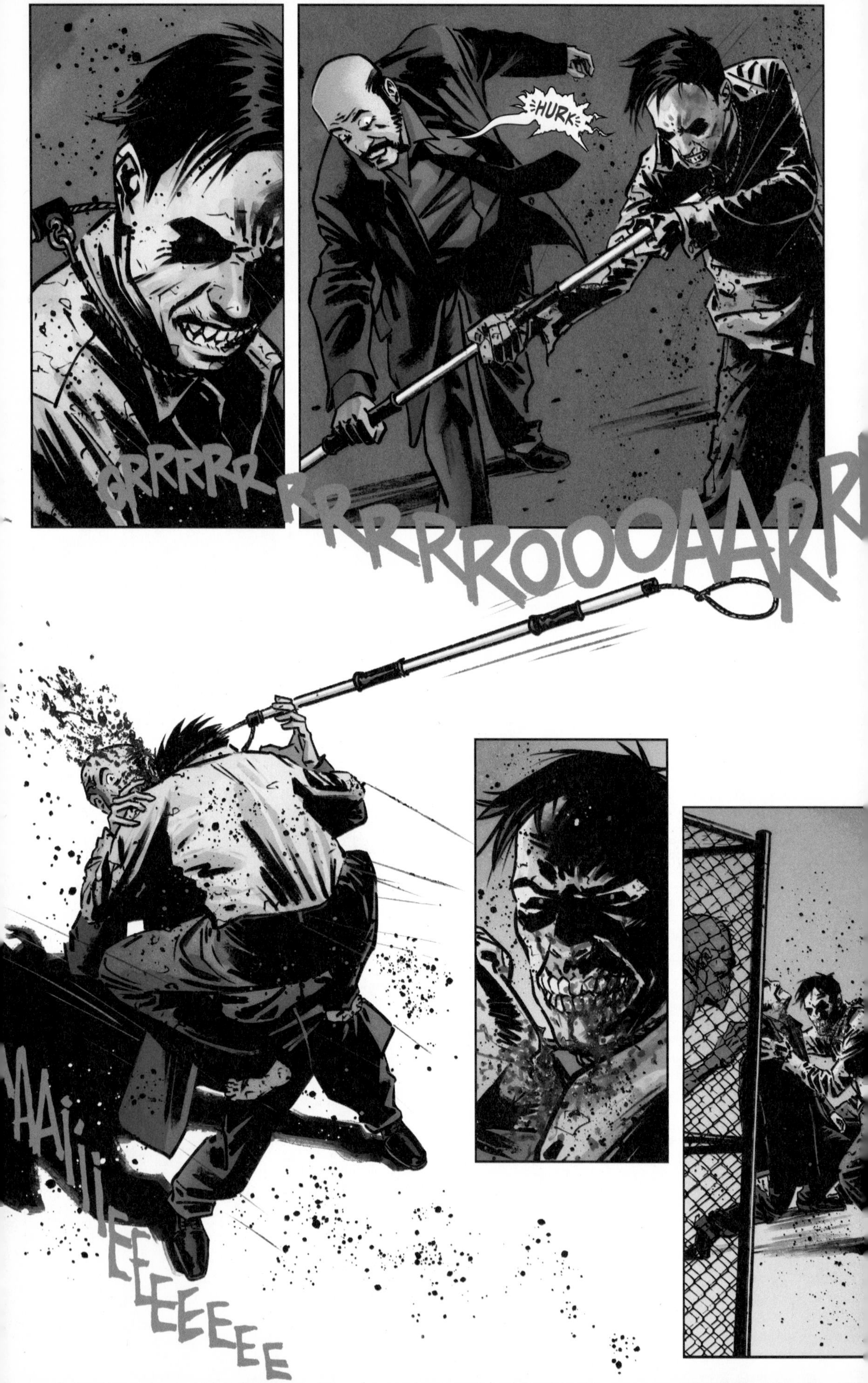

HURK
GRRRRRRRRRROOOAARR
AAIIII EEEEEEEE

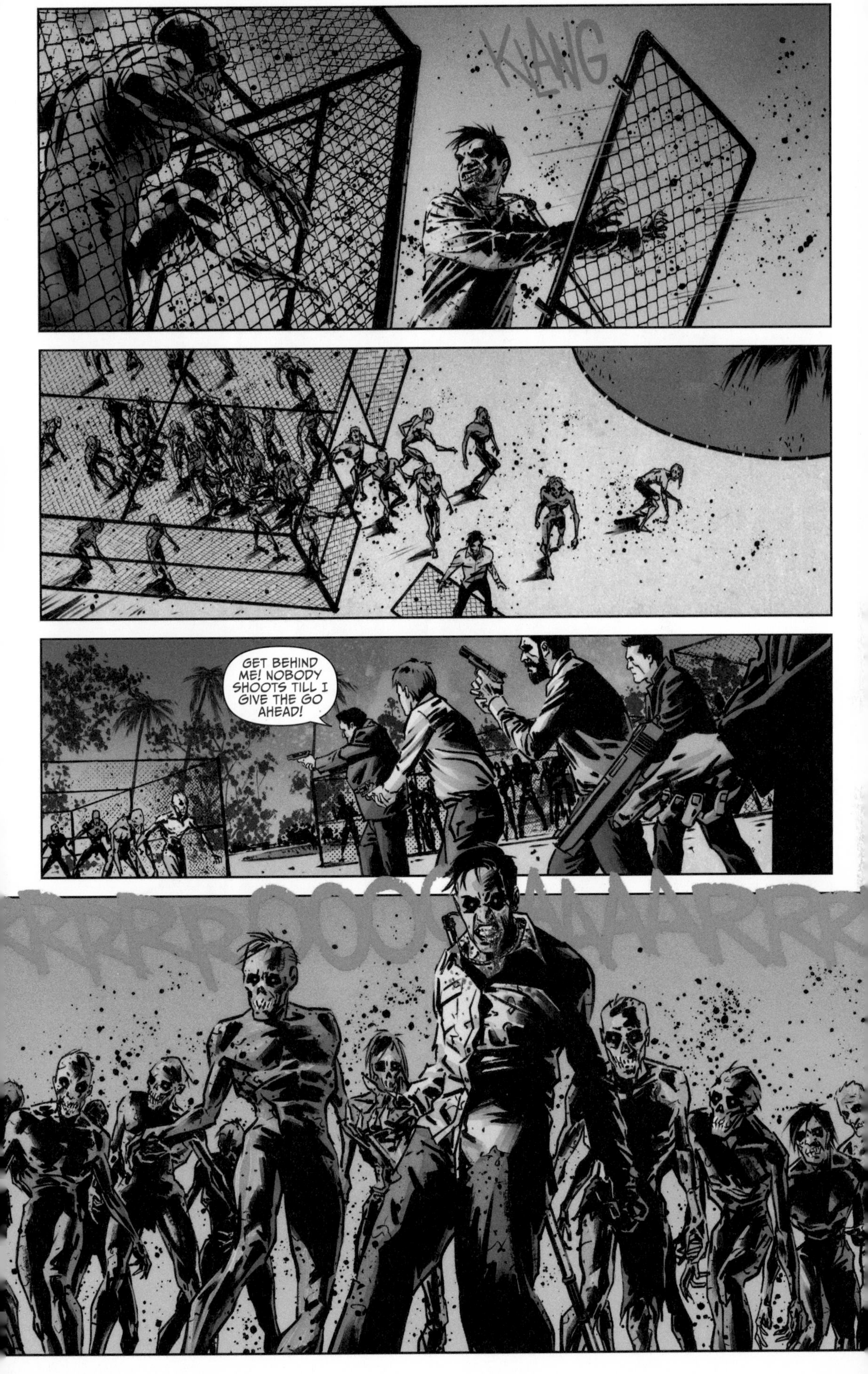
KLANG
GET BEHIND ME! NOBODY SHOOTS TILL I GIVE THE GO AHEAD!

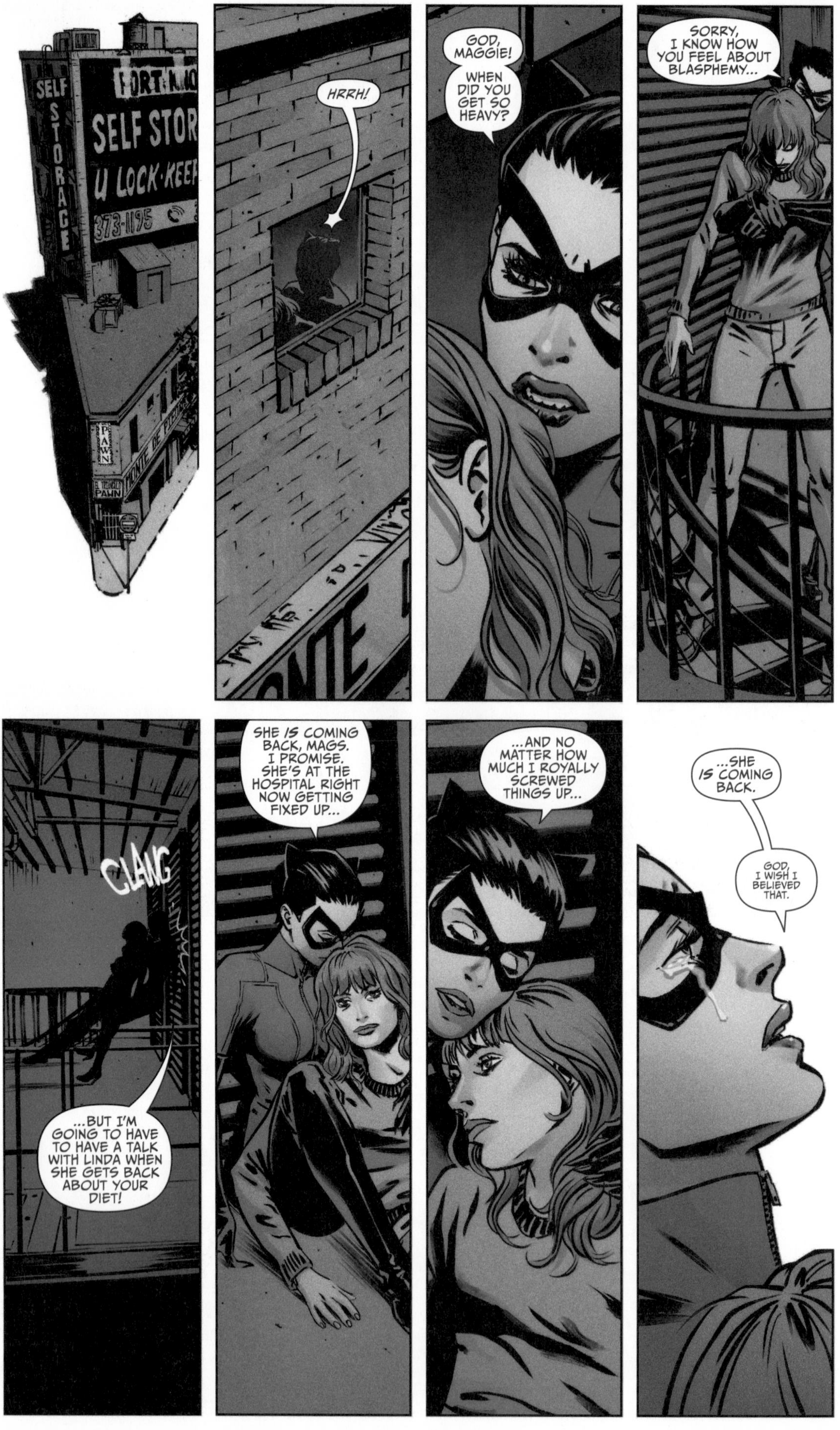
FORT KNO
SELF STORAGE
SELF STOR
U LOCK-KEEP
373-1195
PAWN
MONTE DE PIEDAD
PAWN
HRRH!
MONTE
GOD, MAGGIE!
WHEN DID YOU GET SO HEAVY?
SORRY, I KNOW HOW YOU FEEL ABOUT BLASPHEMY...
CLANG
...BUT I'M GOING TO HAVE TO HAVE A TALK WITH LINDA WHEN SHE GETS BACK ABOUT YOUR DIET!
SHE IS COMING BACK, MAGS. I PROMISE. SHE'S AT THE HOSPITAL RIGHT NOW GETTING FIXED UP...
...AND NO MATTER HOW MUCH I ROYALLY SCREWED THINGS UP...
...SHE IS COMING BACK.
GOD, I WISH I BELIEVED THAT.

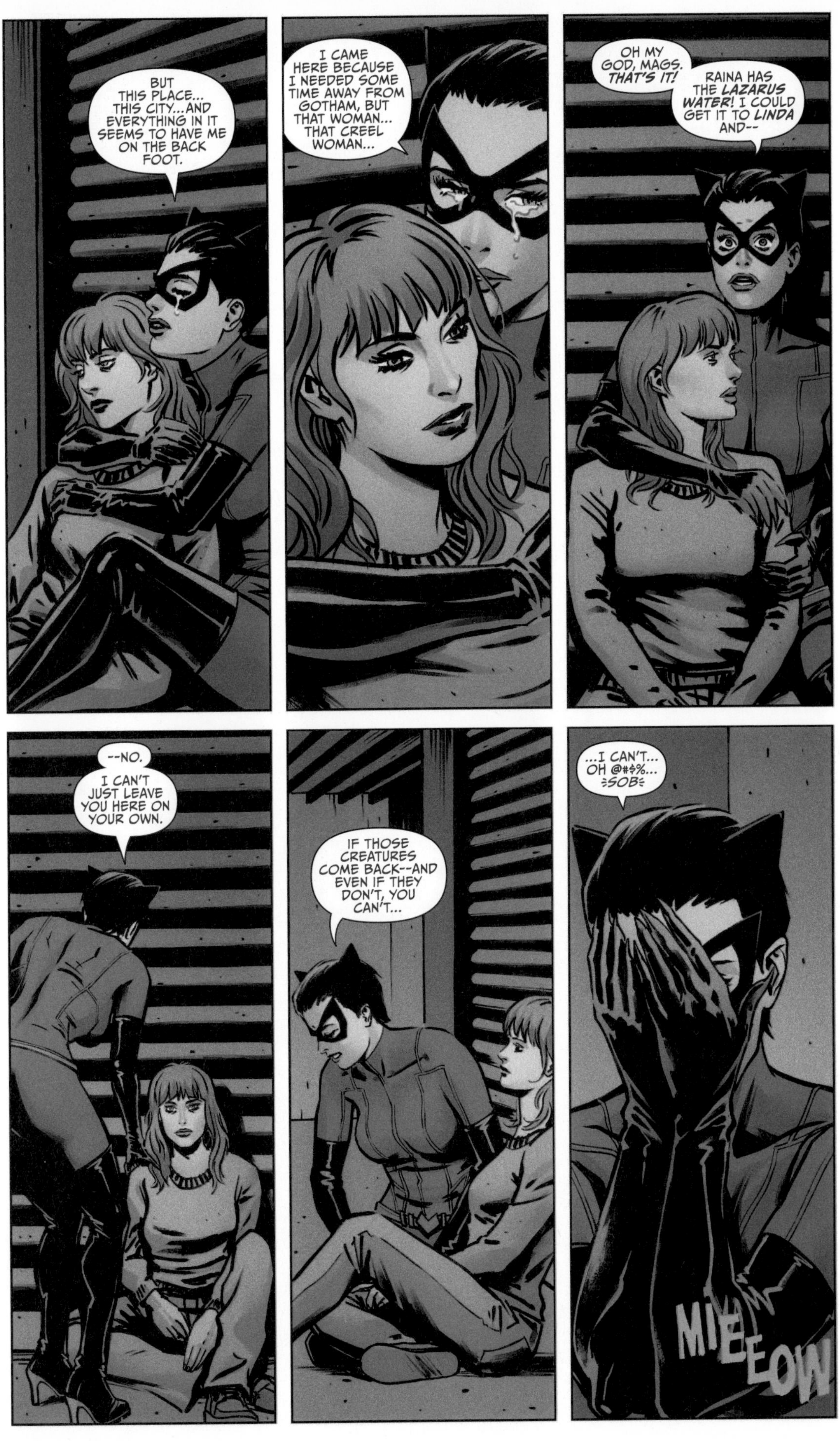
BUT THIS PLACE... THIS CITY...AND EVERYTHING IN IT SEEMS TO HAVE ME ON THE BACK FOOT.
I CAME HERE BECAUSE I NEEDED SOME TIME AWAY FROM GOTHAM, BUT THAT WOMAN... THAT CREEL WOMAN...
OH MY GOD, MAGS. THAT'S IT!
RAINA HAS THE LAZARUS WATER! I COULD GET IT TO LINDA AND--
--NO.
I CAN'T JUST LEAVE YOU HERE ON YOUR OWN.
IF THOSE CREATURES COME BACK--AND EVEN IF THEY DON'T, YOU CAN'T...
...I CAN'T... OH @#$%... SOB
MIEEEOW

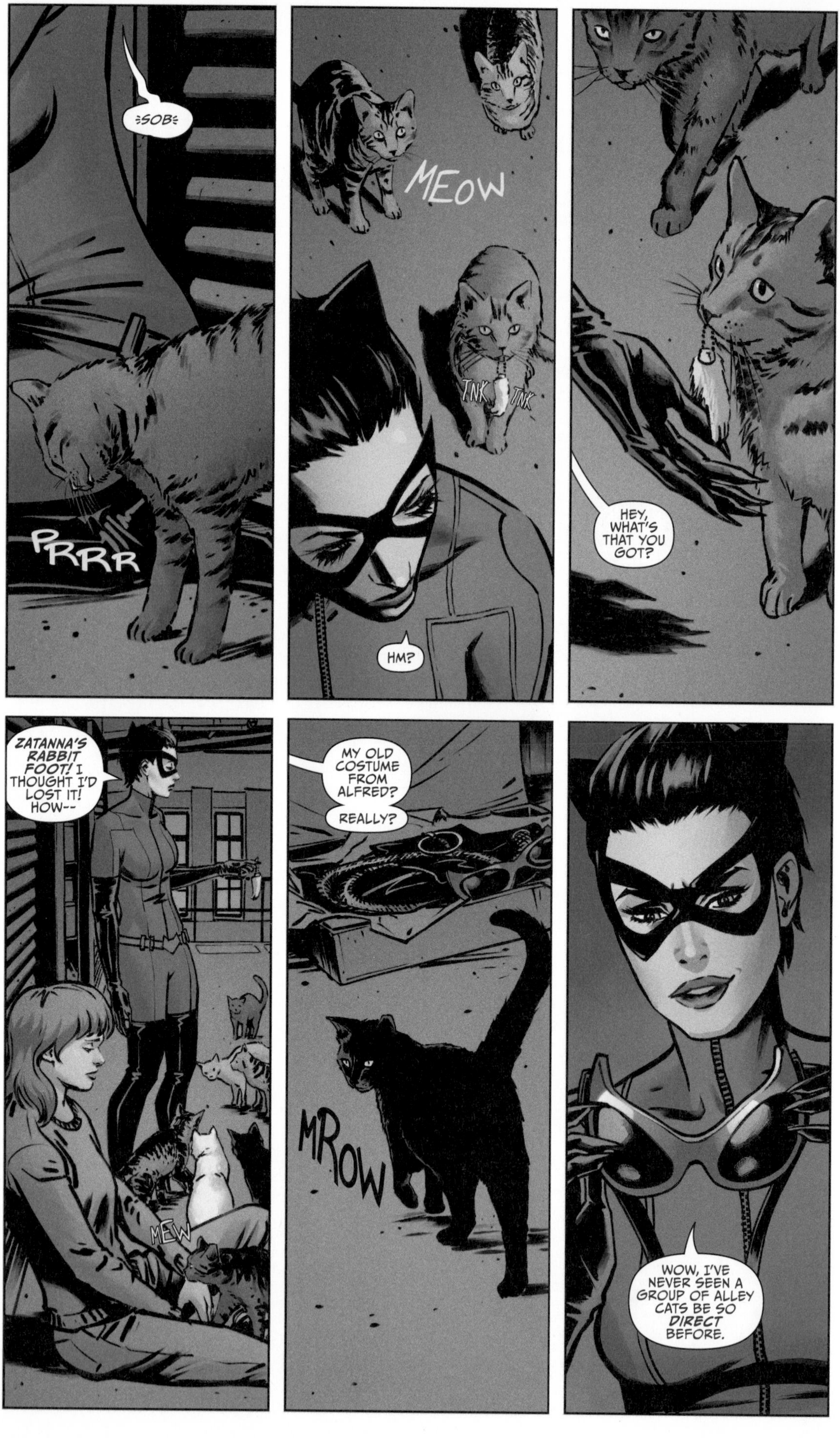

SOB
PRRR
MEOW
TNK TNK
HM?
HEY, WHAT'S THAT YOU GOT?
ZATANNA'S RABBIT FOOT! I THOUGHT I'D LOST IT! HOW--
MEW
MY OLD COSTUME FROM ALFRED?
REALLY?
MROW
WOW, I'VE NEVER SEEN A GROUP OF ALLEY CATS BE SO DIRECT BEFORE.

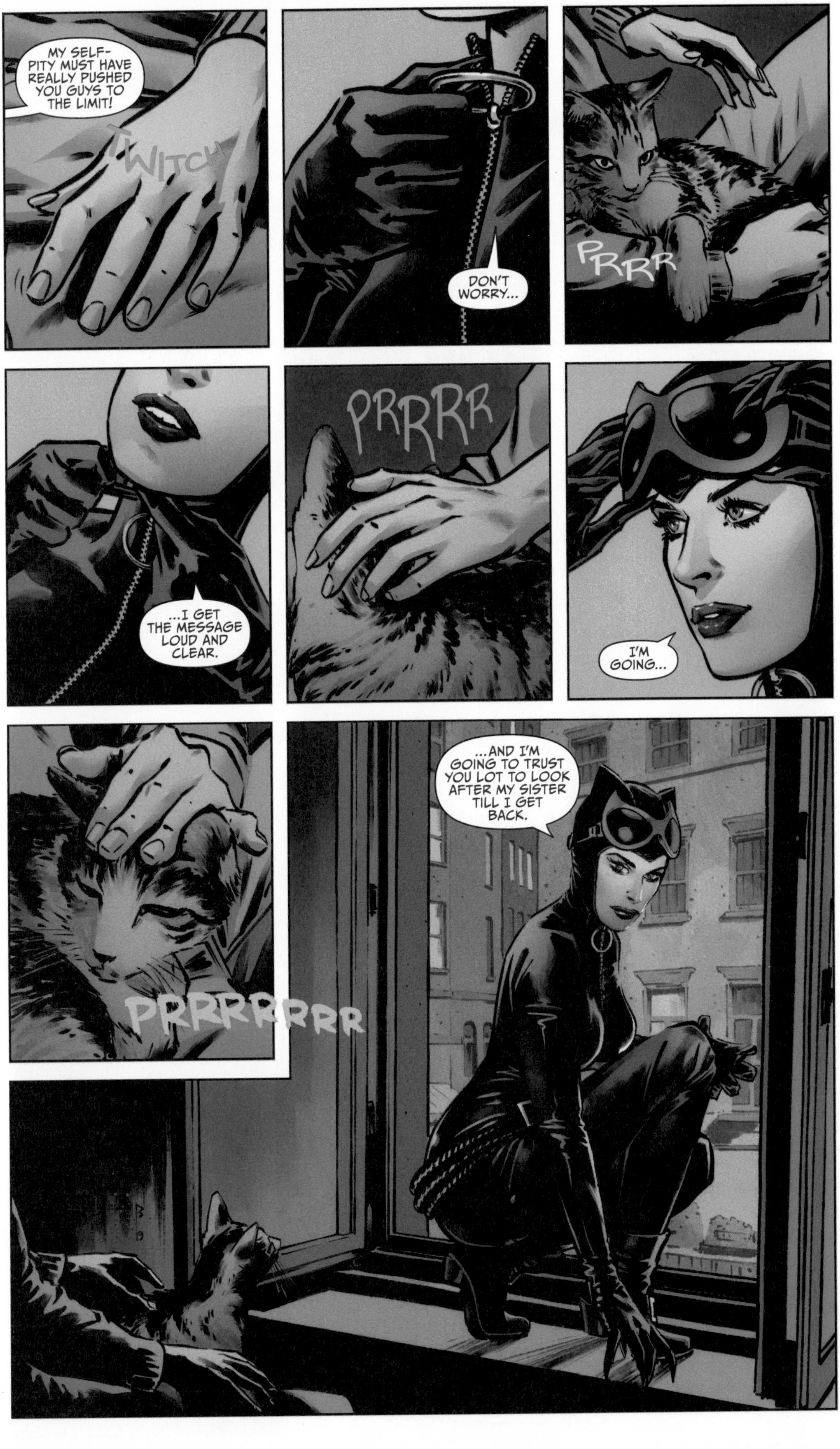
MY SELF-PITY MUST HAVE REALLY PUSHED YOU GUYS TO THE LIMIT!
TWITCH
DON'T WORRY...
PRRRR
...I GET THE MESSAGE LOUD AND CLEAR.
PRRRR
I'M GOING...
PRRRRRRRR
...AND I'M GOING TO TRUST YOU LOT TO LOOK AFTER MY SISTER TILL I GET BACK.

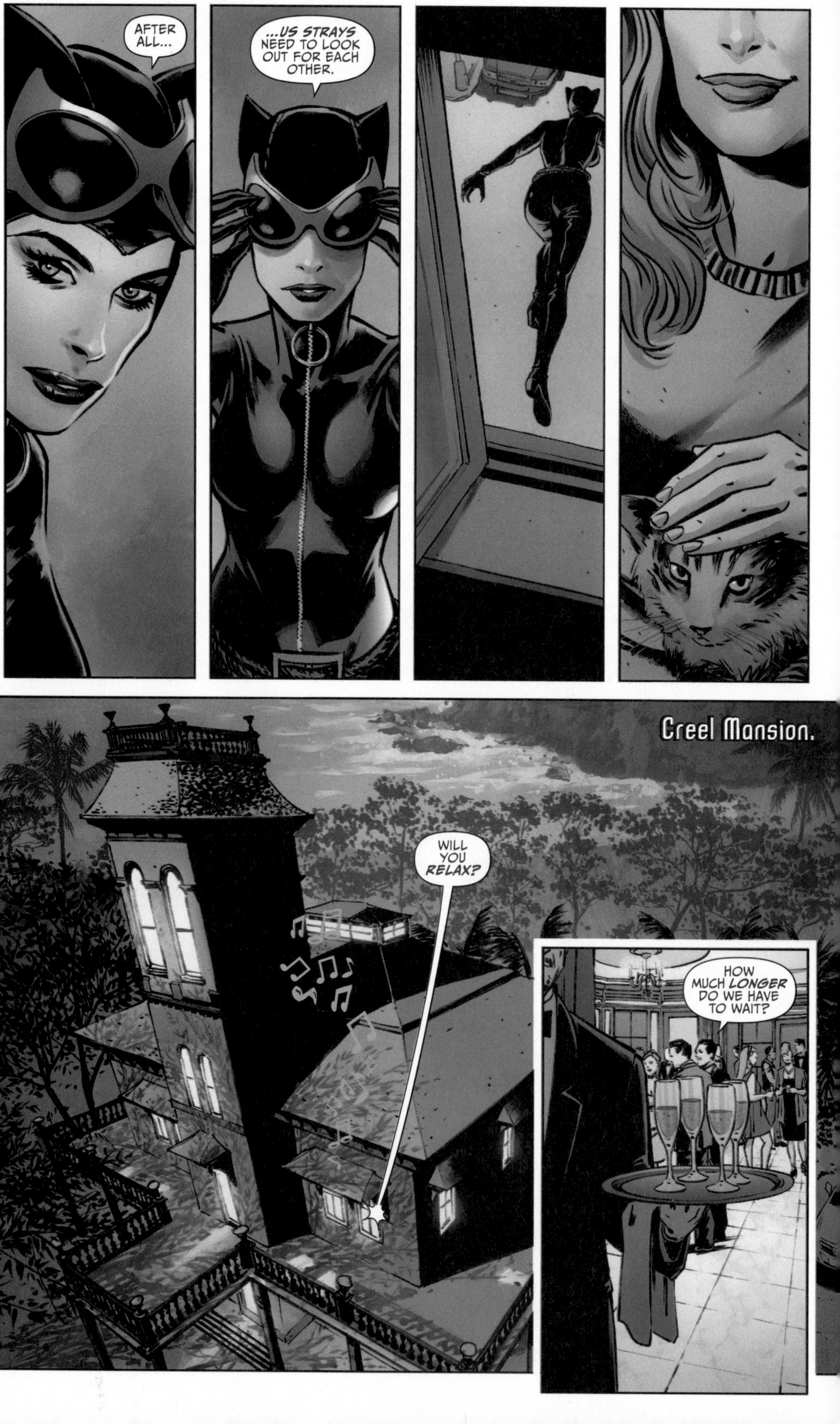
AFTER ALL...
...US STRAYS NEED TO LOOK OUT FOR EACH OTHER.
Creel Mansion.
WILL YOU RELAX?
HOW MUCH LONGER DO WE HAVE TO WAIT?

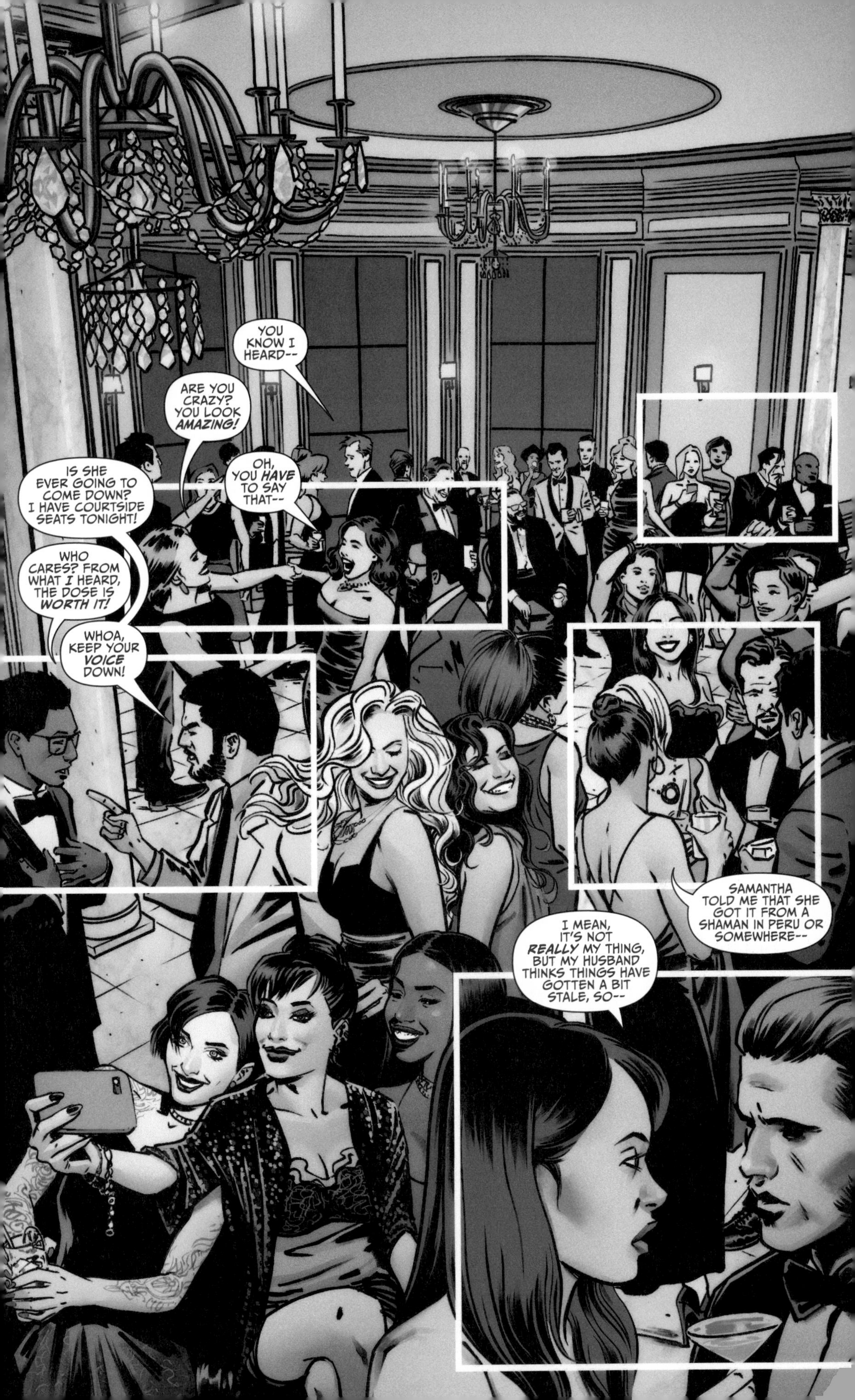
YOU KNOW I HEARD--
ARE YOU CRAZY? YOU LOOK AMAZING!
OH, YOU HAVE TO SAY THAT--
IS SHE EVER GOING TO COME DOWN? I HAVE COURTSIDE SEATS TONIGHT!
WHO CARES? FROM WHAT I HEARD, THE DOSE IS WORTH IT!
WHOA, KEEP YOUR VOICE DOWN!
SAMANTHA TOLD ME THAT SHE GOT IT FROM A SHAMAN IN PERU OR SOMEWHERE--
I MEAN, IT'S NOT REALLY MY THING, BUT MY HUSBAND THINKS THINGS HAVE GOTTEN A BIT STALE, SO--

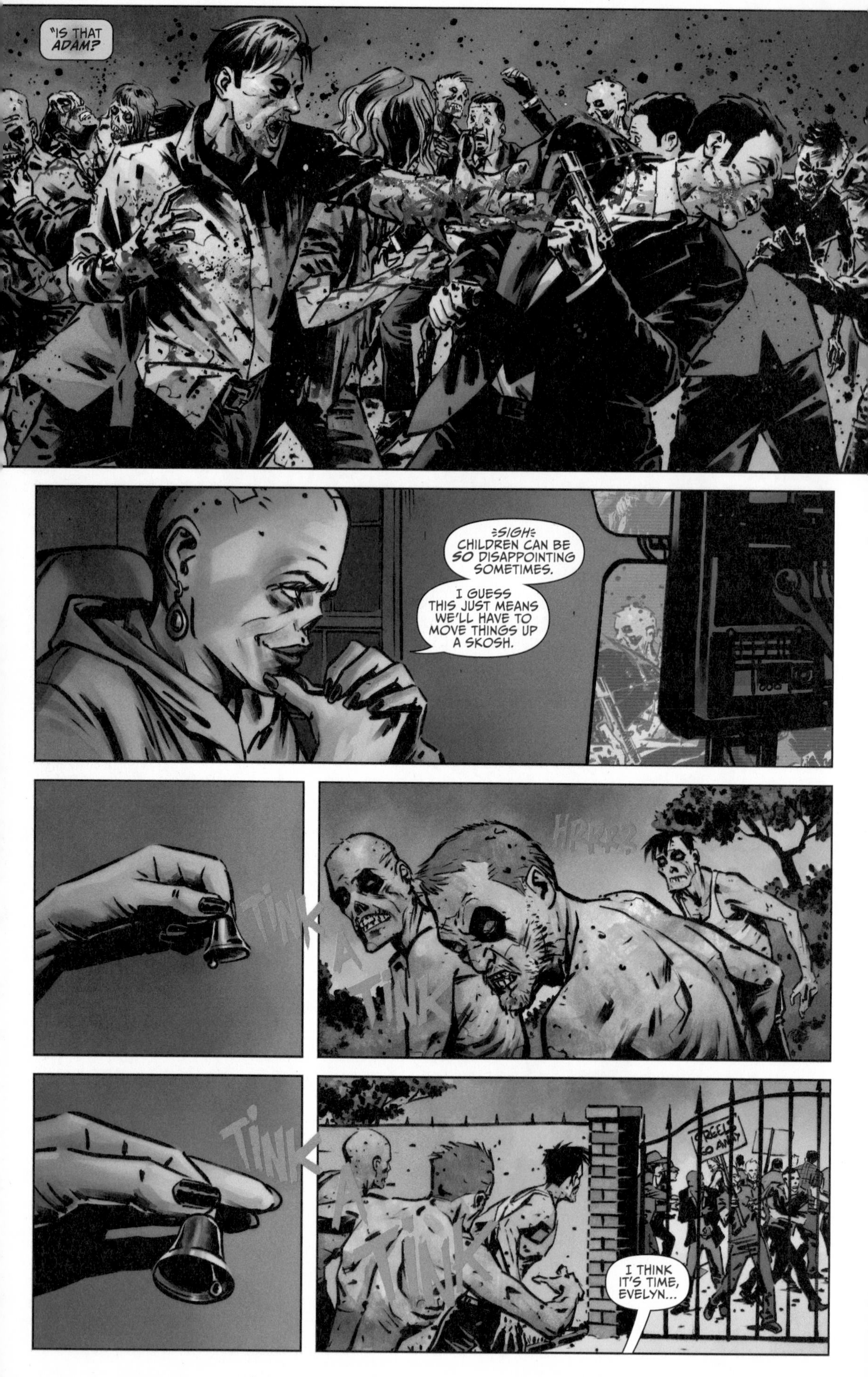
"IS THAT ADAM?
SIGH CHILDREN CAN BE SO DISAPPOINTING SOMETIMES.
I GUESS THIS JUST MEANS WE'LL HAVE TO MOVE THINGS UP A SKOSH.
TINK A TINK
HRRR??
TINK A TINK
I THINK IT'S TIME, EVELYN...

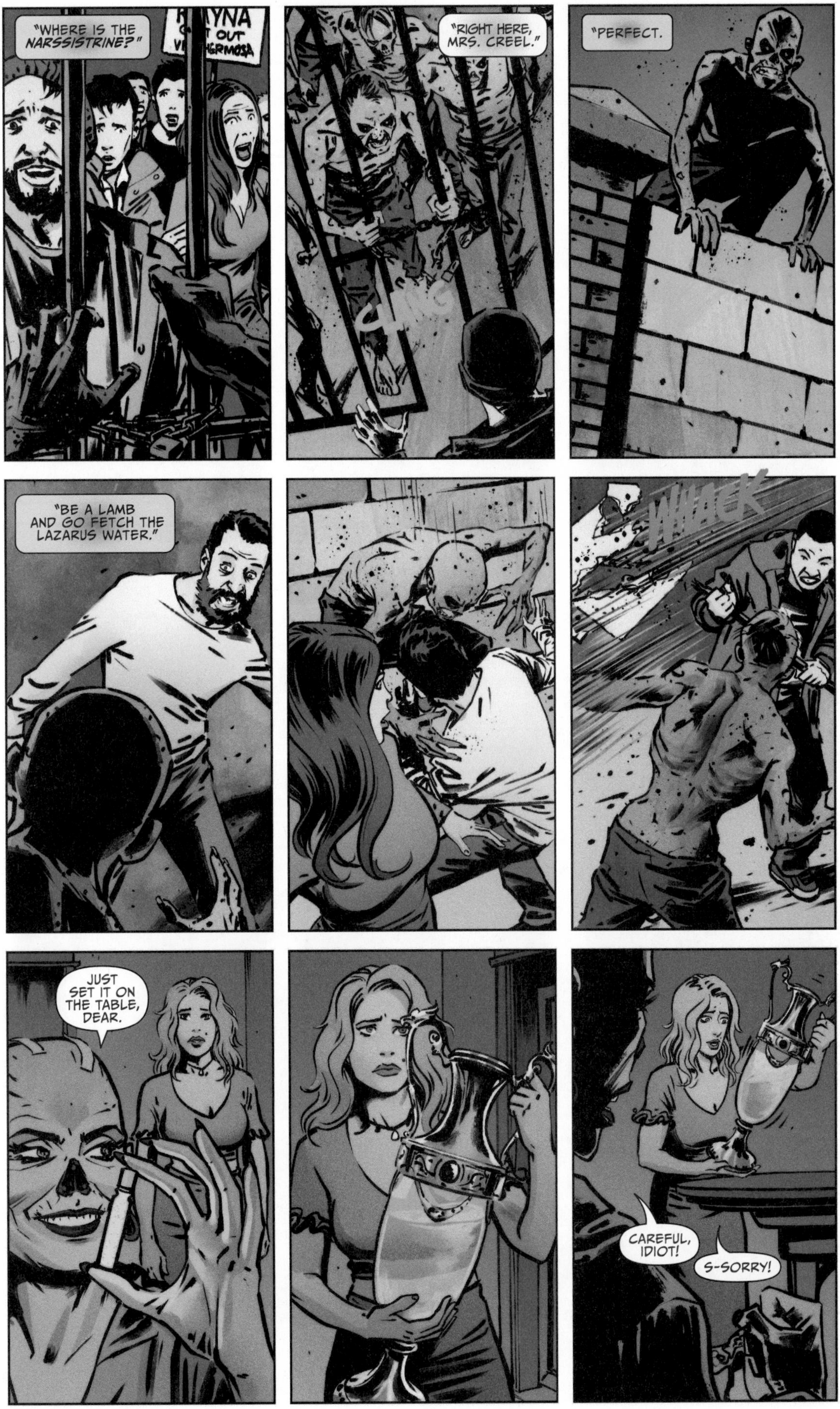
"WHERE IS THE *NARSSISTRINE?*"
"RIGHT HERE, MRS. CREEL."
"PERFECT.
"BE A LAMB AND GO FETCH THE LAZARUS WATER."
WHACK
JUST SET IT ON THE TABLE, DEAR.
CAREFUL, IDIOT!
S-SORRY!

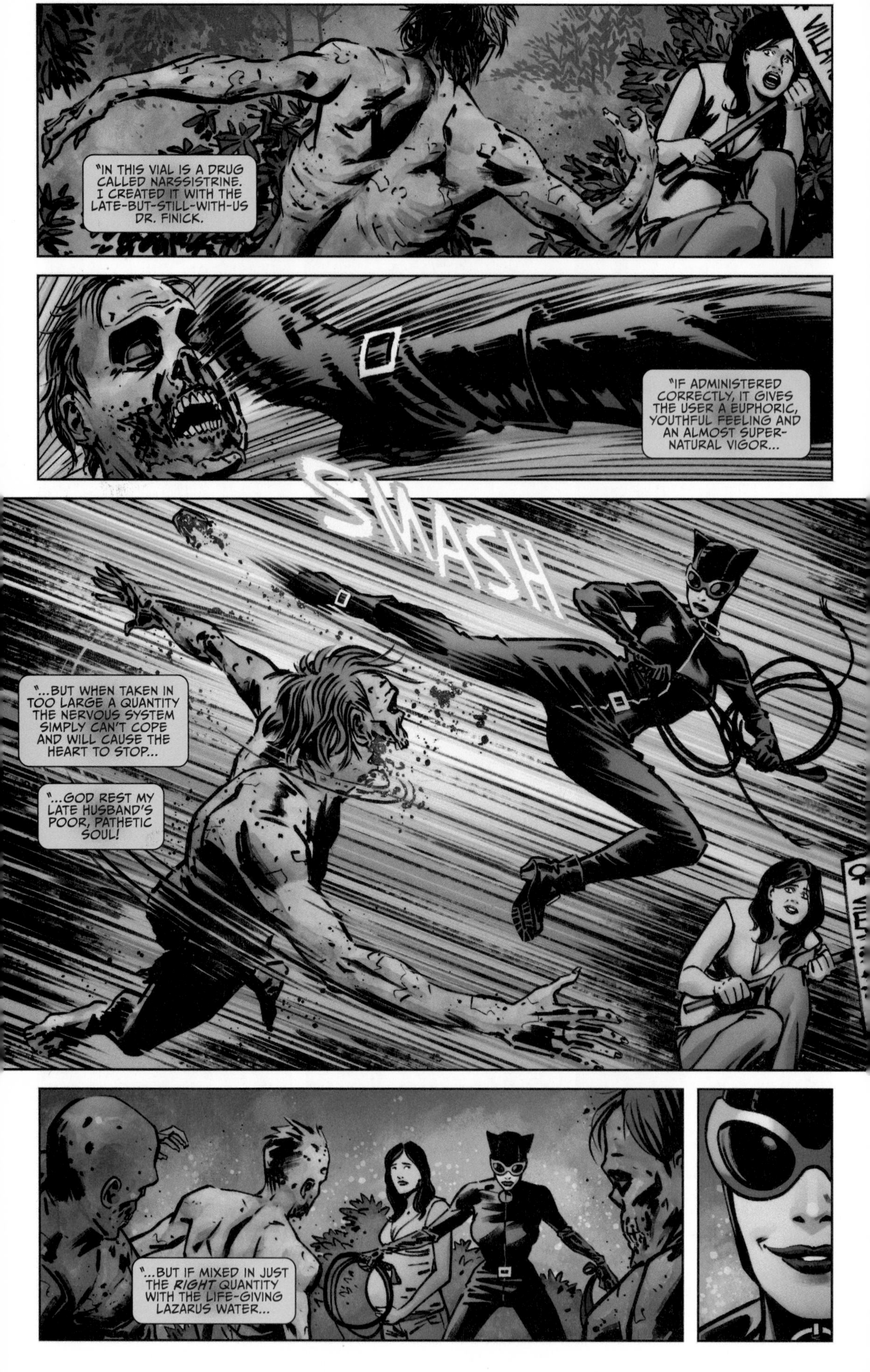
"IN THIS VIAL IS A DRUG CALLED NARSSISTRINE. I CREATED IT WITH THE LATE-BUT-STILL-WITH-US DR. FINICK.
"IF ADMINISTERED CORRECTLY, IT GIVES THE USER A EUPHORIC, YOUTHFUL FEELING AND AN ALMOST SUPER-NATURAL VIGOR...
SMASH
"...BUT WHEN TAKEN IN TOO LARGE A QUANTITY THE NERVOUS SYSTEM SIMPLY CAN'T COPE AND WILL CAUSE THE HEART TO STOP...
"...GOD REST MY LATE HUSBAND'S POOR, PATHETIC SOUL!
"...BUT IF MIXED IN JUST THE *RIGHT* QUANTITY WITH THE LIFE-GIVING LAZARUS WATER...

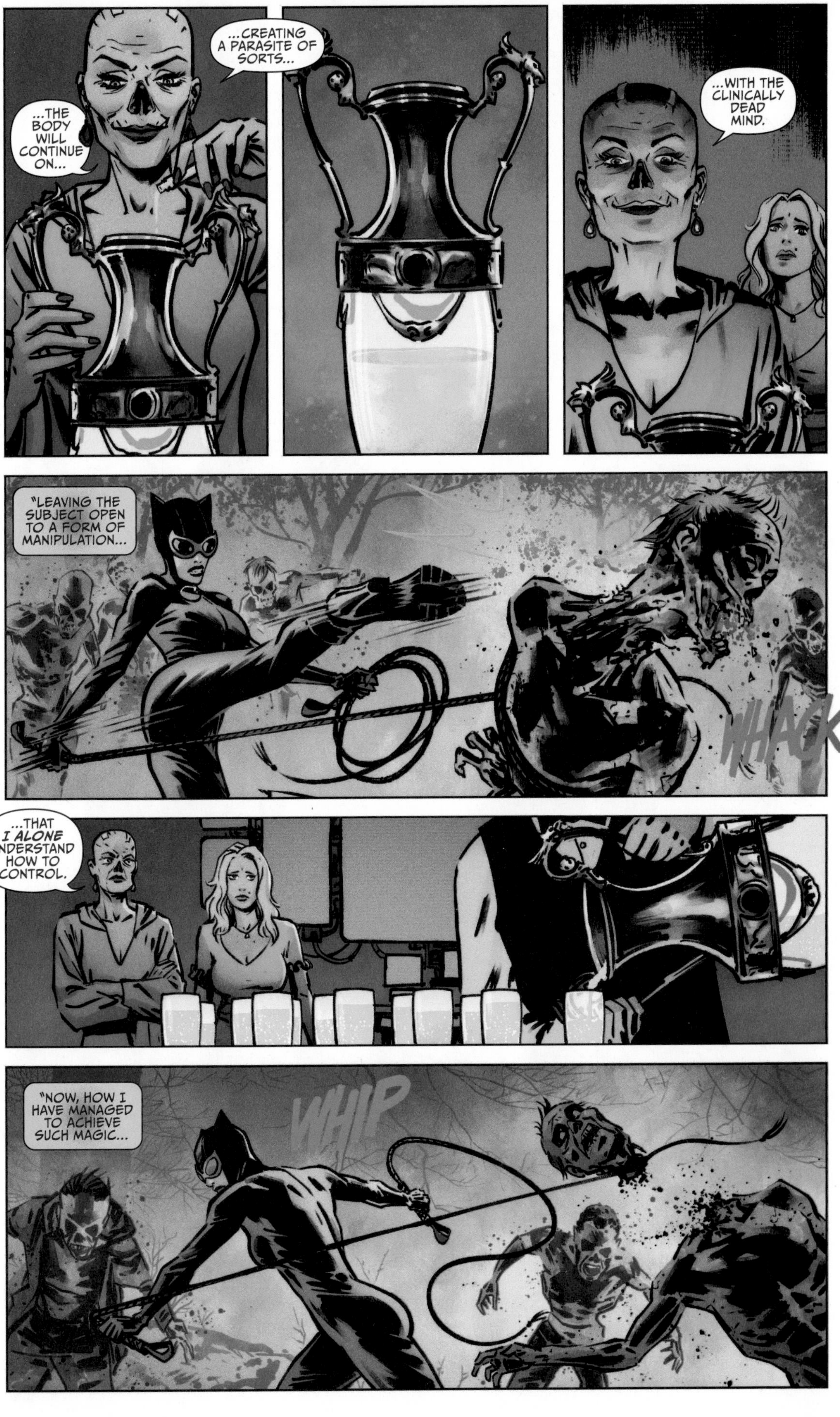
...THE BODY WILL CONTINUE ON...
...CREATING A PARASITE OF SORTS...
...WITH THE CLINICALLY DEAD MIND.
"LEAVING THE SUBJECT OPEN TO A FORM OF MANIPULATION...
WHACK
...THAT I ALONE UNDERSTAND HOW TO CONTROL.
"NOW, HOW I HAVE MANAGED TO ACHIEVE SUCH MAGIC...
WHIP

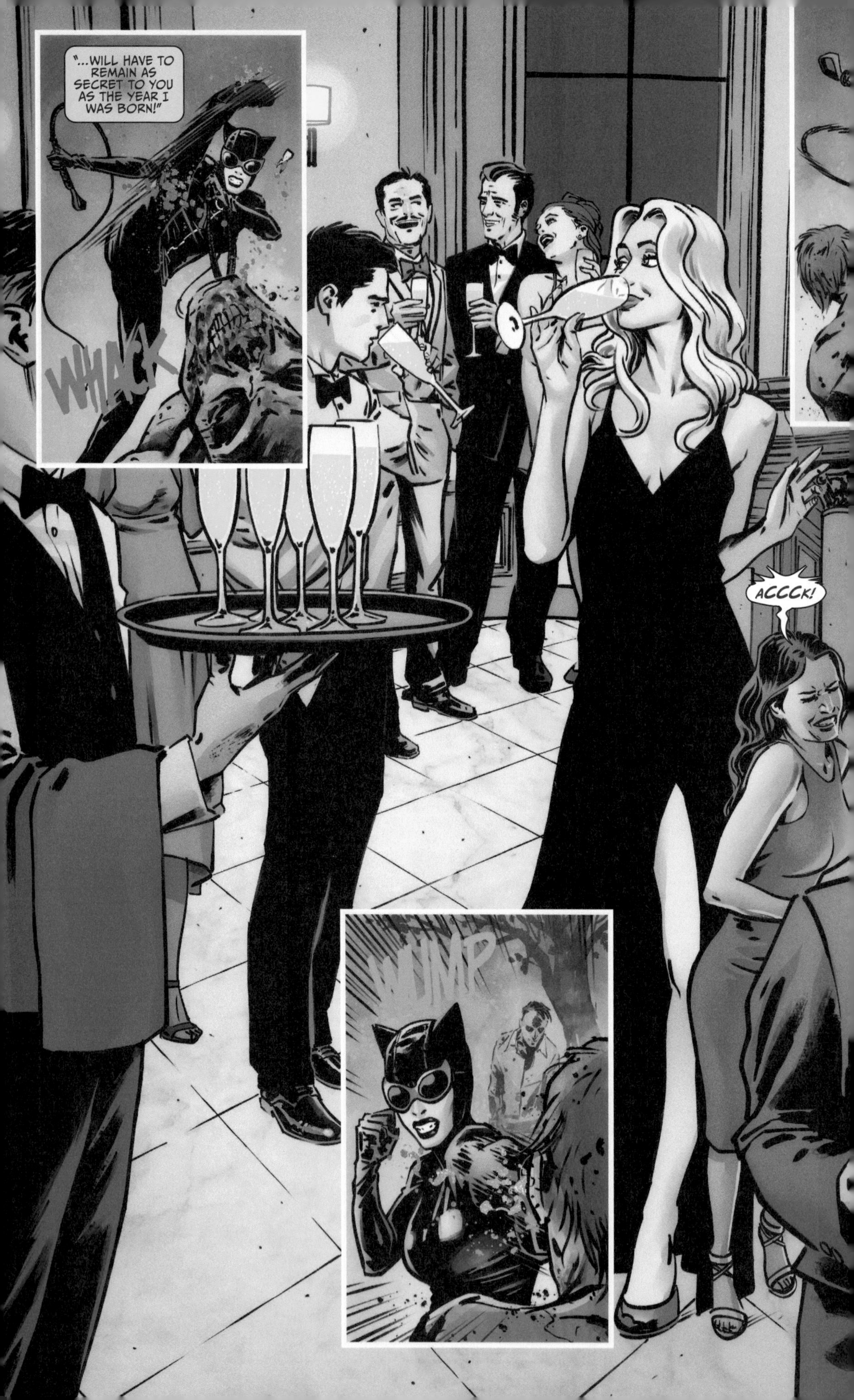
"...WILL HAVE TO REMAIN AS SECRET TO YOU AS THE YEAR I WAS BORN!"
WHACK
ACCCK!
WUMP

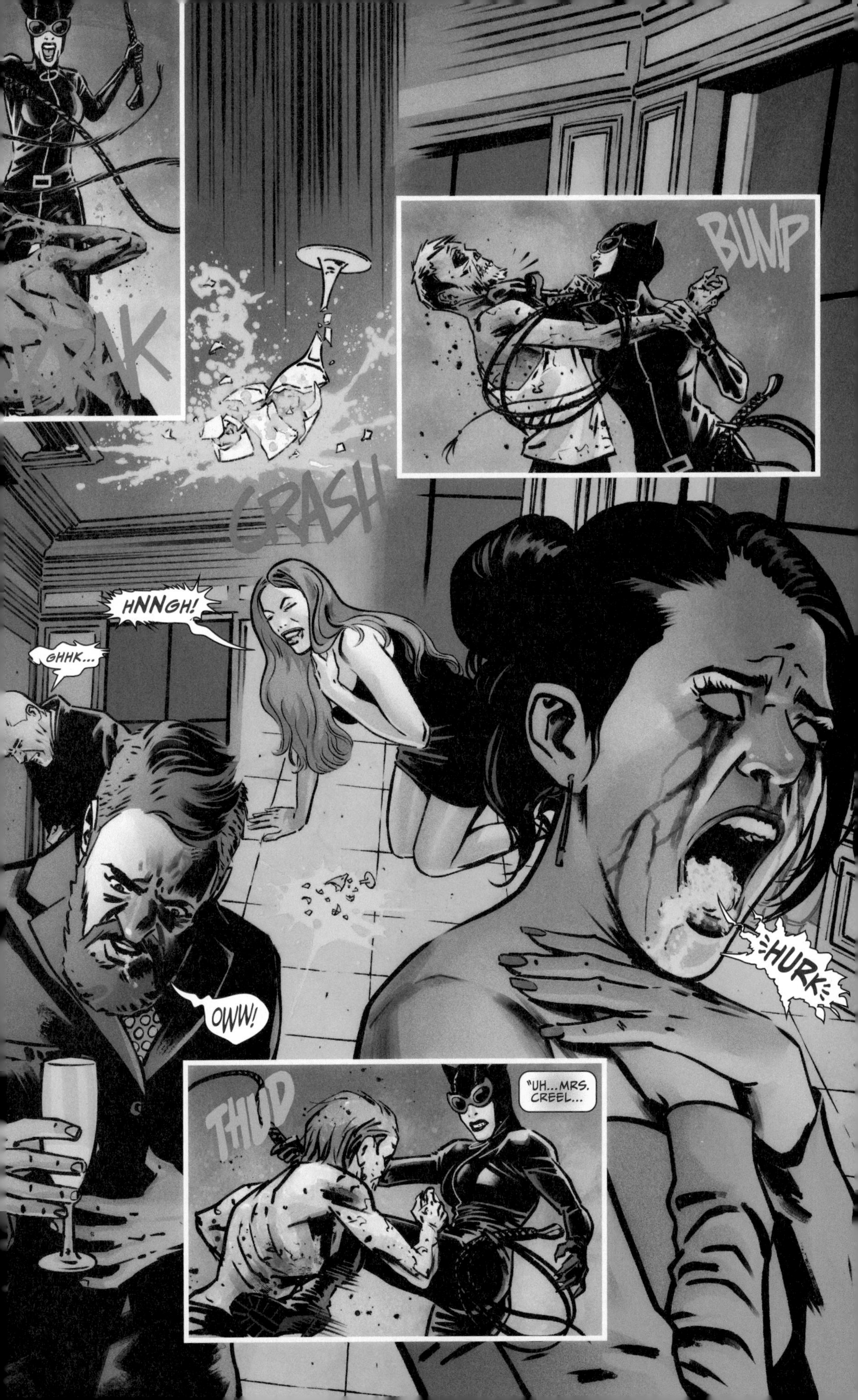
KRAK
CRASH
BUMP
HNNGH!
GHHK...
HURK
OWW!
THUD
"UH...MRS. CREEL...

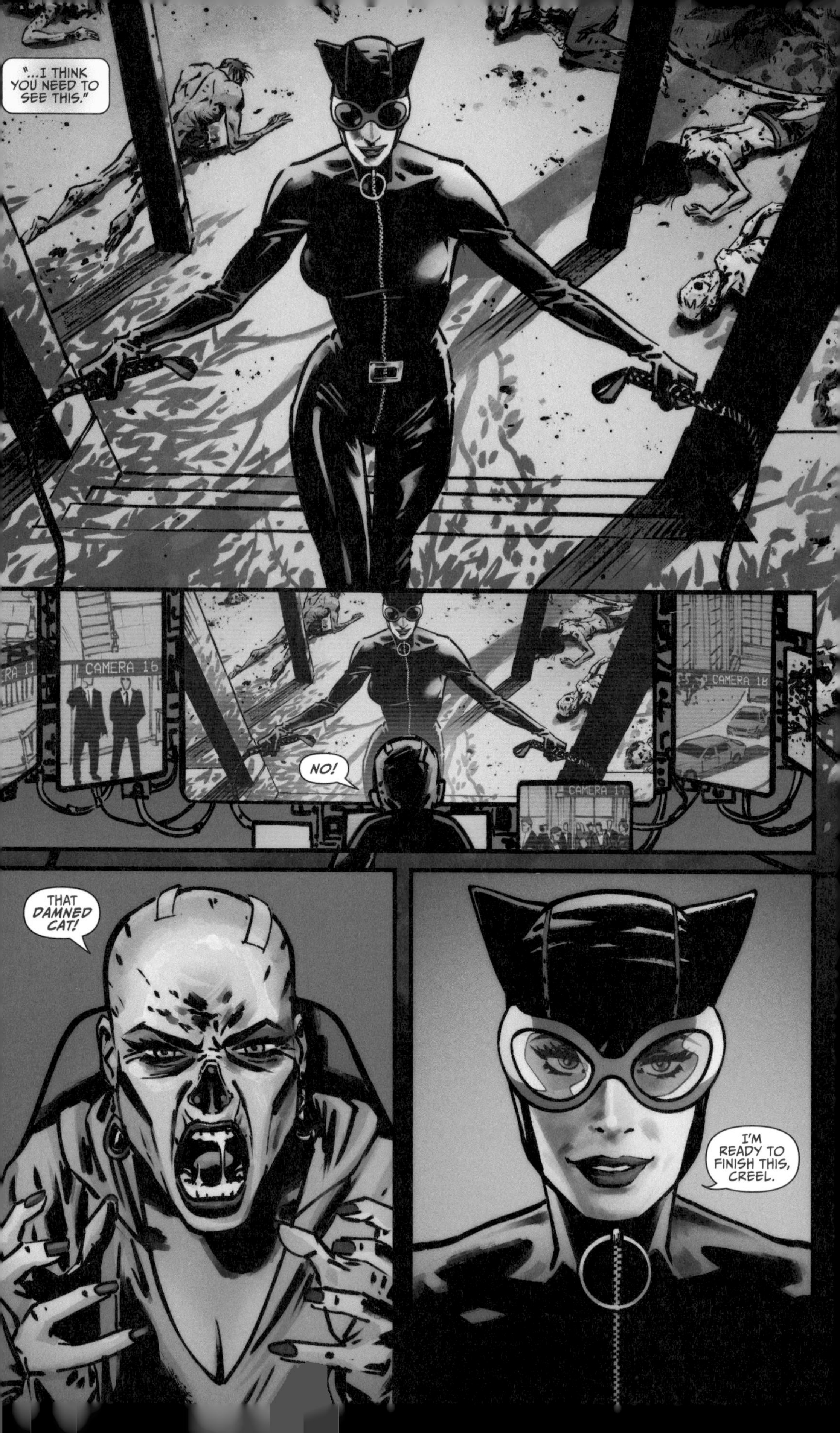
"...I THINK YOU NEED TO SEE THIS."
CAMERA 16
CAMERA 18
NO!
CAMERA 17
THAT DAMNED CAT!
I'M READY TO FINISH THIS, CREEL.

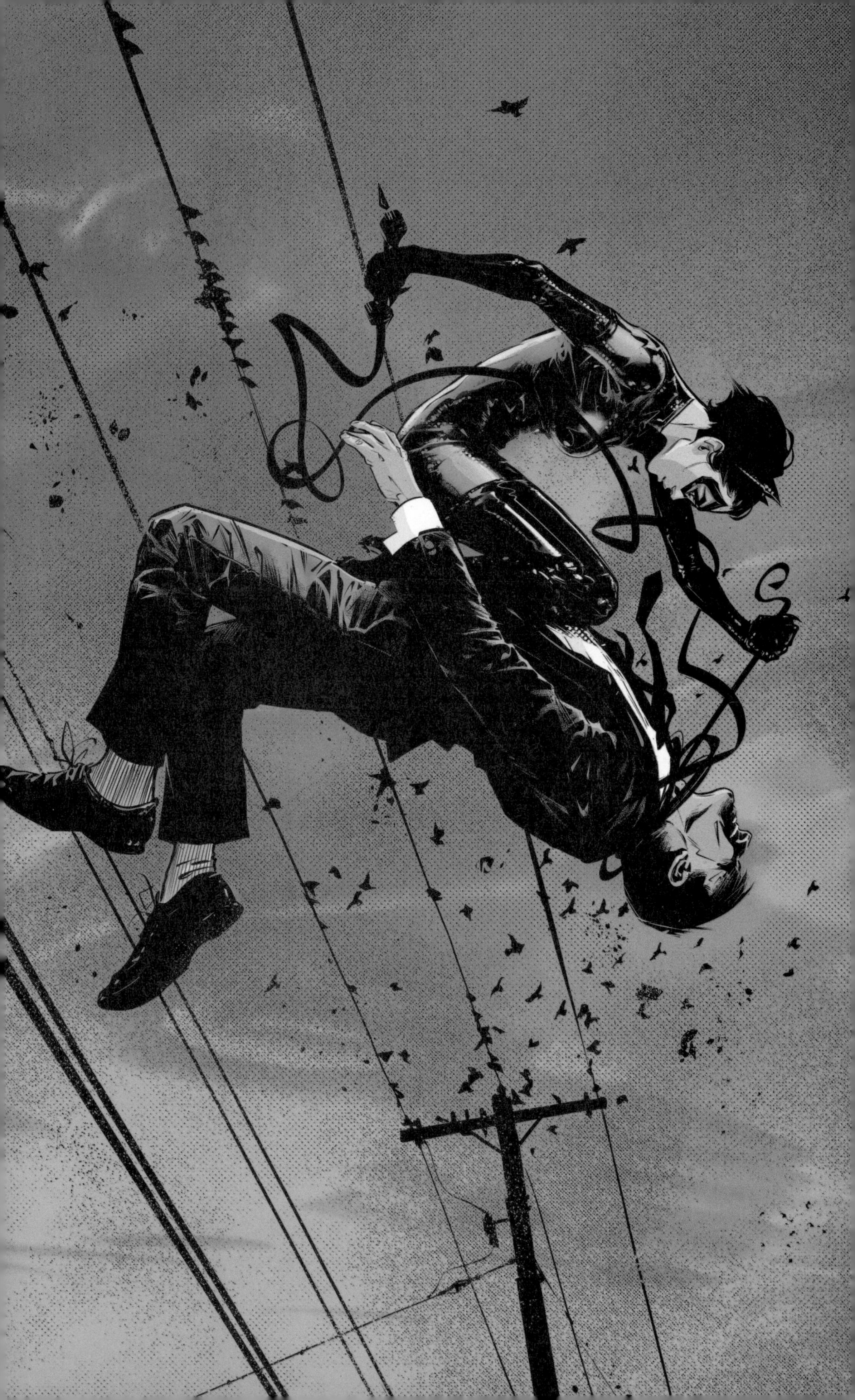

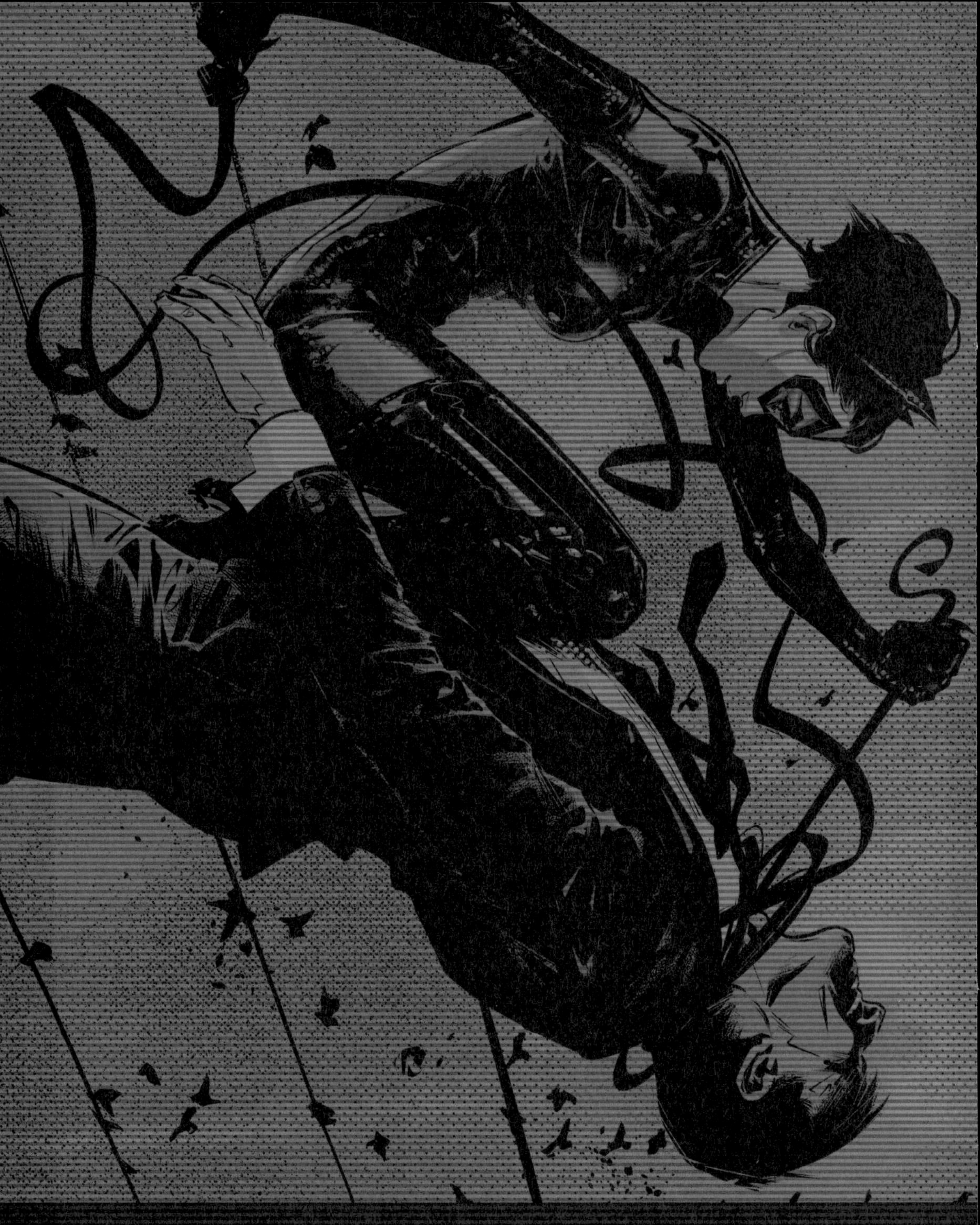

CATWOMAN
#21

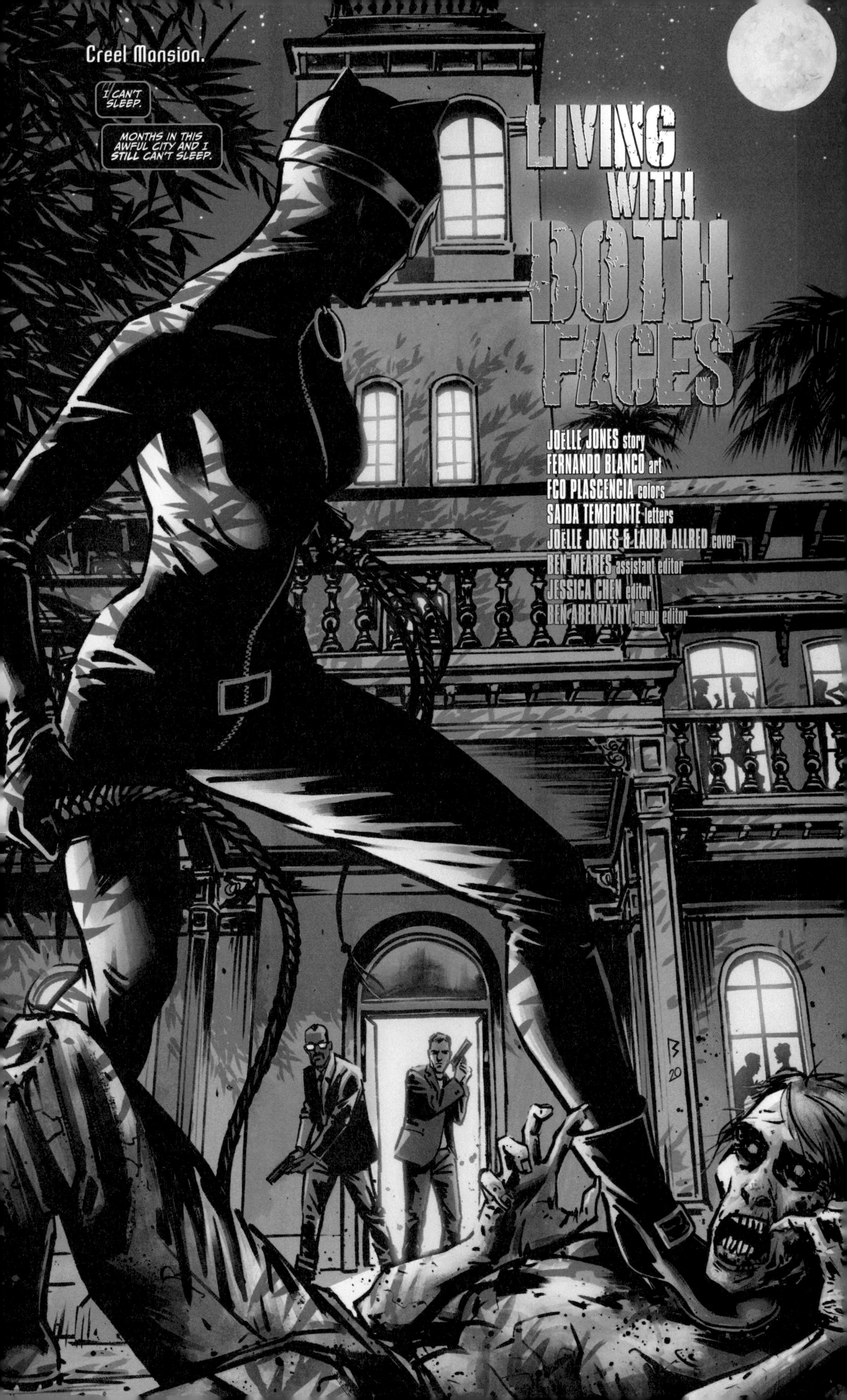

Creel Mansion.
I CAN'T SLEEP.
MONTHS IN THIS AWFUL CITY AND I STILL CAN'T SLEEP.
LIVING WITH BOTH FACES
JOËLLE JONES story
FERNANDO BLANCO art
FCO PLASCENCIA colors
SAIDA TEMOFONTE letters
JOËLLE JONES & LAURA ALLRED cover
BEN MEARES assistant editor
JESSICA CHEN editor
BEN ABERNATHY group editor

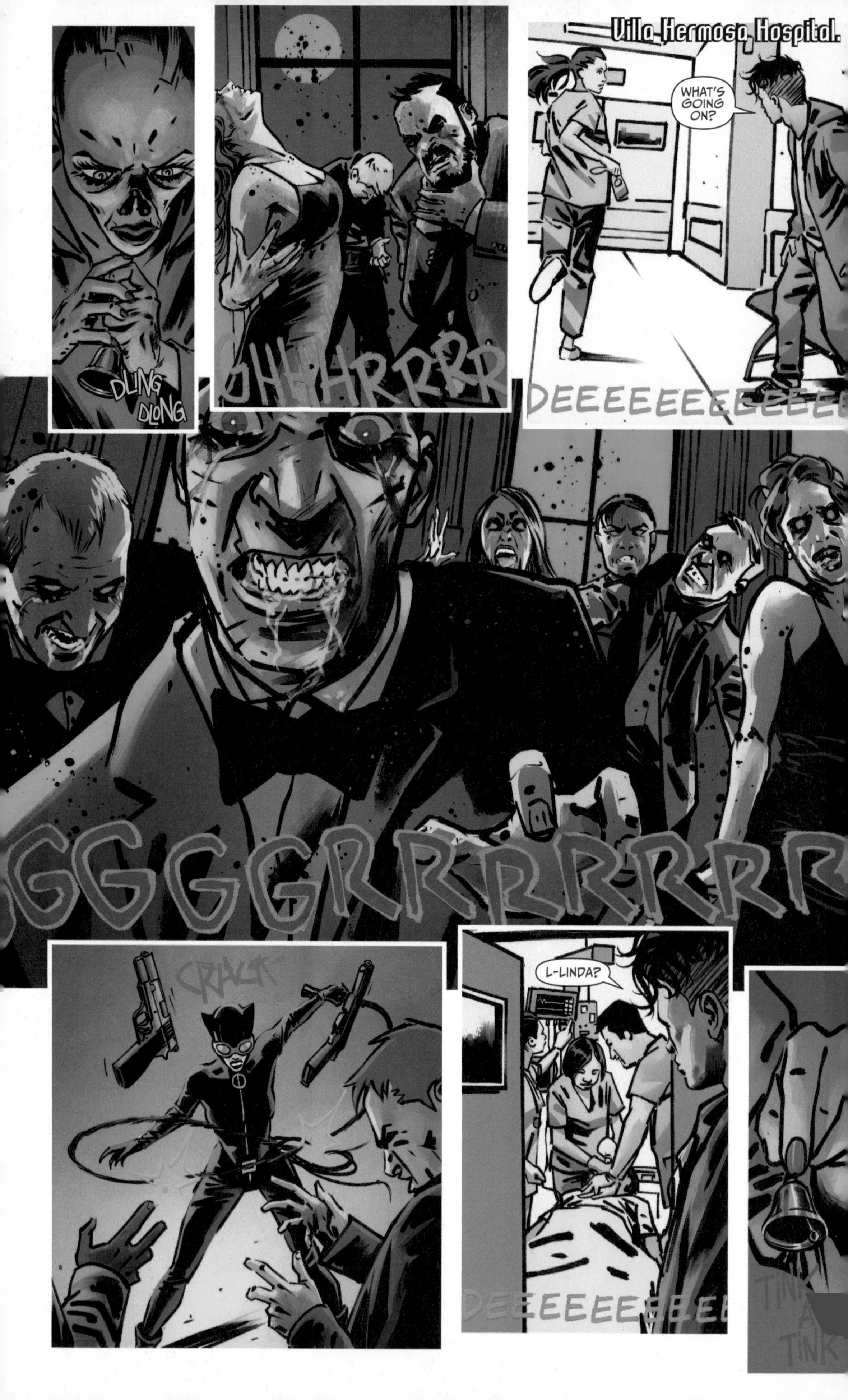
Villa Hermosa Hospital.
DLING DLONG
OHHHRRRR
WHAT'S GOING ON?
DEEEEEEEEEEEE
GGGGRRRRRRR
CRACK
L-LINDA?
DEEEEEEEEEE
TINK A TINK

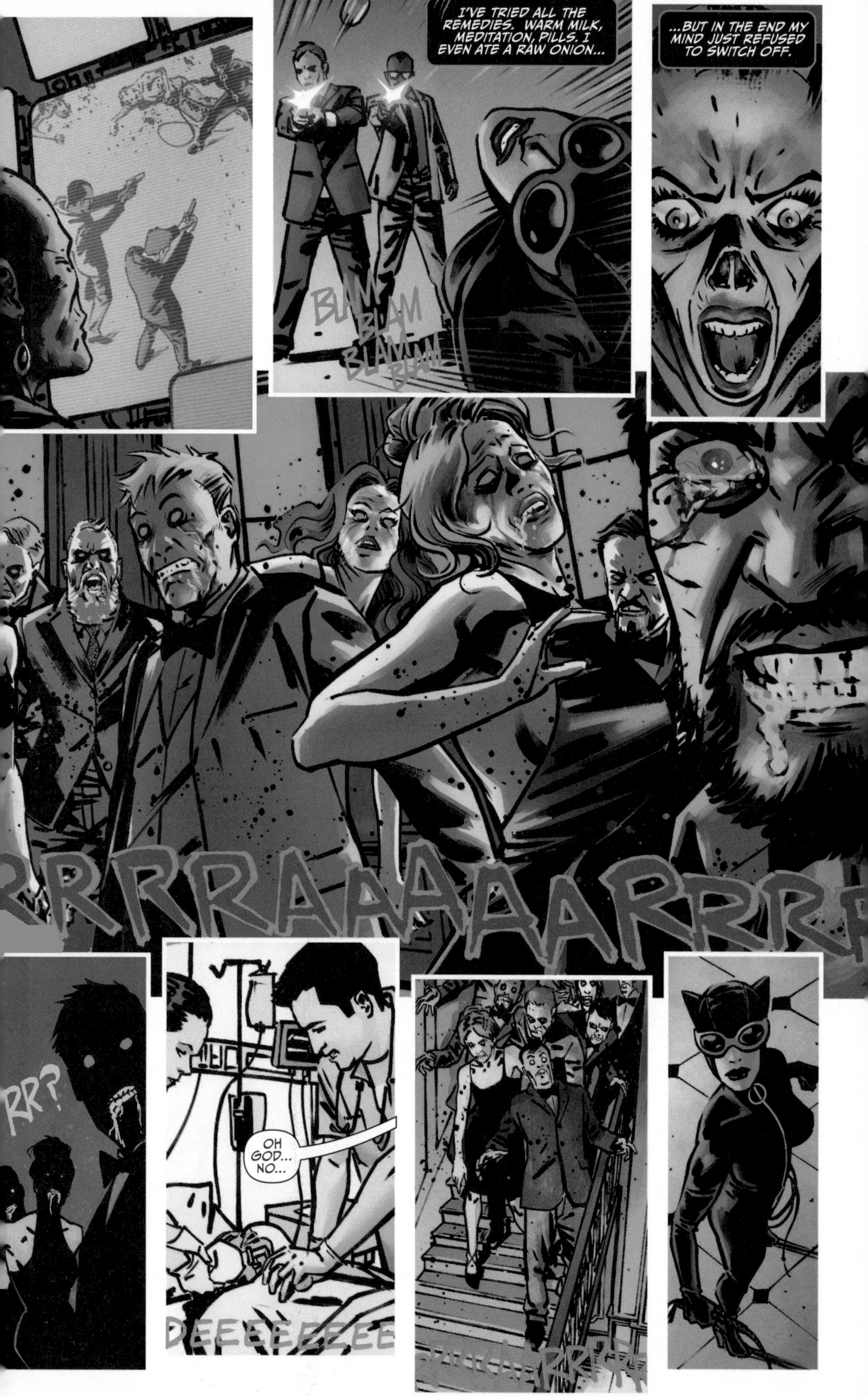
I'VE TRIED ALL THE REMEDIES. WARM MILK, MEDITATION, PILLS. I EVEN ATE A RAW ONION...
BLAM BLAM BLAM BLAM
...BUT IN THE END MY MIND JUST REFUSED TO SWITCH OFF.
RRRRAAAAAARRRR
RR?
OH GOD... NO...
DEEEEEEEEE

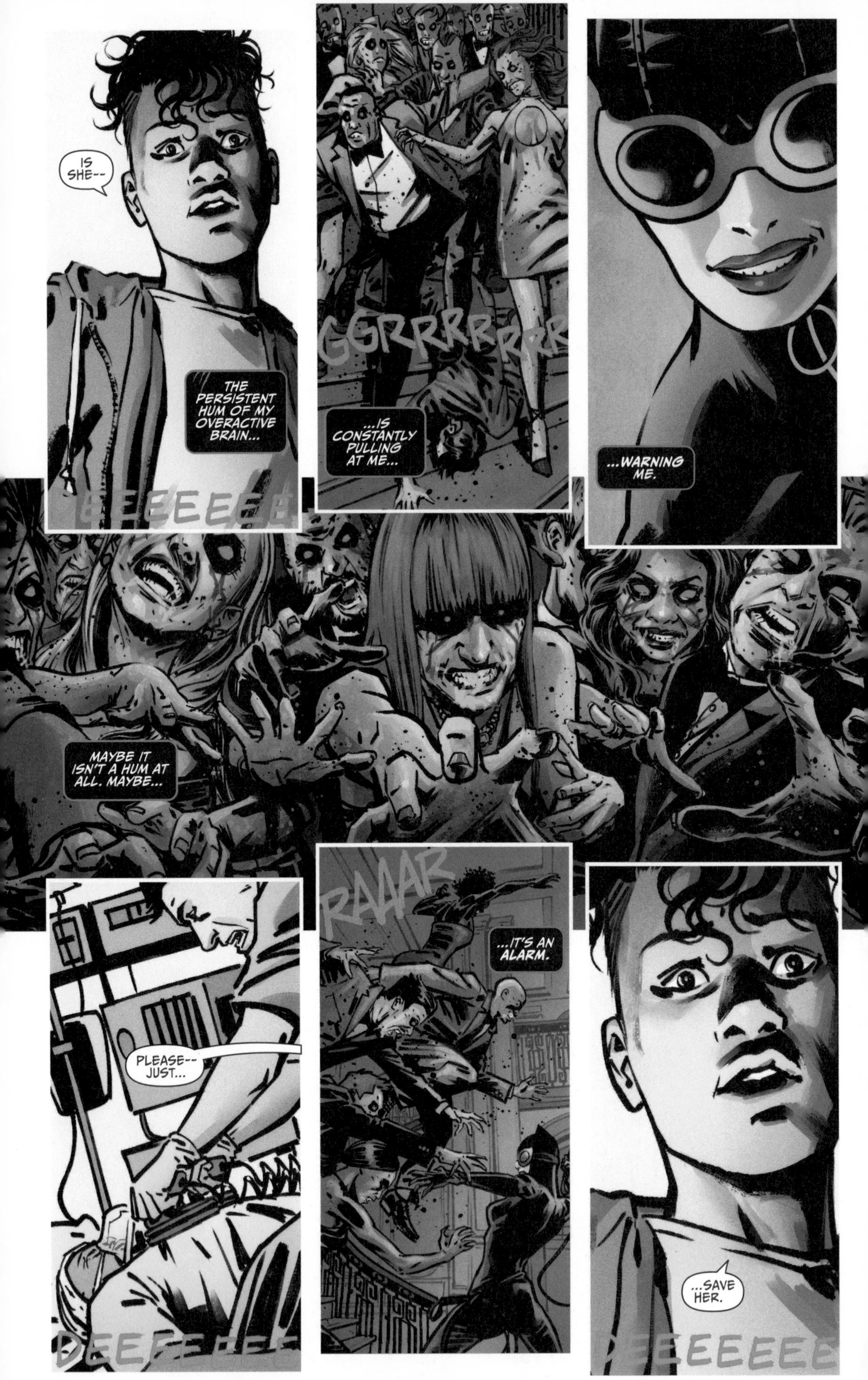
IS SHE--
THE PERSISTENT HUM OF MY OVERACTIVE BRAIN...
GGRRRRRRRRR
...IS CONSTANTLY PULLING AT ME...
...WARNING ME.
EEEEEEEE
MAYBE IT ISN'T A HUM AT ALL. MAYBE...
PLEASE-- JUST...
DEEEEEEE
RAAAR
...IT'S AN ALARM.
...SAVE HER.
DEEEEEEE

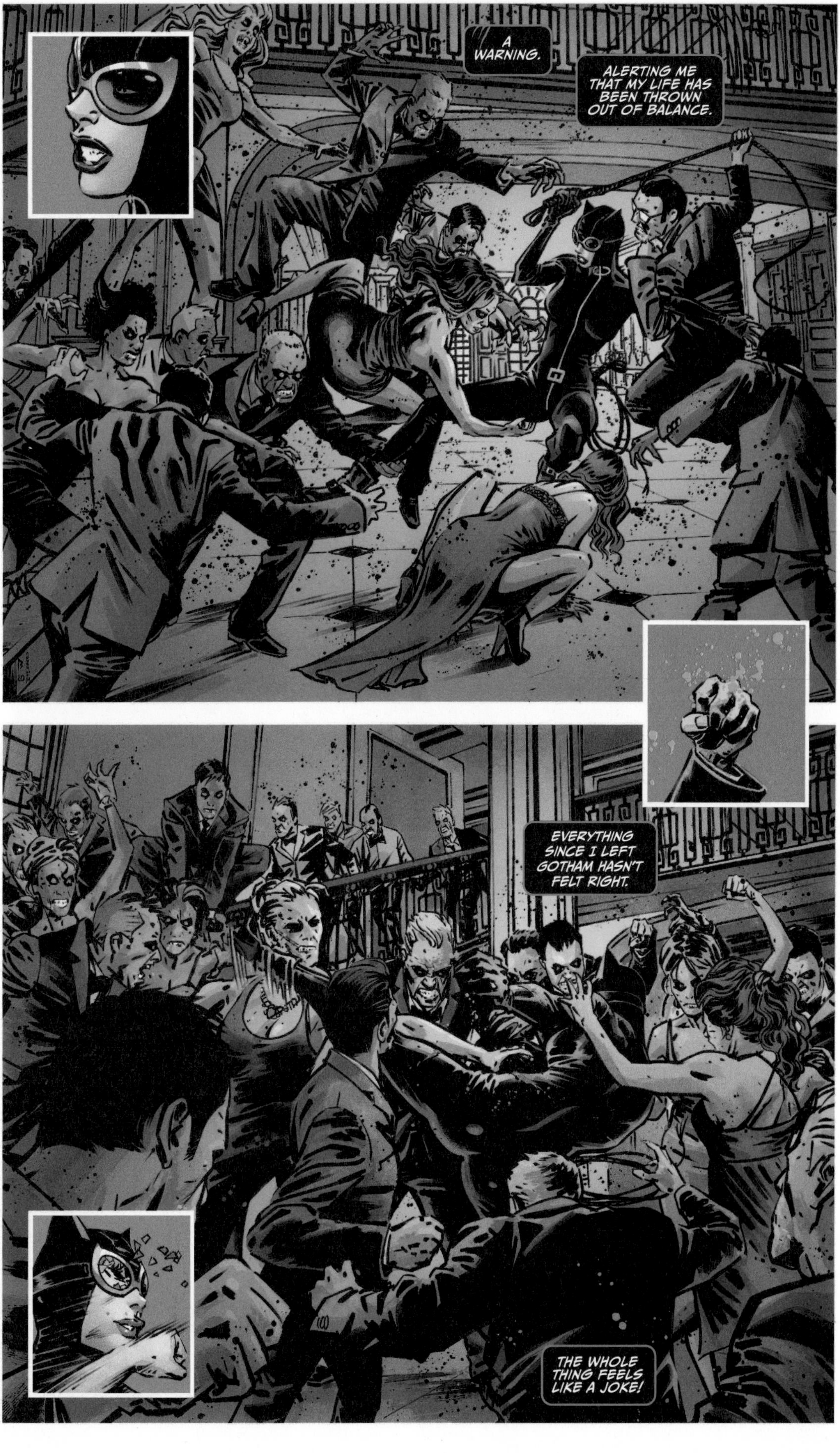
A WARNING.
ALERTING ME THAT MY LIFE HAS BEEN THROWN OUT OF BALANCE.
EVERYTHING SINCE I LEFT GOTHAM HASN'T FELT RIGHT.
THE WHOLE THING FEELS LIKE A JOKE!

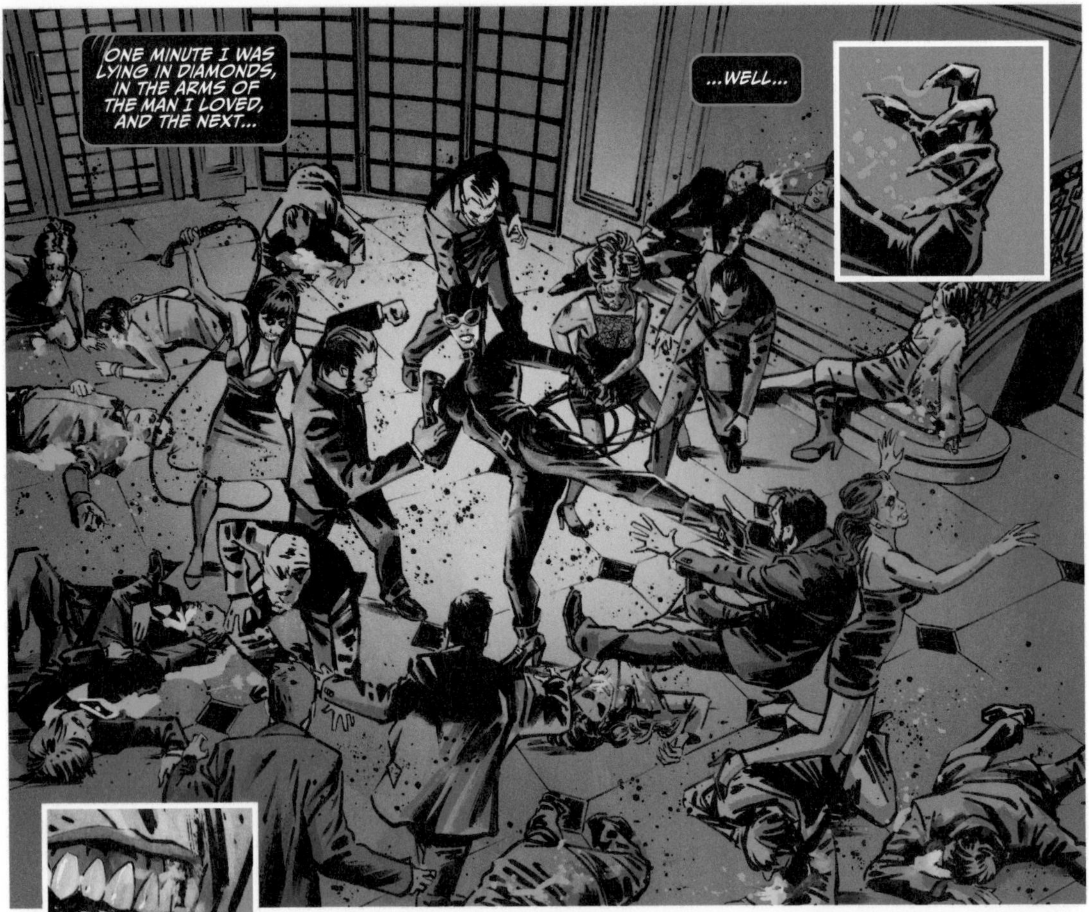
ONE MINUTE I WAS LYING IN DIAMONDS, IN THE ARMS OF THE MAN I LOVED, AND THE NEXT...
...WELL...

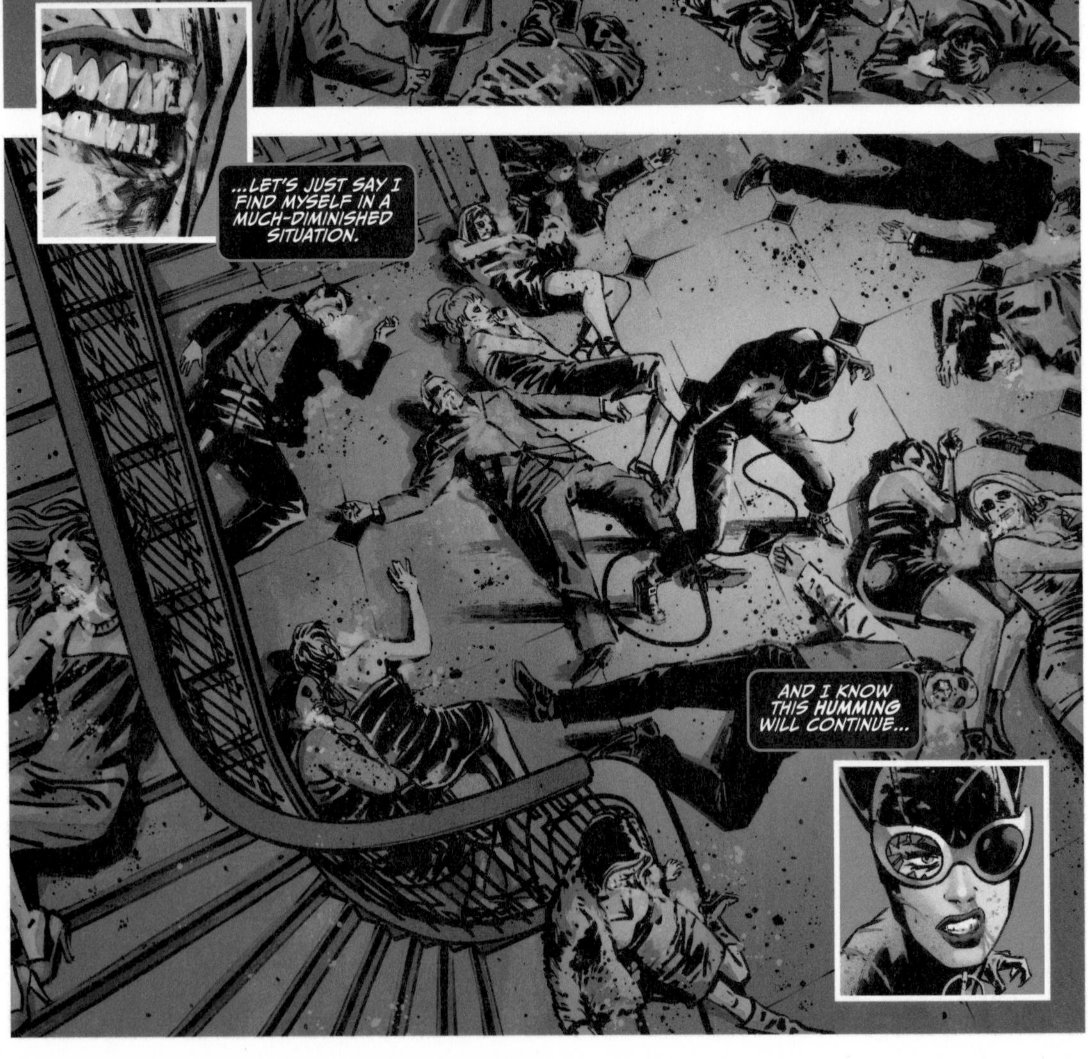
...LET'S JUST SAY I FIND MYSELF IN A MUCH-DIMINISHED SITUATION.
AND I KNOW THIS HUMMING WILL CONTINUE...

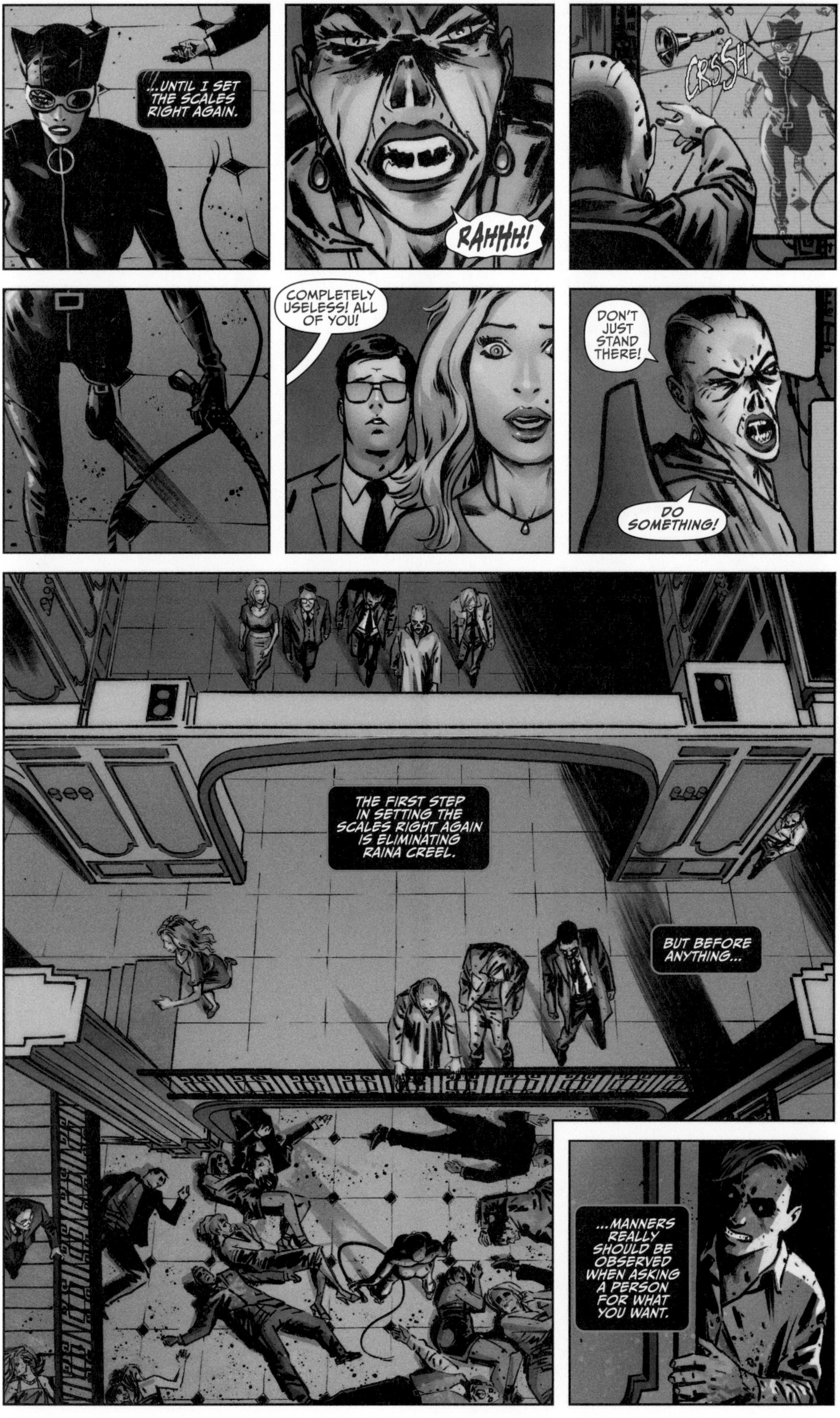
...UNTIL I SET THE SCALES RIGHT AGAIN.
RAHHH!
CRSSH
COMPLETELY USELESS! ALL OF YOU!
DON'T JUST STAND THERE!
DO SOMETHING!
THE FIRST STEP IN SETTING THE SCALES RIGHT AGAIN IS ELIMINATING RAINA CREEL.
BUT BEFORE ANYTHING...
...MANNERS REALLY SHOULD BE OBSERVED WHEN ASKING A PERSON FOR WHAT YOU WANT.

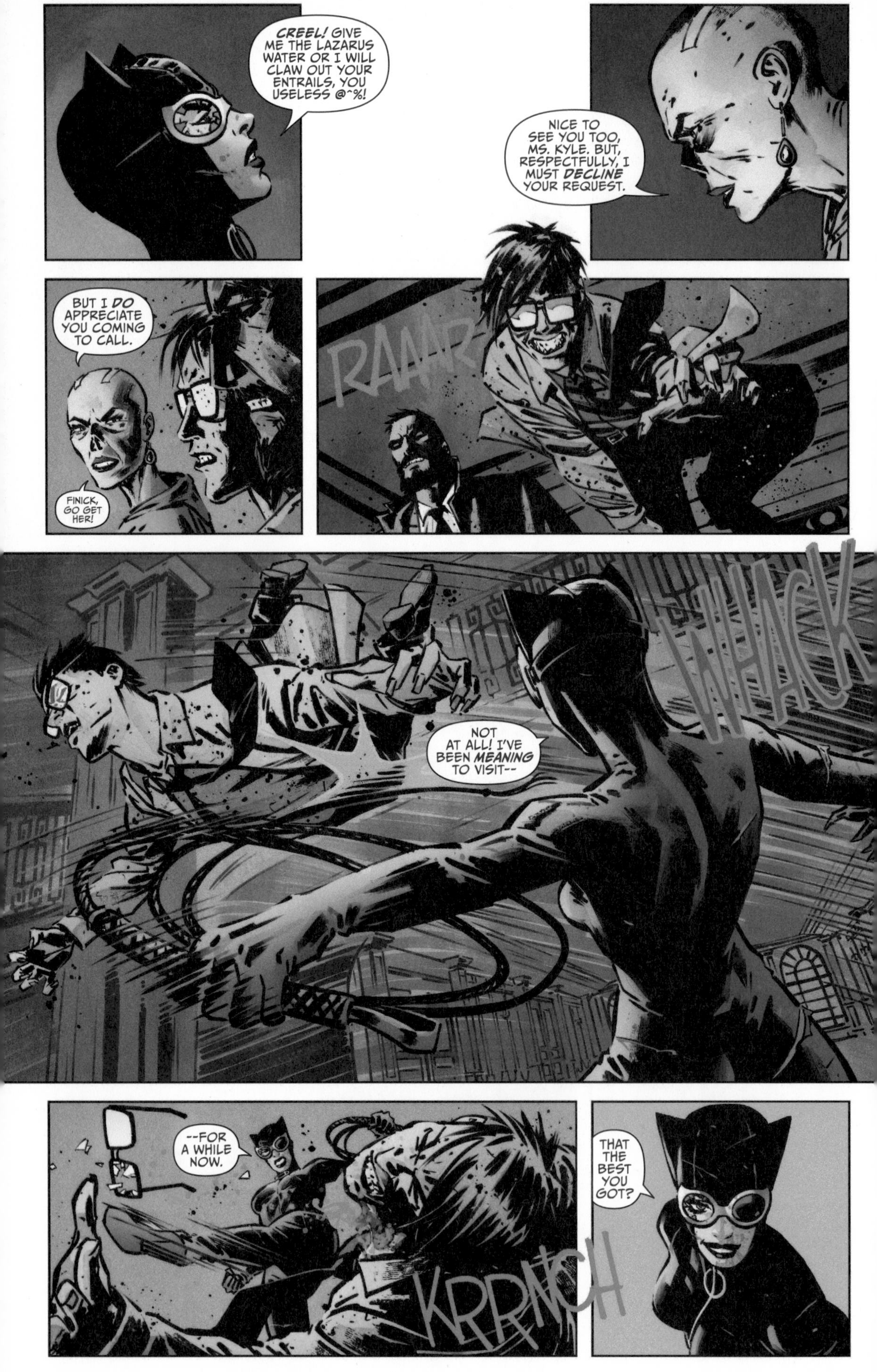

CREEL! GIVE ME THE LAZARUS WATER OR I WILL CLAW OUT YOUR ENTRAILS, YOU USELESS @^%!
NICE TO SEE YOU TOO, MS. KYLE. BUT, RESPECTFULLY, I MUST DECLINE YOUR REQUEST.
BUT I DO APPRECIATE YOU COMING TO CALL.
FINICK, GO GET HER!
RAAAR
WHACK
NOT AT ALL! I'VE BEEN MEANING TO VISIT--
--FOR A WHILE NOW.
KRRNCH
THAT THE BEST YOU GOT?

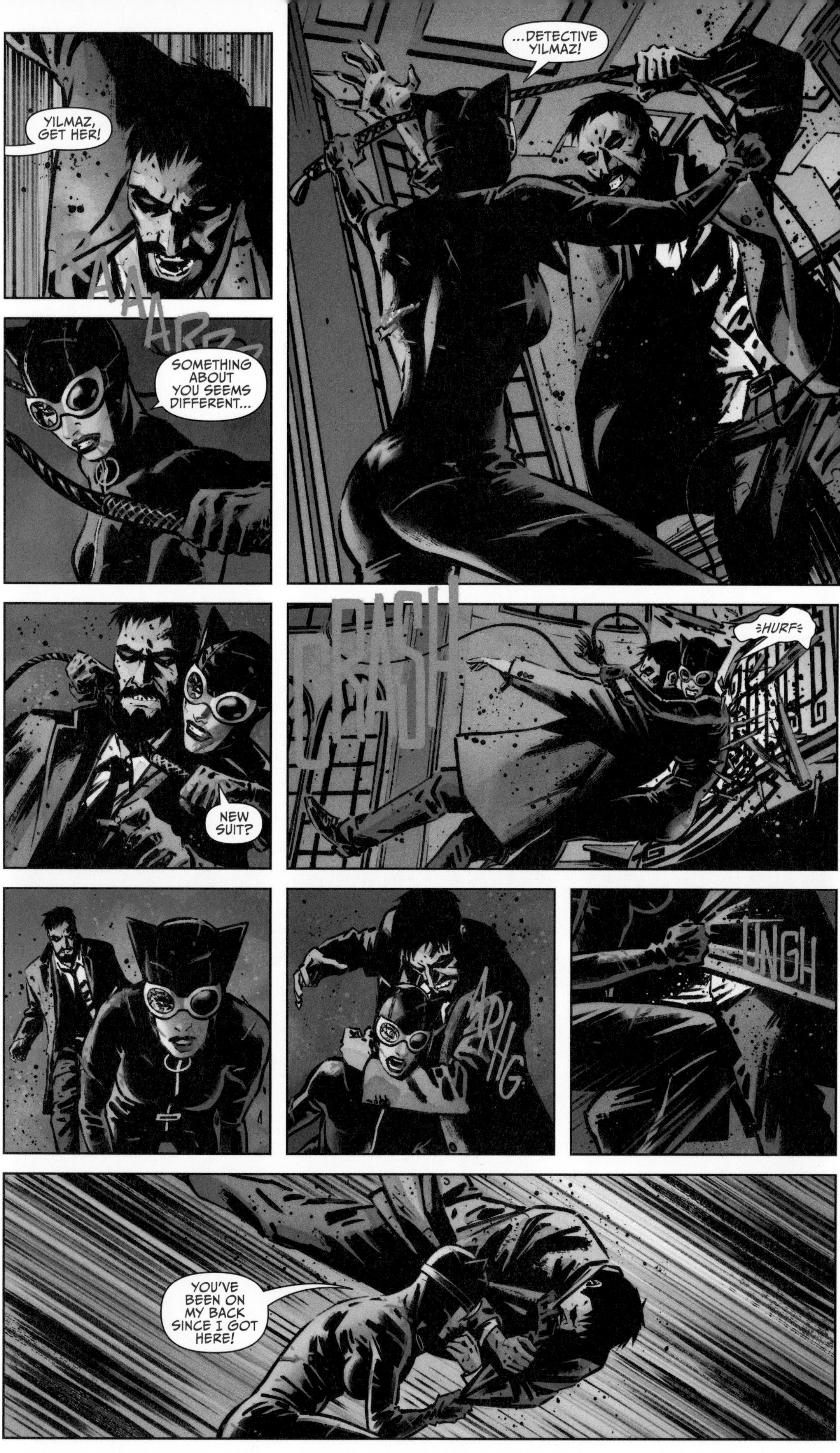
YILMAZ, GET HER!
SOMETHING ABOUT YOU SEEMS DIFFERENT...
...DETECTIVE YILMAZ!
NEW SUIT?
CRASH
HURF
ARHG
UNGH
YOU'VE BEEN ON MY BACK SINCE I GOT HERE!

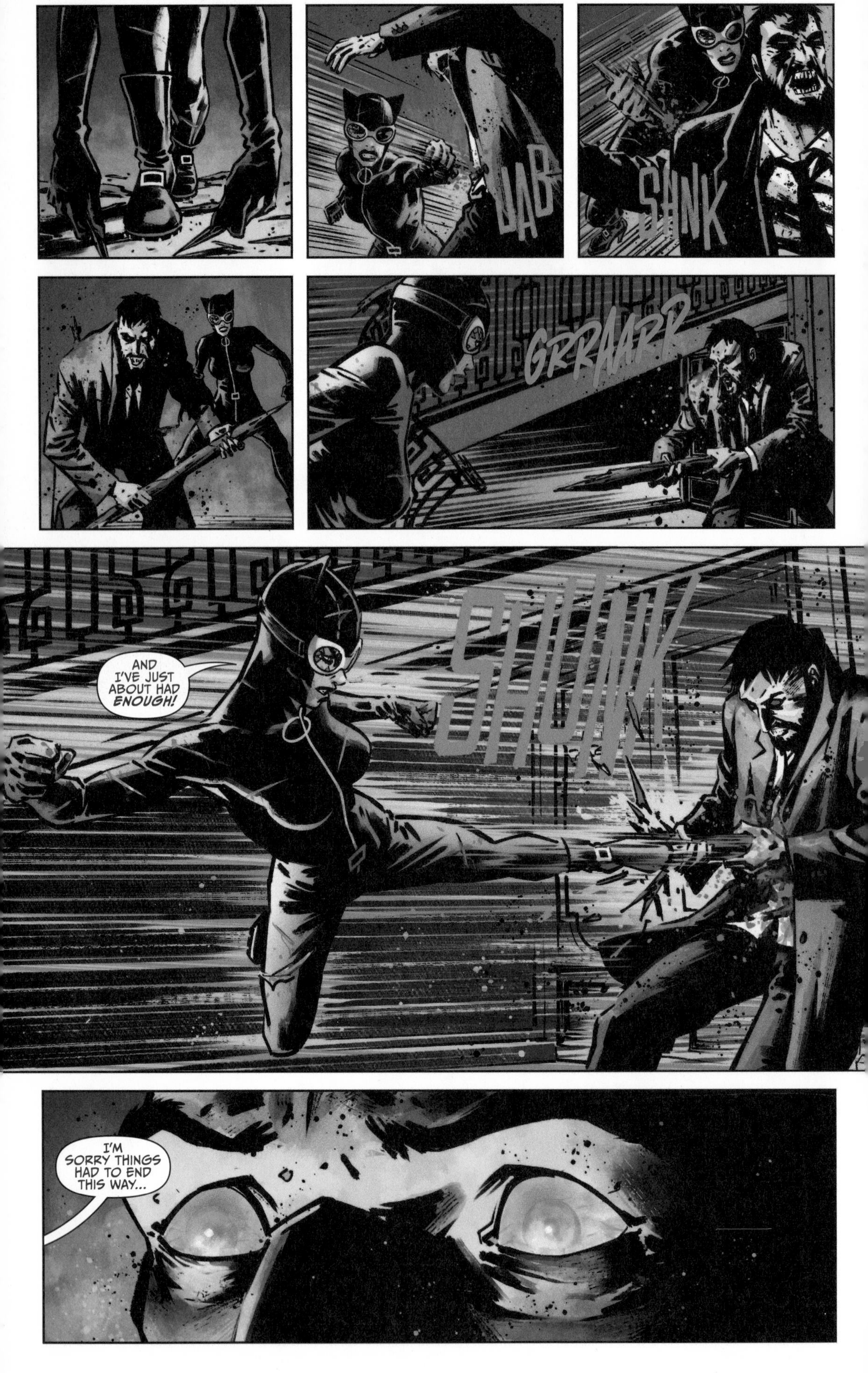
JAB
SHNK
GRRAARR
AND I'VE JUST ABOUT HAD ENOUGH!
SHUNK
I'M SORRY THINGS HAD TO END THIS WAY...

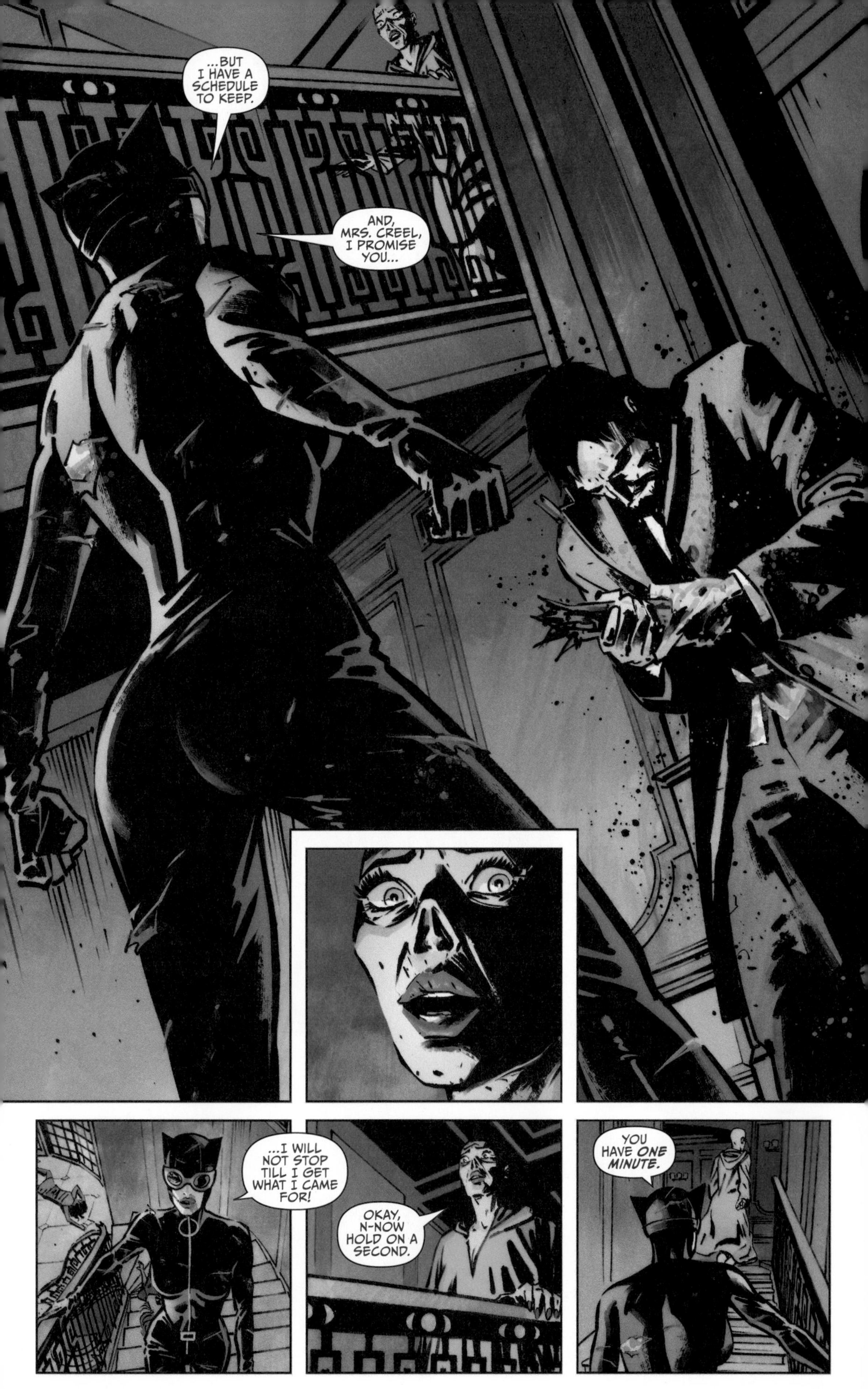
...BUT I HAVE A SCHEDULE TO KEEP.
AND, MRS. CREEL, I PROMISE YOU...
...I WILL NOT STOP TILL I GET WHAT I CAME FOR!
OKAY, N-NOW HOLD ON A SECOND.
YOU HAVE *ONE MINUTE*.

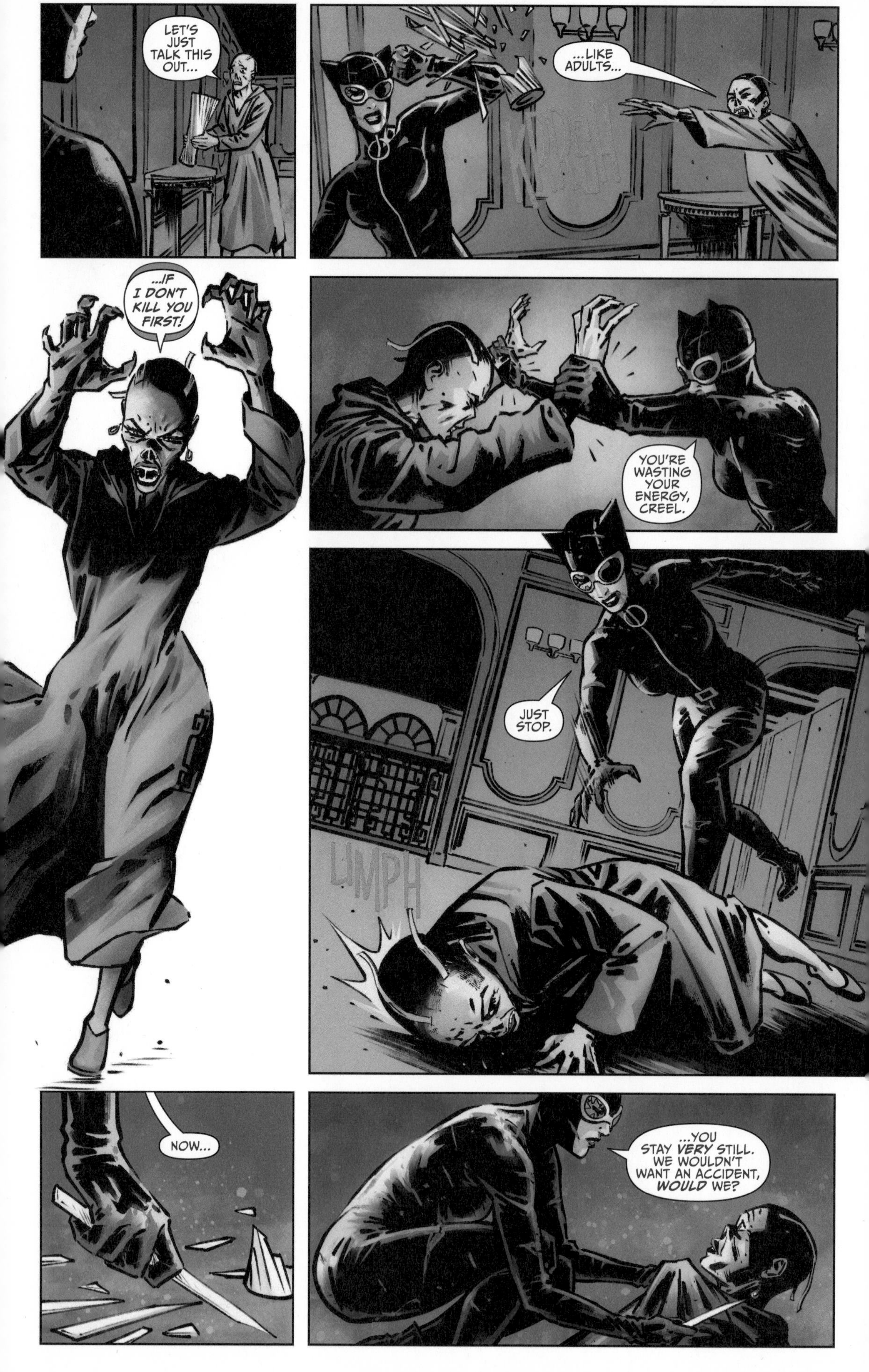
LET'S JUST TALK THIS OUT...
KRASH
...LIKE ADULTS...
...IF I DON'T KILL YOU FIRST!
YOU'RE WASTING YOUR ENERGY, CREEL.
JUST STOP.
LUMPH
NOW...
...YOU STAY VERY STILL. WE WOULDN'T WANT AN ACCIDENT, WOULD WE?

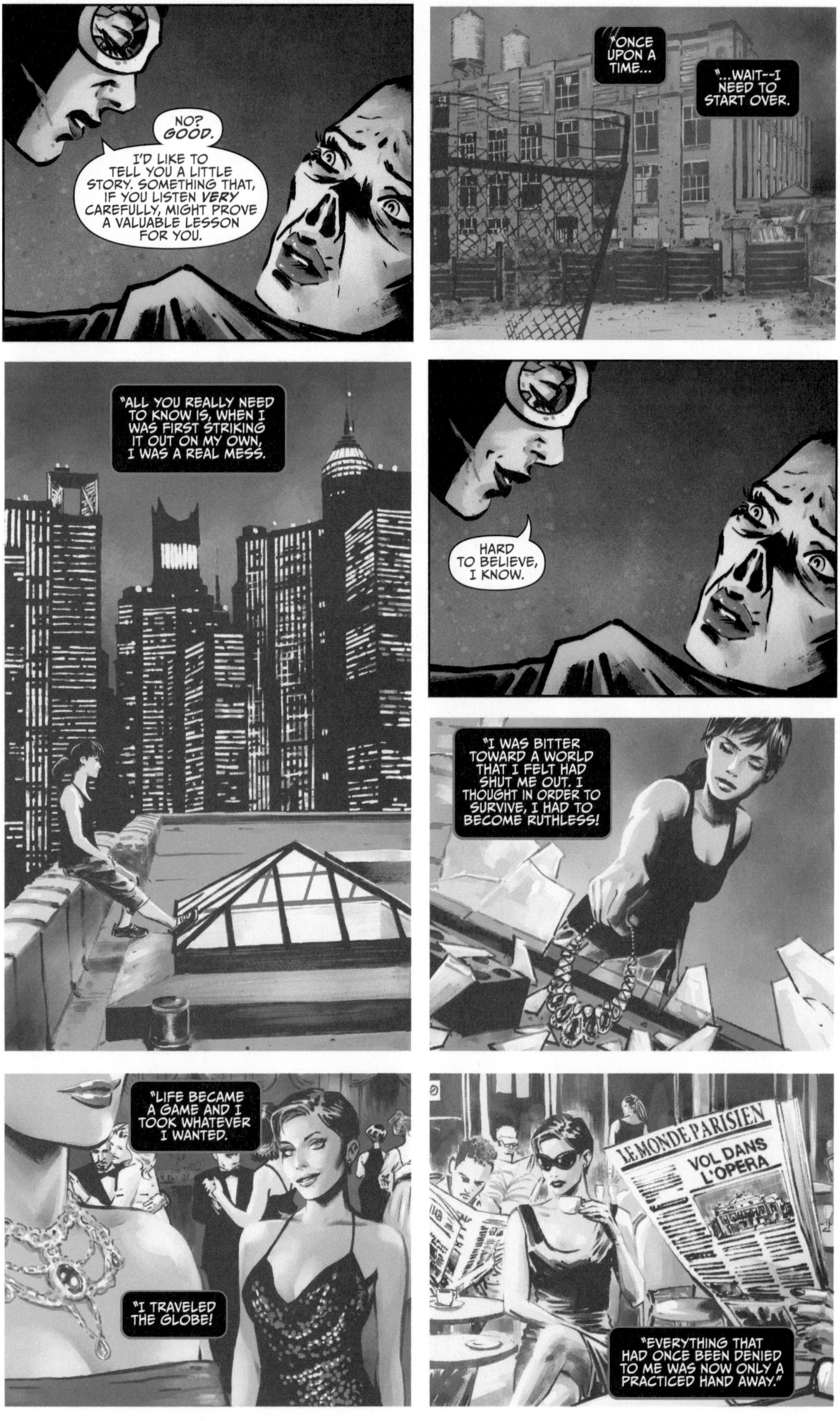
NO? GOOD.
I'D LIKE TO TELL YOU A LITTLE STORY. SOMETHING THAT, IF YOU LISTEN VERY CAREFULLY, MIGHT PROVE A VALUABLE LESSON FOR YOU.
"ONCE UPON A TIME...
"...WAIT--I NEED TO START OVER.
"ALL YOU REALLY NEED TO KNOW IS, WHEN I WAS FIRST STRIKING IT OUT ON MY OWN, I WAS A REAL MESS.
HARD TO BELIEVE, I KNOW.
"I WAS BITTER TOWARD A WORLD THAT I FELT HAD SHUT ME OUT. I THOUGHT IN ORDER TO SURVIVE, I HAD TO BECOME RUTHLESS!
"LIFE BECAME A GAME AND I TOOK WHATEVER I WANTED.
"I TRAVELED THE GLOBE!
LE MONDE PARISIEN
VOL DANS L'OPERA
"EVERYTHING THAT HAD ONCE BEEN DENIED TO ME WAS NOW ONLY A PRACTICED HAND AWAY."

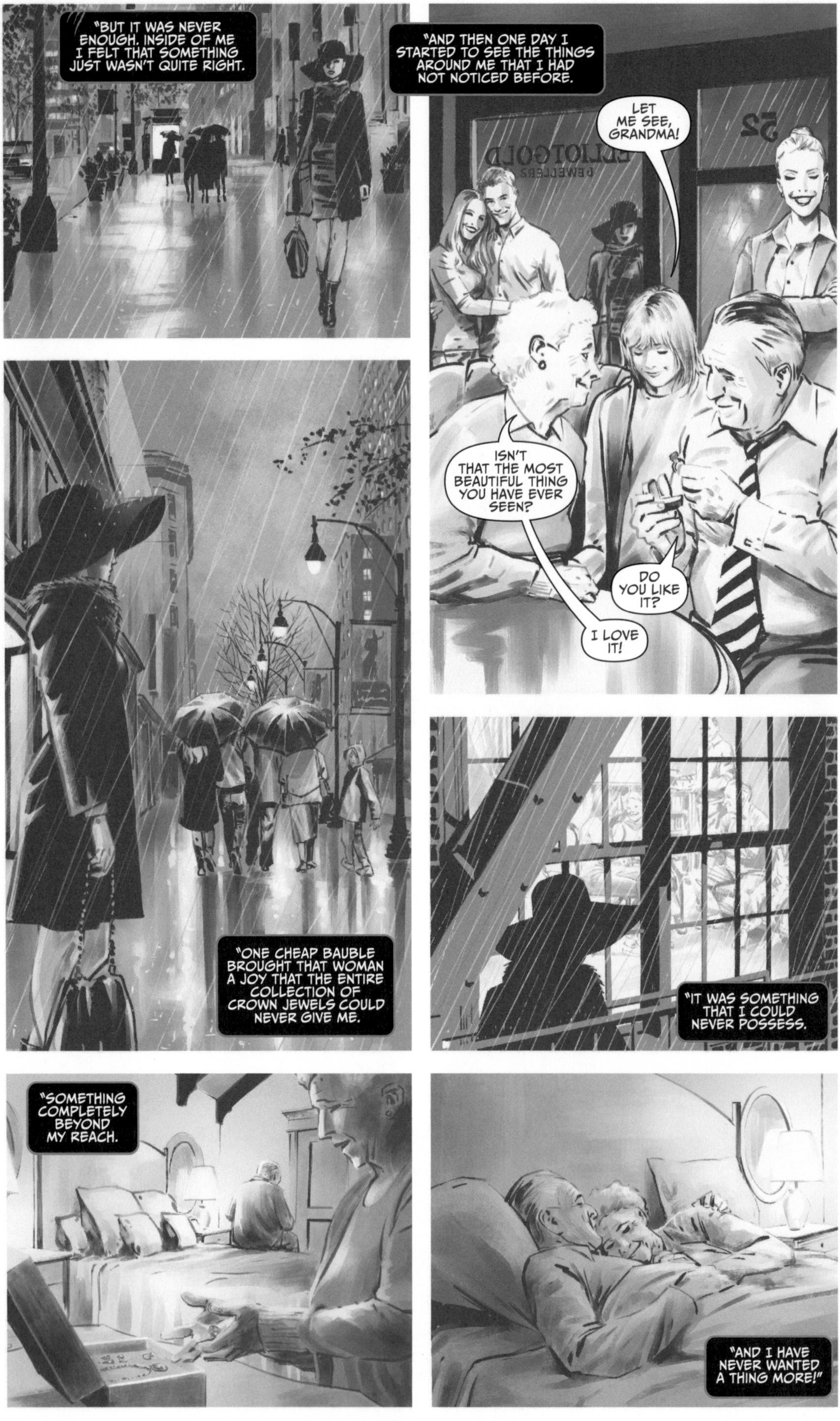

"BUT IT WAS NEVER ENOUGH. INSIDE OF ME I FELT THAT SOMETHING JUST WASN'T QUITE RIGHT.
"AND THEN ONE DAY I STARTED TO SEE THE THINGS AROUND ME THAT I HAD NOT NOTICED BEFORE.
LET ME SEE, GRANDMA!
ISN'T THAT THE MOST BEAUTIFUL THING YOU HAVE EVER SEEN?
DO YOU LIKE IT?
I LOVE IT!
"ONE CHEAP BAUBLE BROUGHT THAT WOMAN A JOY THAT THE ENTIRE COLLECTION OF CROWN JEWELS COULD NEVER GIVE ME.
"IT WAS SOMETHING THAT I COULD NEVER POSSESS.
"SOMETHING COMPLETELY BEYOND MY REACH.
"AND I HAVE NEVER WANTED A THING MORE!"

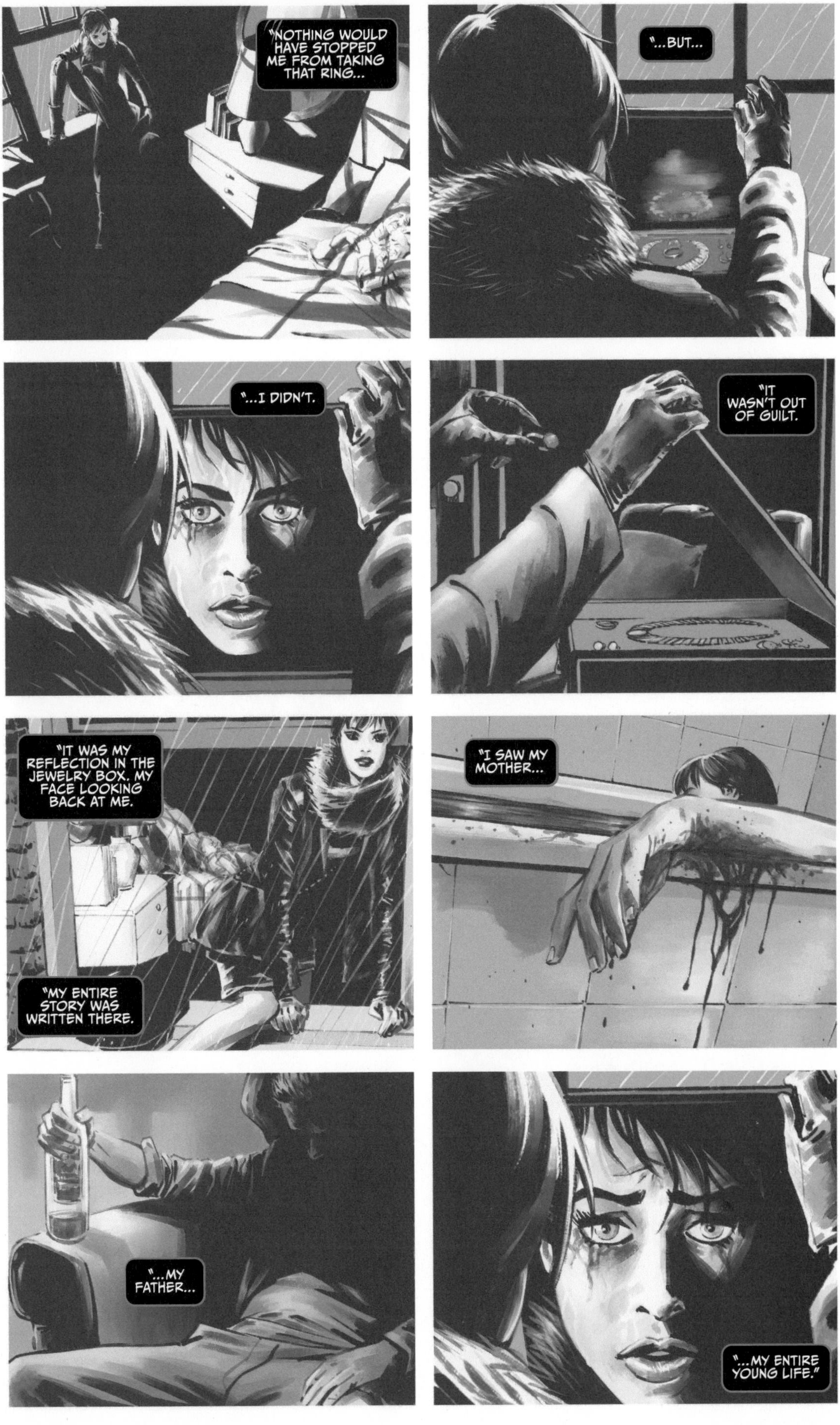
"NOTHING WOULD HAVE STOPPED ME FROM TAKING THAT RING...
"...BUT...
"...I DIDN'T.
"IT WASN'T OUT OF GUILT.
"IT WAS MY REFLECTION IN THE JEWELRY BOX. MY FACE LOOKING BACK AT ME.
"MY ENTIRE STORY WAS WRITTEN THERE.
"I SAW MY MOTHER...
"...MY FATHER...
"...MY ENTIRE YOUNG LIFE."

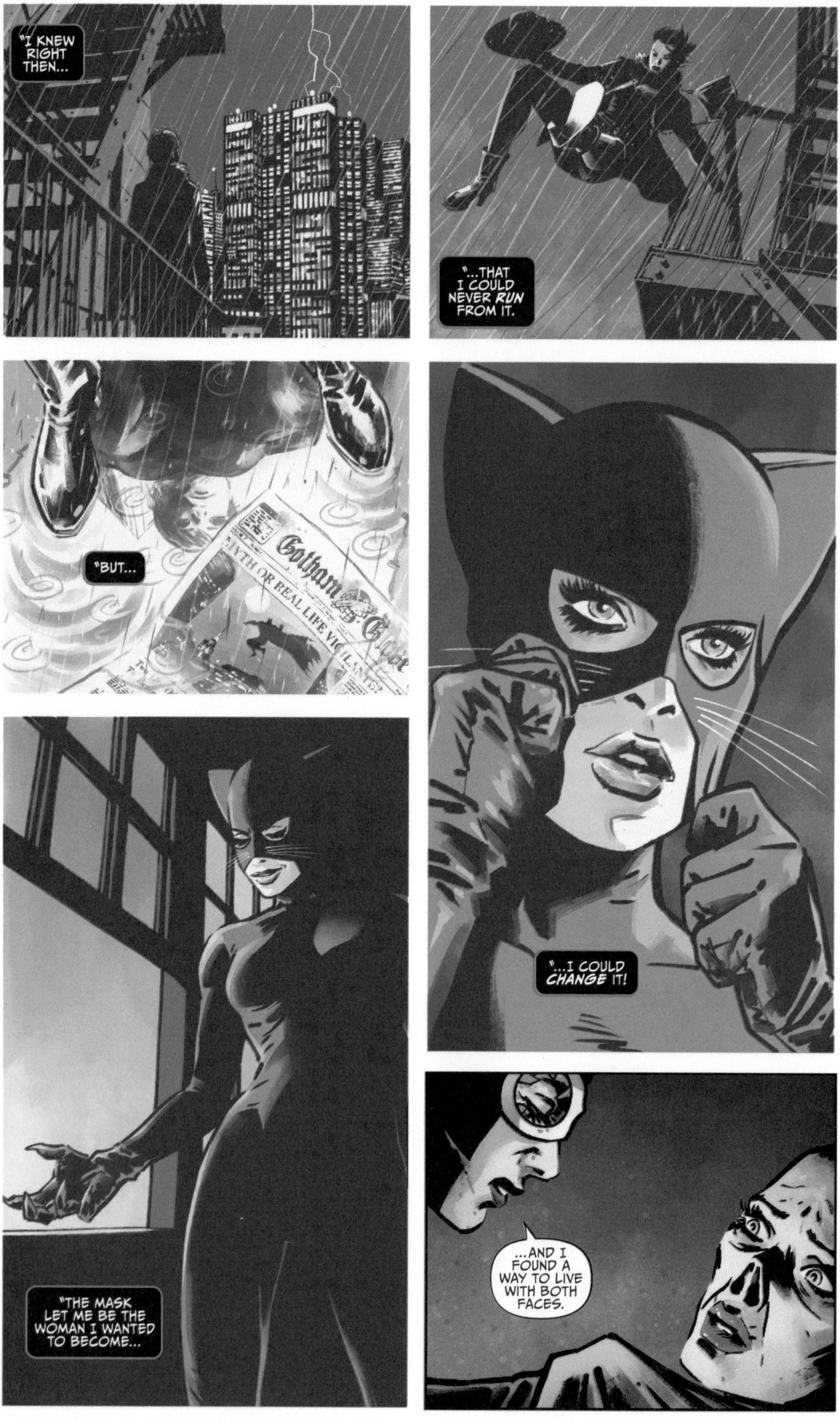
"I KNEW RIGHT THEN...
"...THAT I COULD NEVER *RUN* FROM IT.
Gotham
MYTH OR REAL LIFE VIGILANTE?
"BUT...
"...I COULD *CHANGE* IT!
"THE MASK LET ME BE THE WOMAN I WANTED TO BECOME...
...AND I FOUND A WAY TO LIVE WITH BOTH FACES.

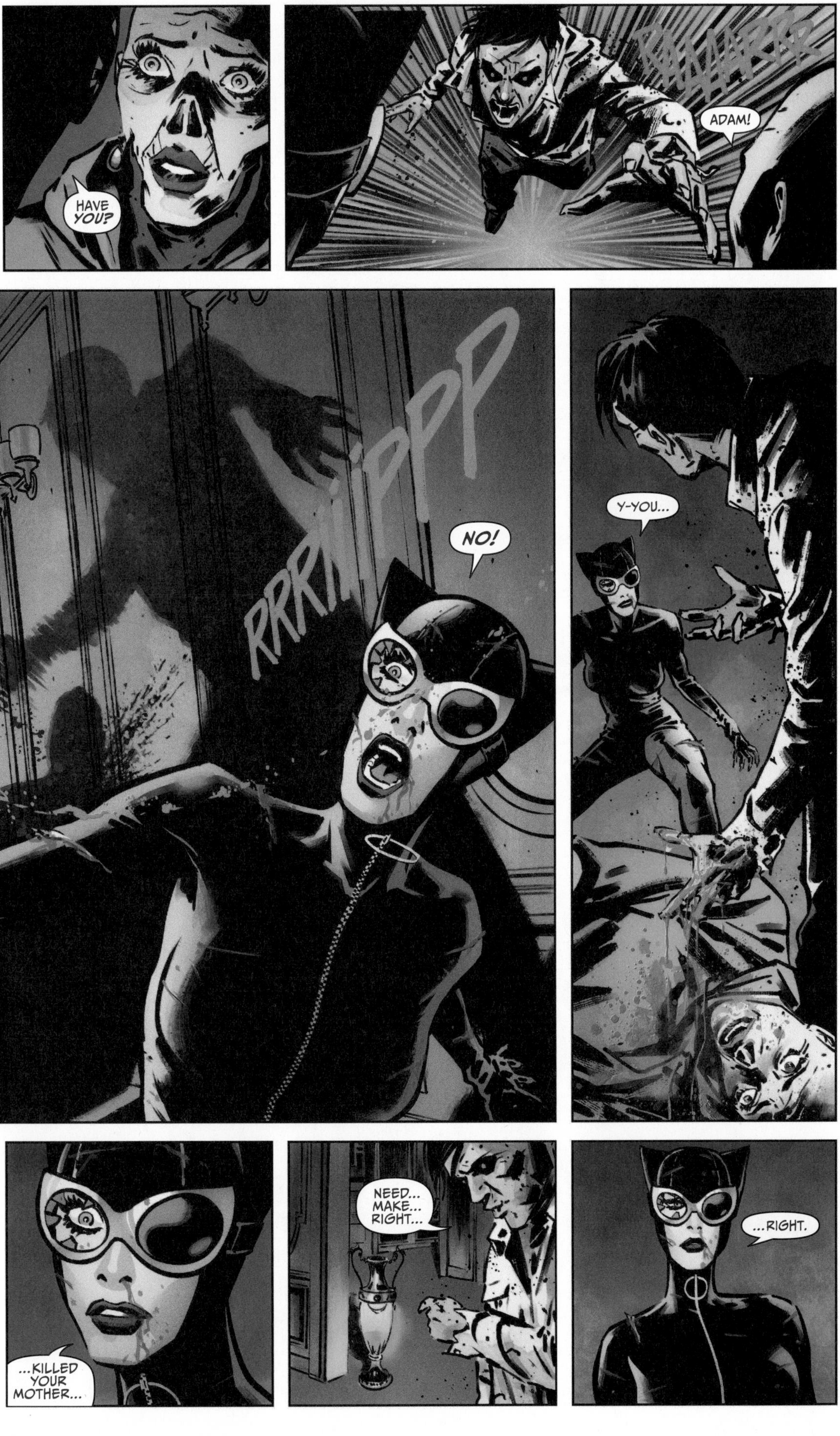
HAVE YOU?
ADAM!
RRRIIPPP
NO!
Y-YOU...
...KILLED YOUR MOTHER...
NEED... MAKE... RIGHT...
...RIGHT.

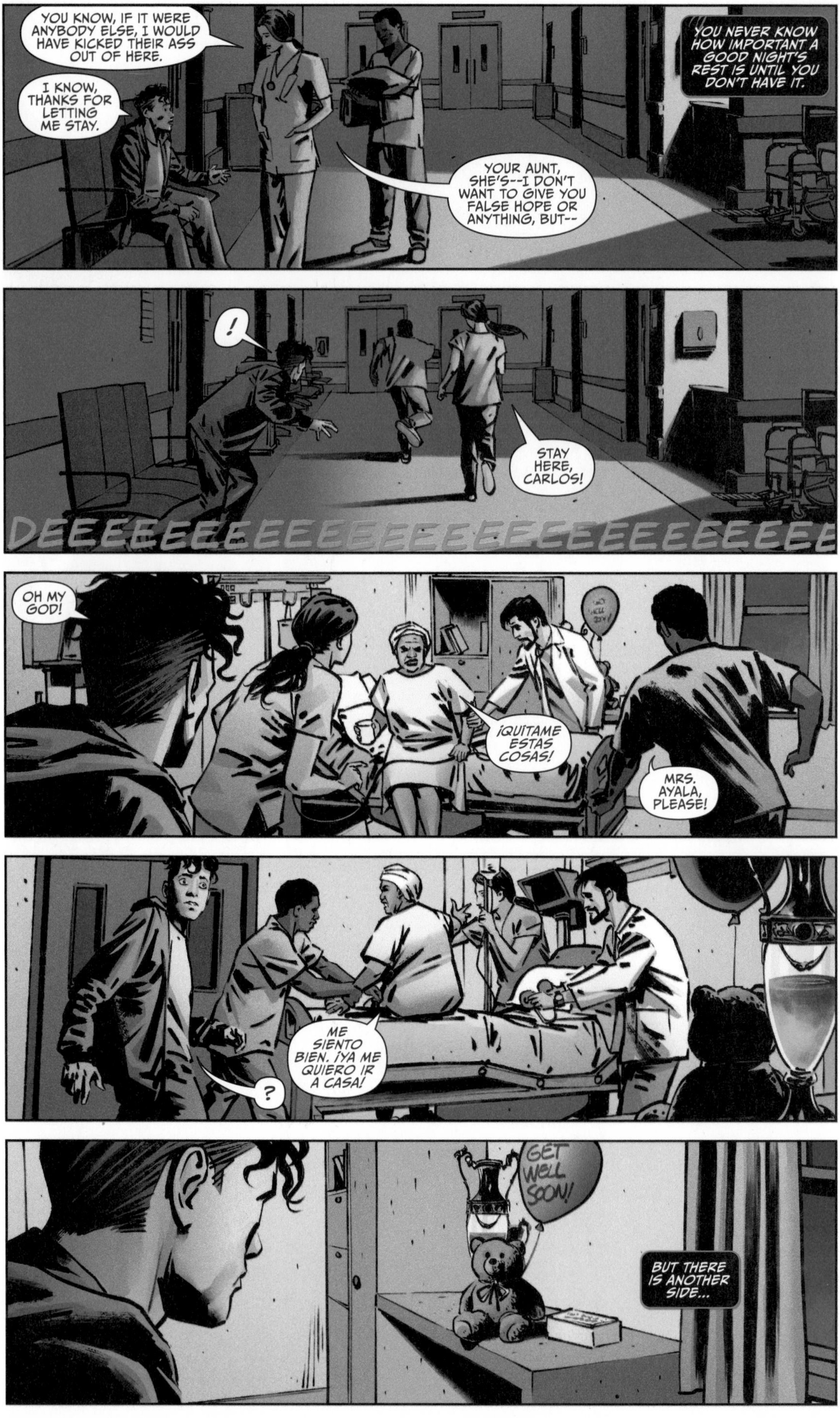
YOU KNOW, IF IT WERE ANYBODY ELSE, I WOULD HAVE KICKED THEIR ASS OUT OF HERE.
I KNOW, THANKS FOR LETTING ME STAY.
YOU NEVER KNOW HOW IMPORTANT A GOOD NIGHT'S REST IS UNTIL YOU DON'T HAVE IT.
YOUR AUNT, SHE'S--I DON'T WANT TO GIVE YOU FALSE HOPE OR ANYTHING, BUT--
!
STAY HERE, CARLOS!
DEEEEEEEEEEEEEEEEEEEEEEEEEEEEE
OH MY GOD!
¡QUITAME ESTAS COSAS!
MRS. AYALA, PLEASE!
ME SIENTO BIEN. ¡YA ME QUIERO IR A CASA!
?
GET WELL SOON!
BUT THERE IS ANOTHER SIDE...

...AND WHILE I DON'T WANT TO BE TOO POLLYANNA ABOUT IT...

TO CARLOS AYALA FROM A MYSTERIOUS ADMIRER

...IT COULD ALL BE A GOOD THING.

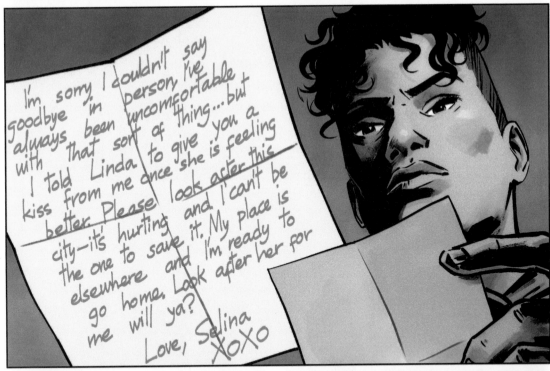

I'm sorry I couldn't say goodbye in person. I've always been uncomfortable with that sort of thing....but I told Linda to give you a kiss from me once she is feeling better. Please look after this city—it's hurting and I can't be the one to save it. My place is elsewhere and I'm ready to go home. Look after her for me will ya?
Love, Selina
XOXO

A WAY OF LETTING YOU KNOW THAT THINGS ARE JUST NOT RIGHT...

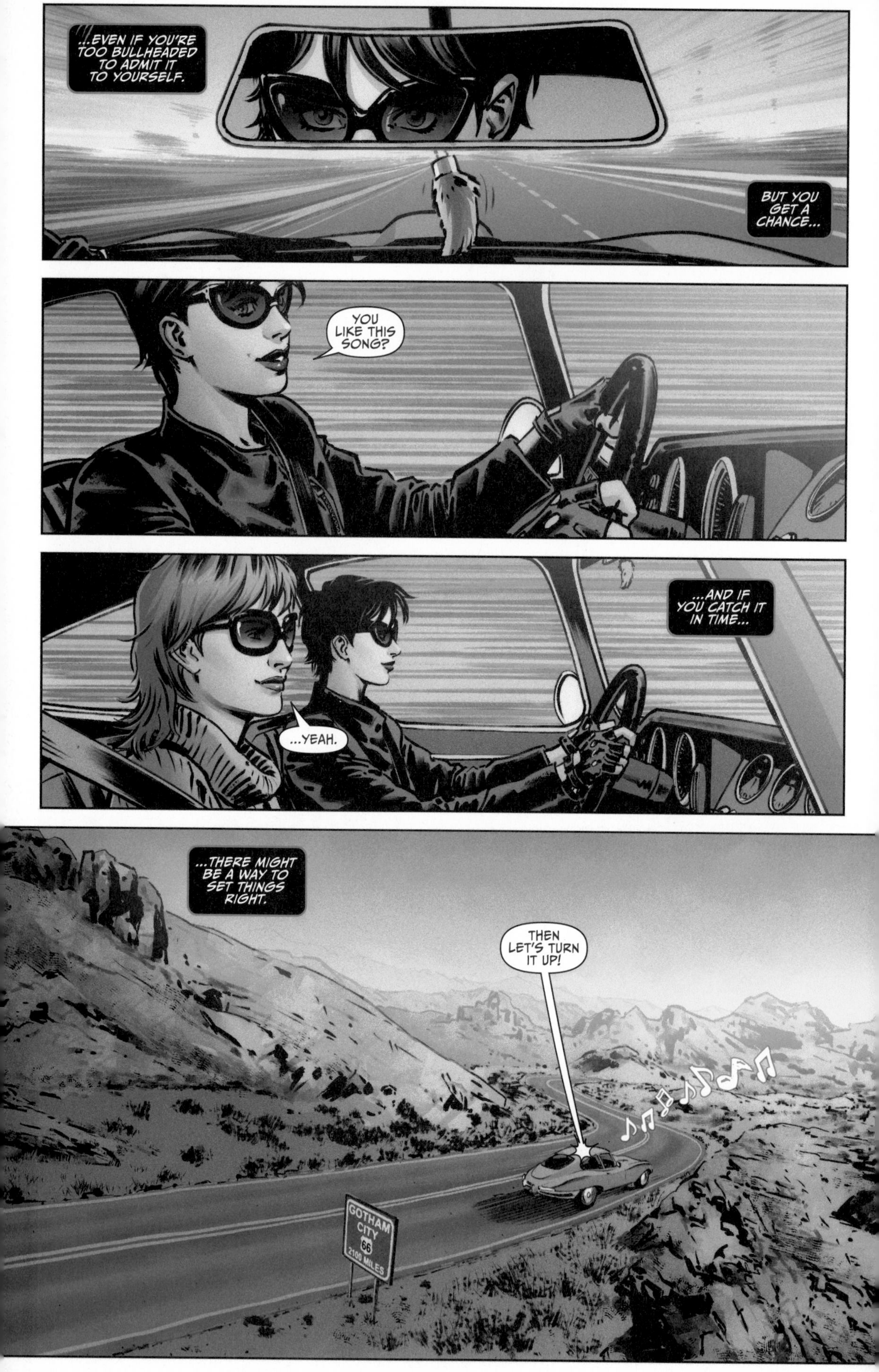
...EVEN IF YOU'RE TOO BULLHEADED TO ADMIT IT TO YOURSELF.
BUT YOU GET A CHANCE...
YOU LIKE THIS SONG?
...AND IF YOU CATCH IT IN TIME...
...YEAH.
...THERE MIGHT BE A WAY TO SET THINGS RIGHT.
THEN LET'S TURN IT UP!
GOTHAM CITY
66
2100 MILES

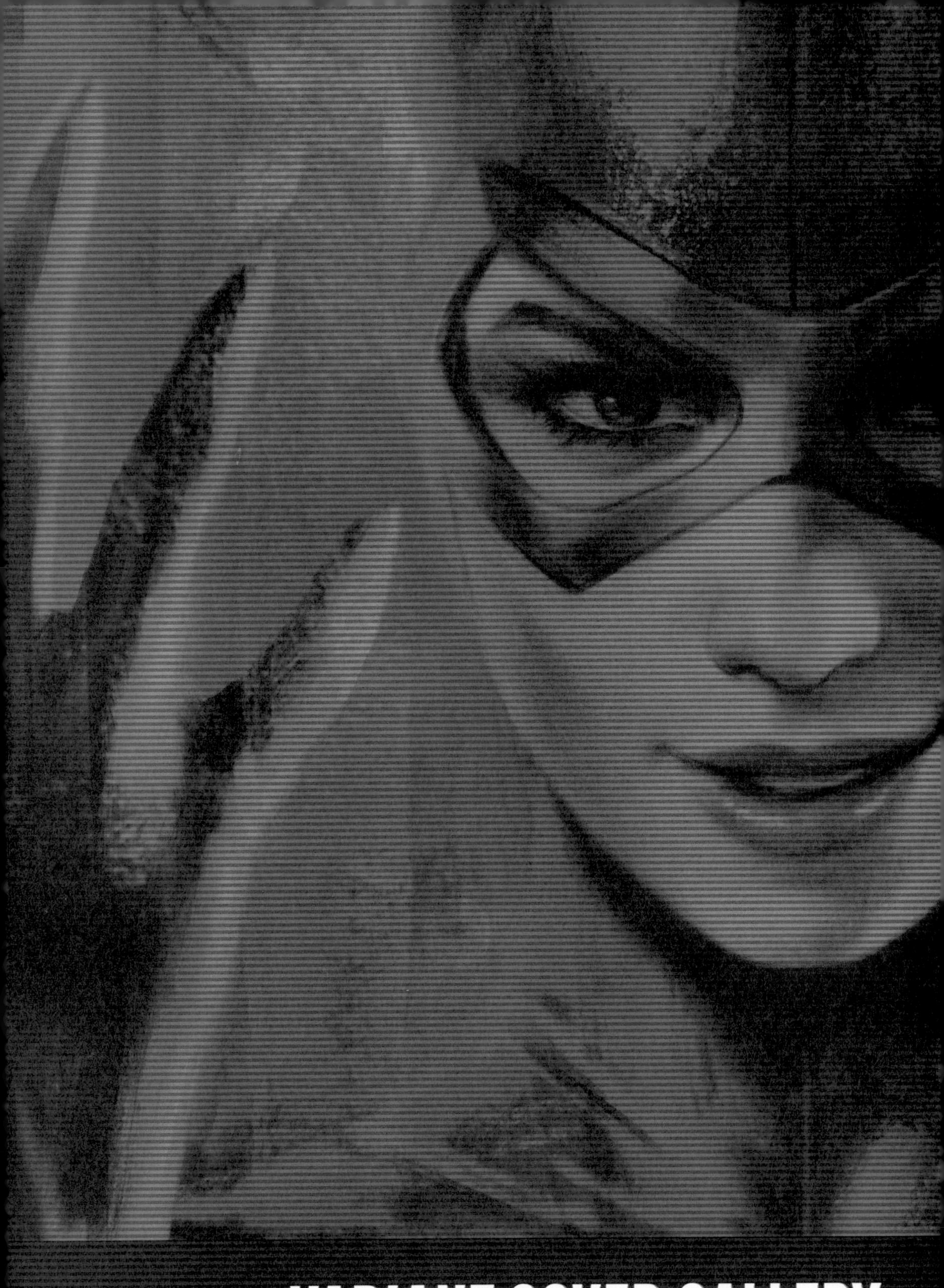

VARIANT COVER GALLERY

***Catwoman* #16**
variant cover by VIKTOR KALVACHEV

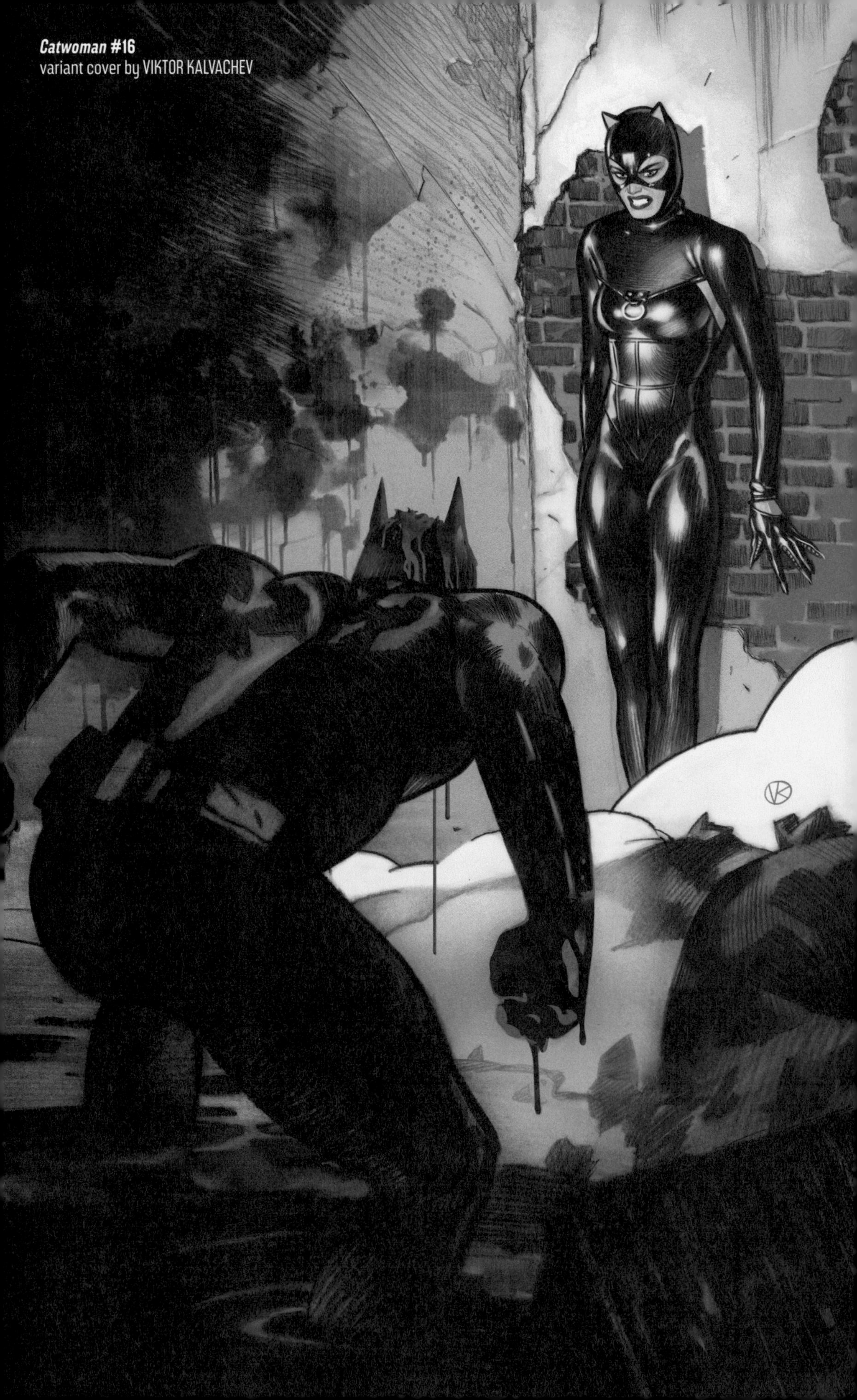

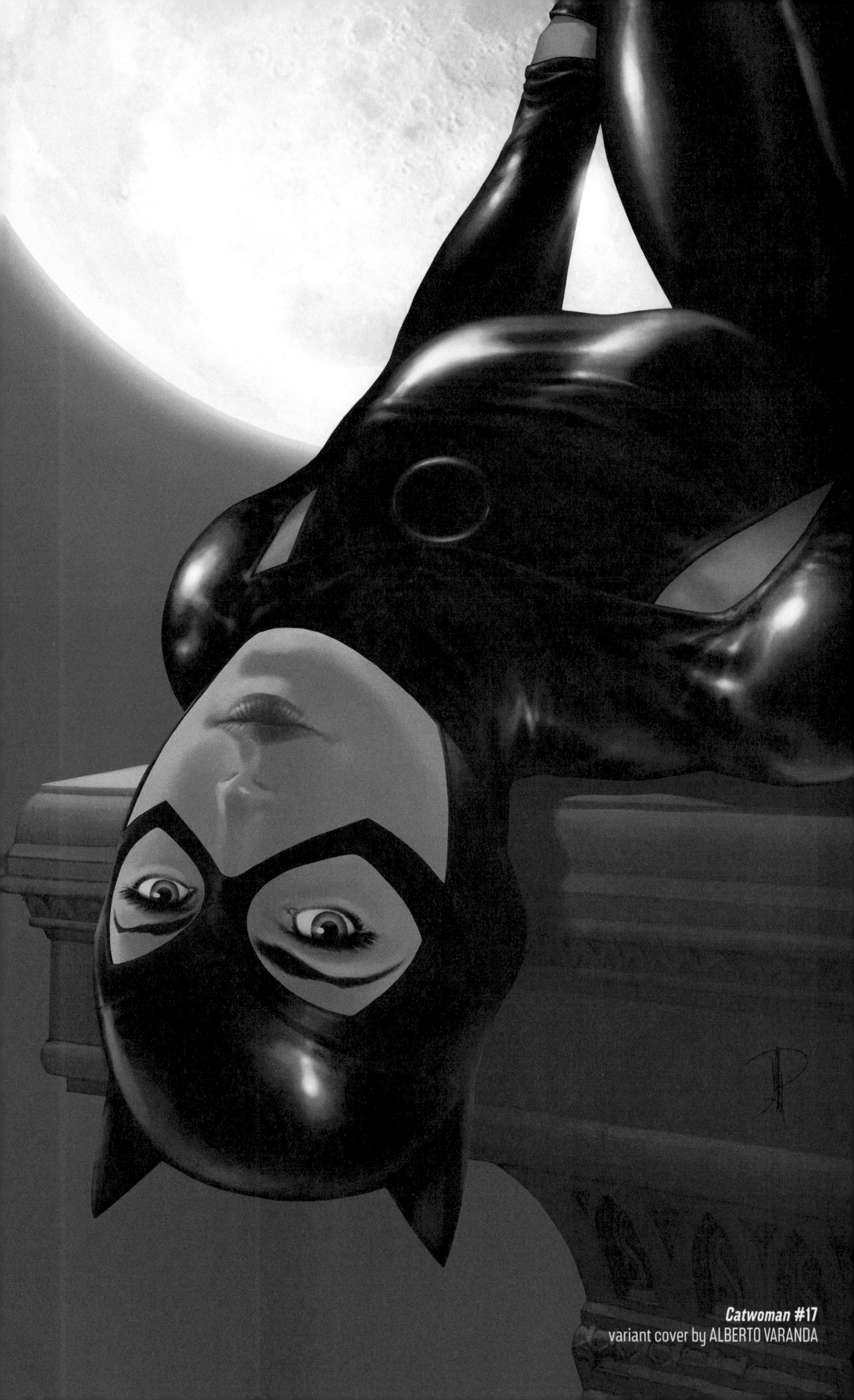

***Catwoman* #17**
variant cover by ALBERTO VARANDA

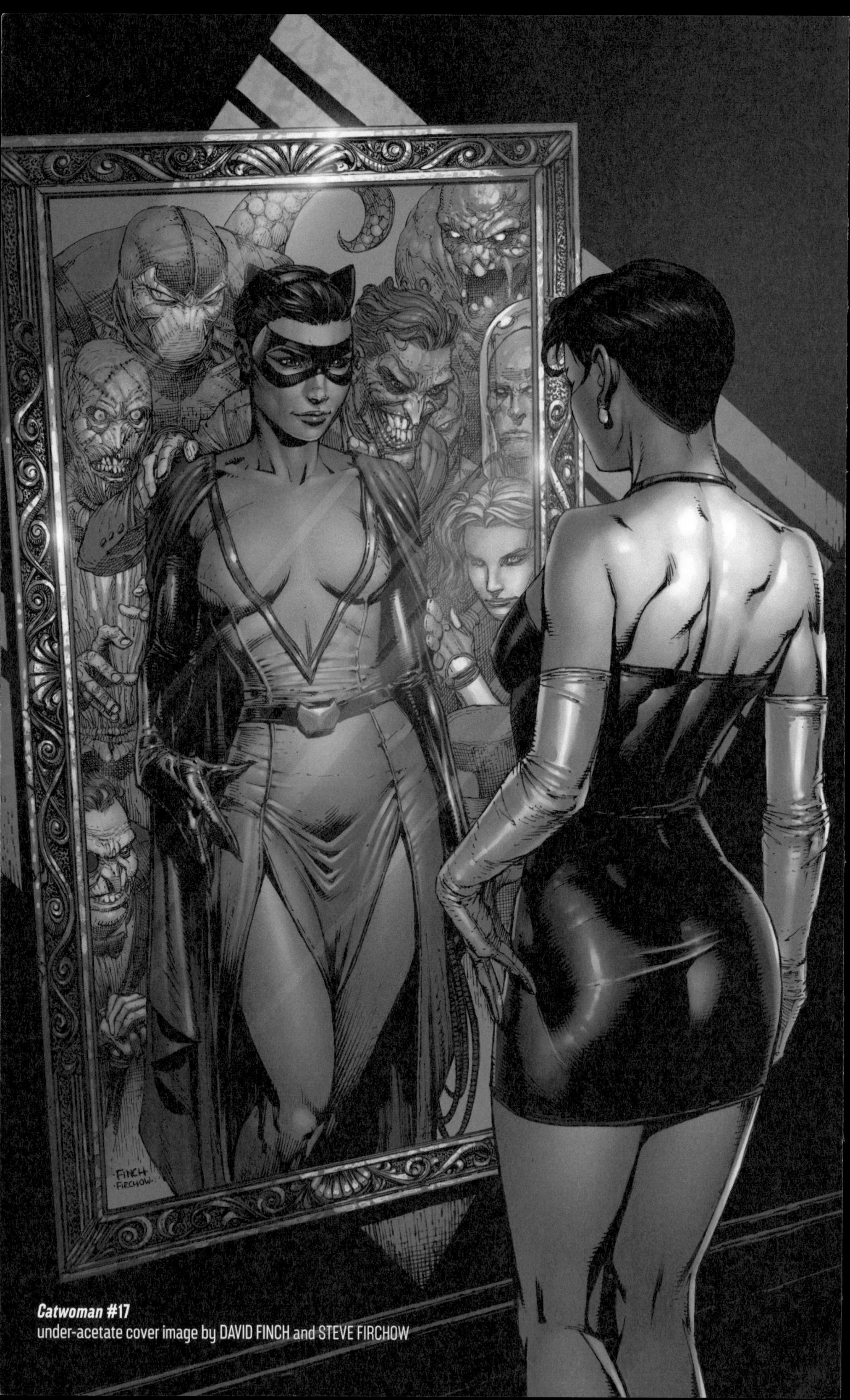
FINCH
FIRCHOW

Catwoman #17
under-acetate cover image by DAVID FINCH and STEVE FIRCHOW

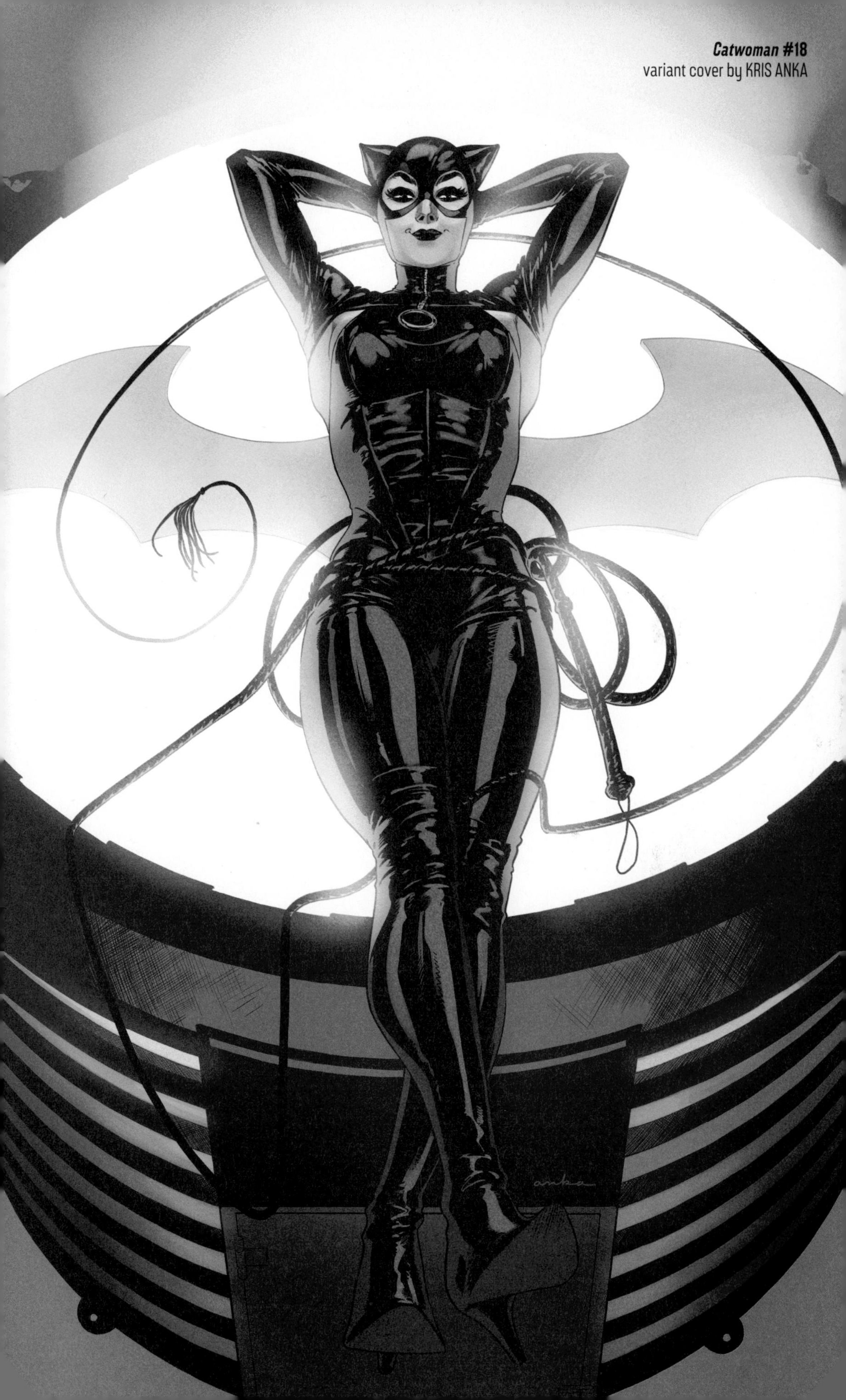

***Catwoman* #18**
variant cover by KRIS ANKA

Catwoman #19
variant cover by IAN MACDONALD

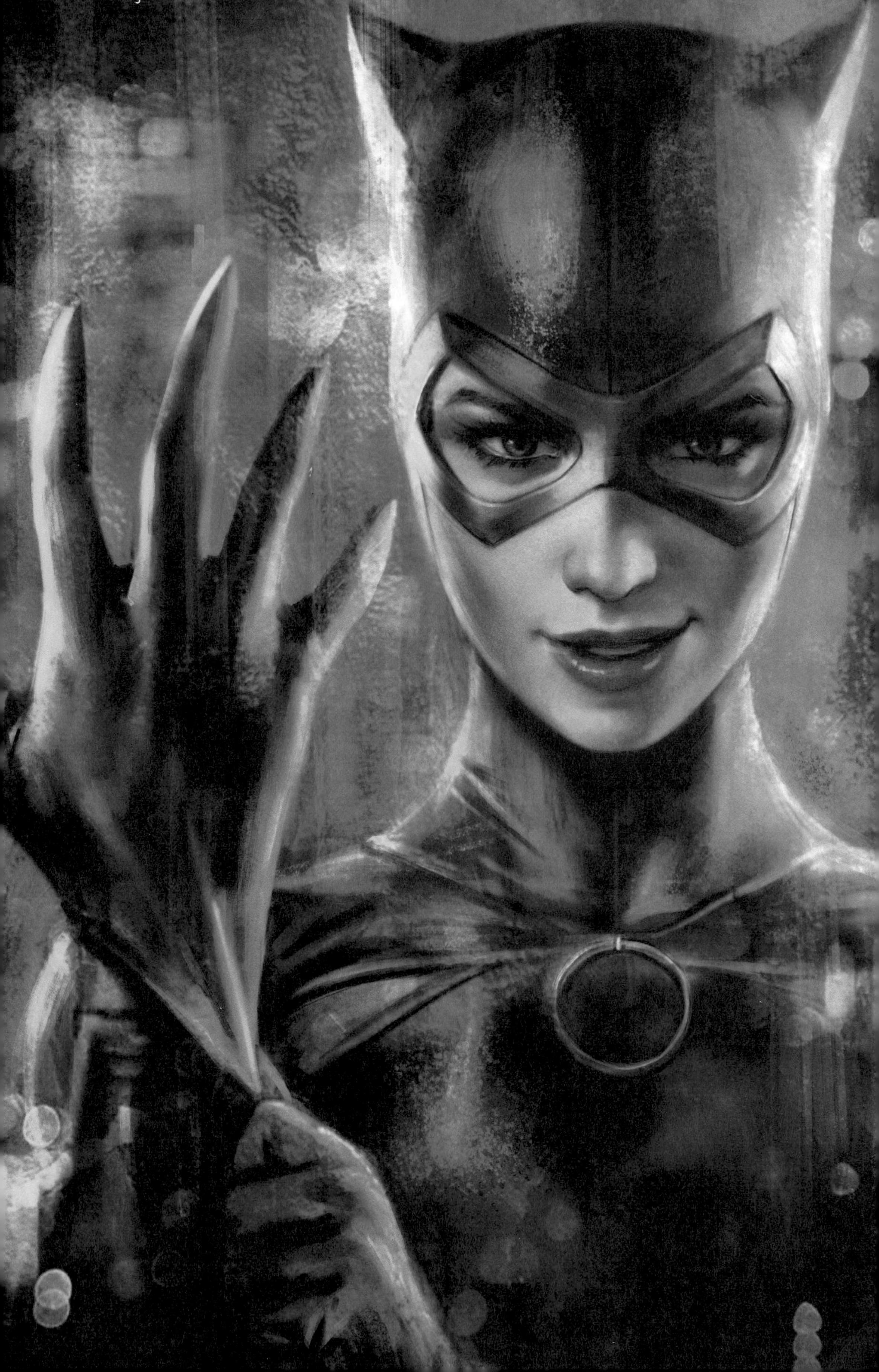

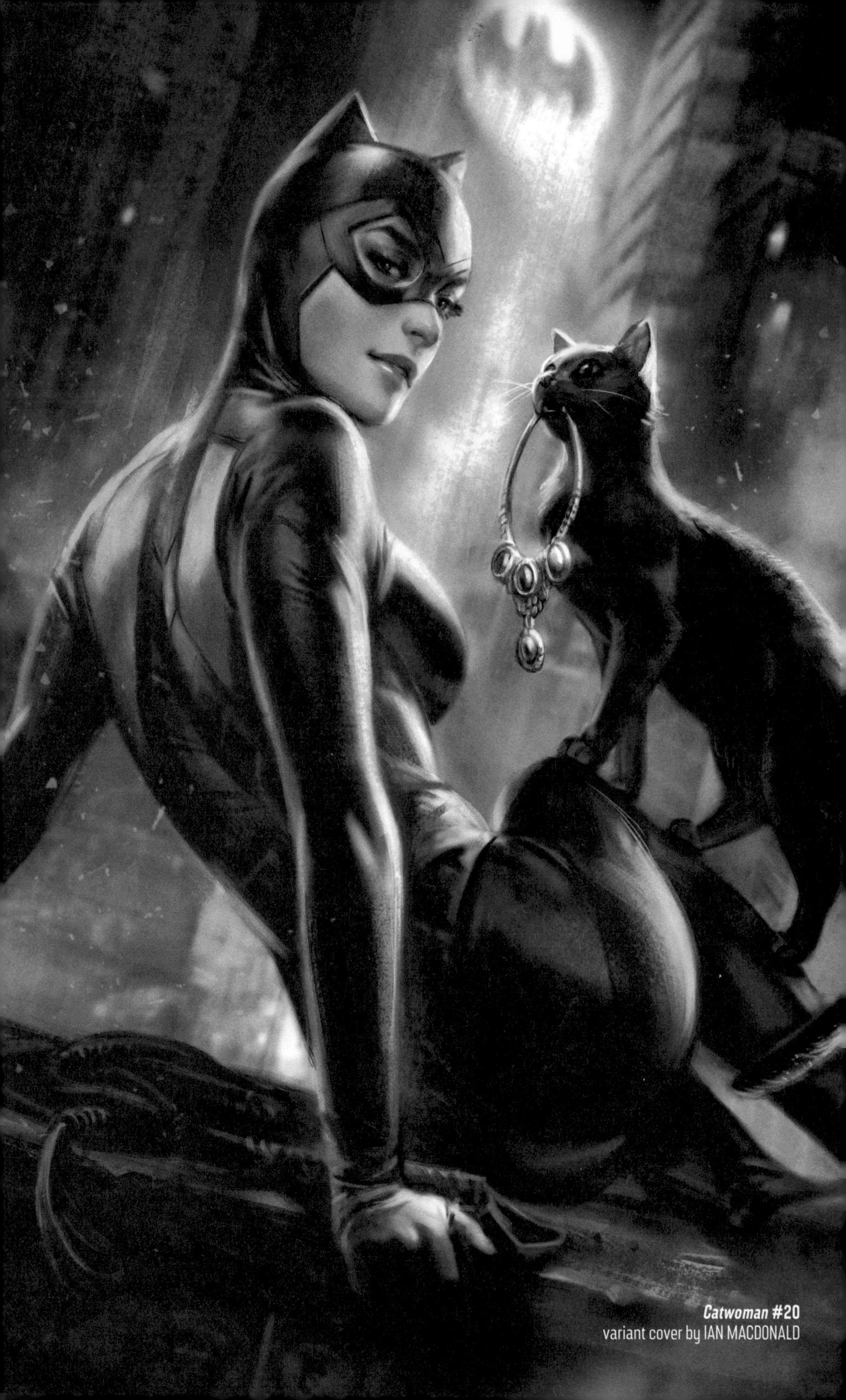

***Catwoman* #20**
variant cover by IAN MACDONALD

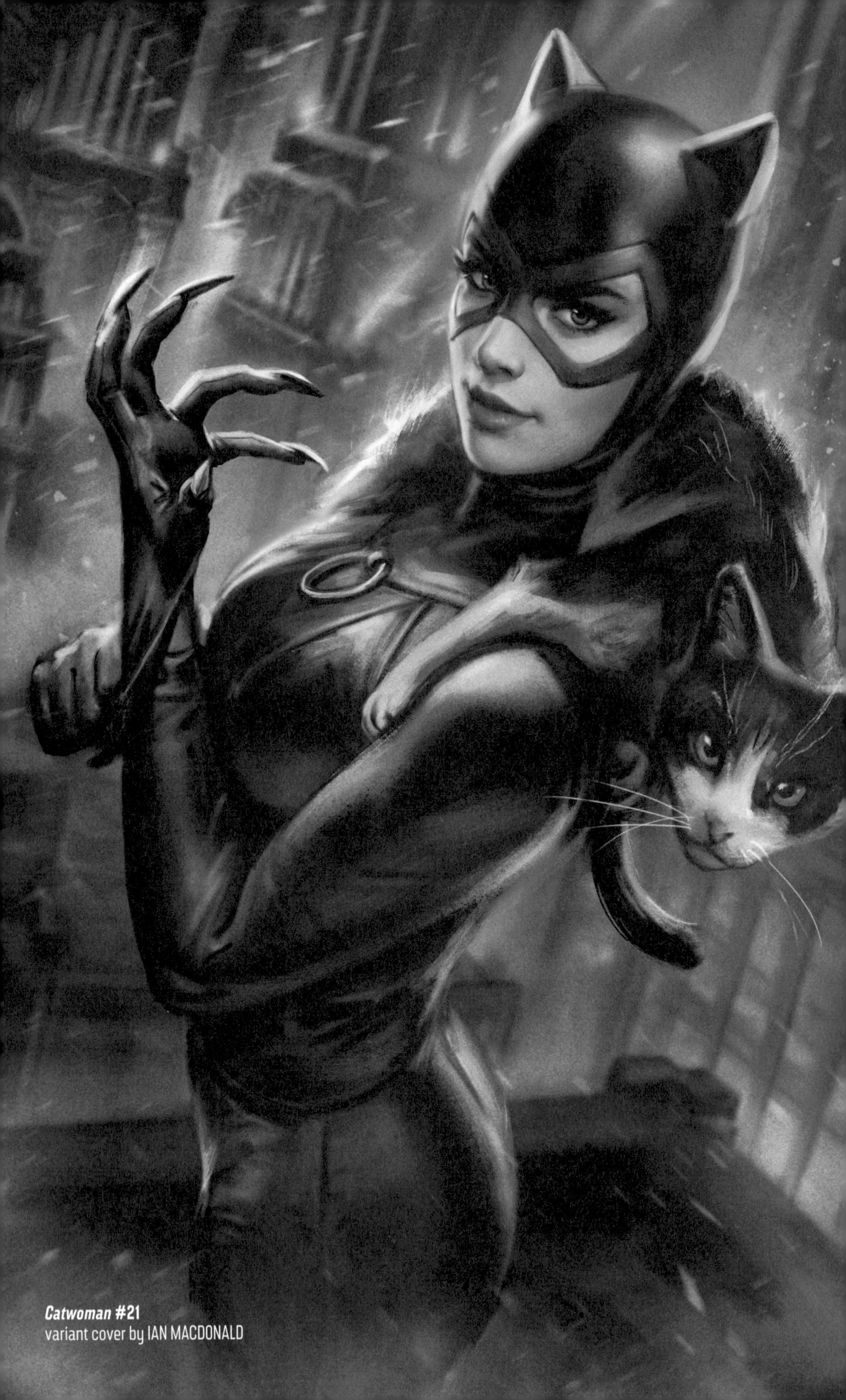

***Catwoman* #21**
variant cover by IAN MACDONALD

***Catwoman* #17**
page 5 line art by Joëlle Jones

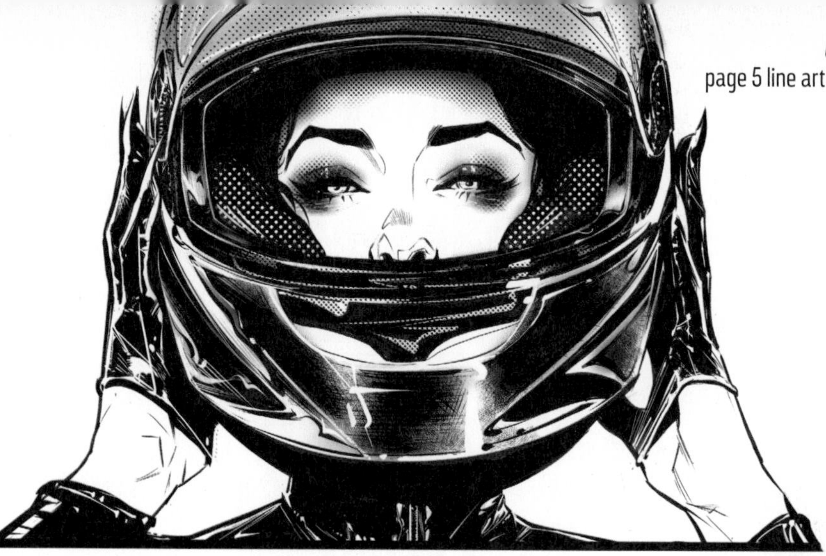

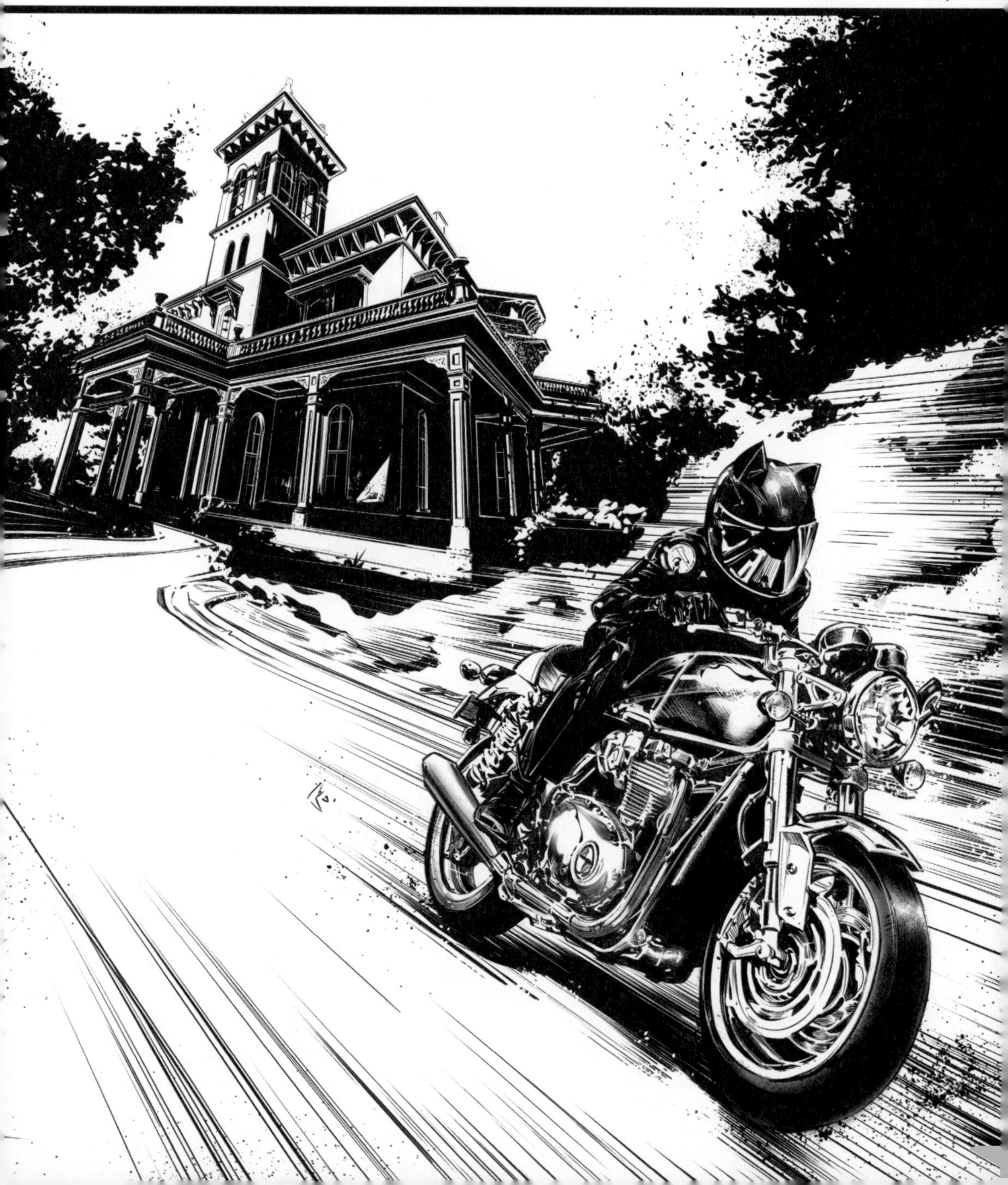

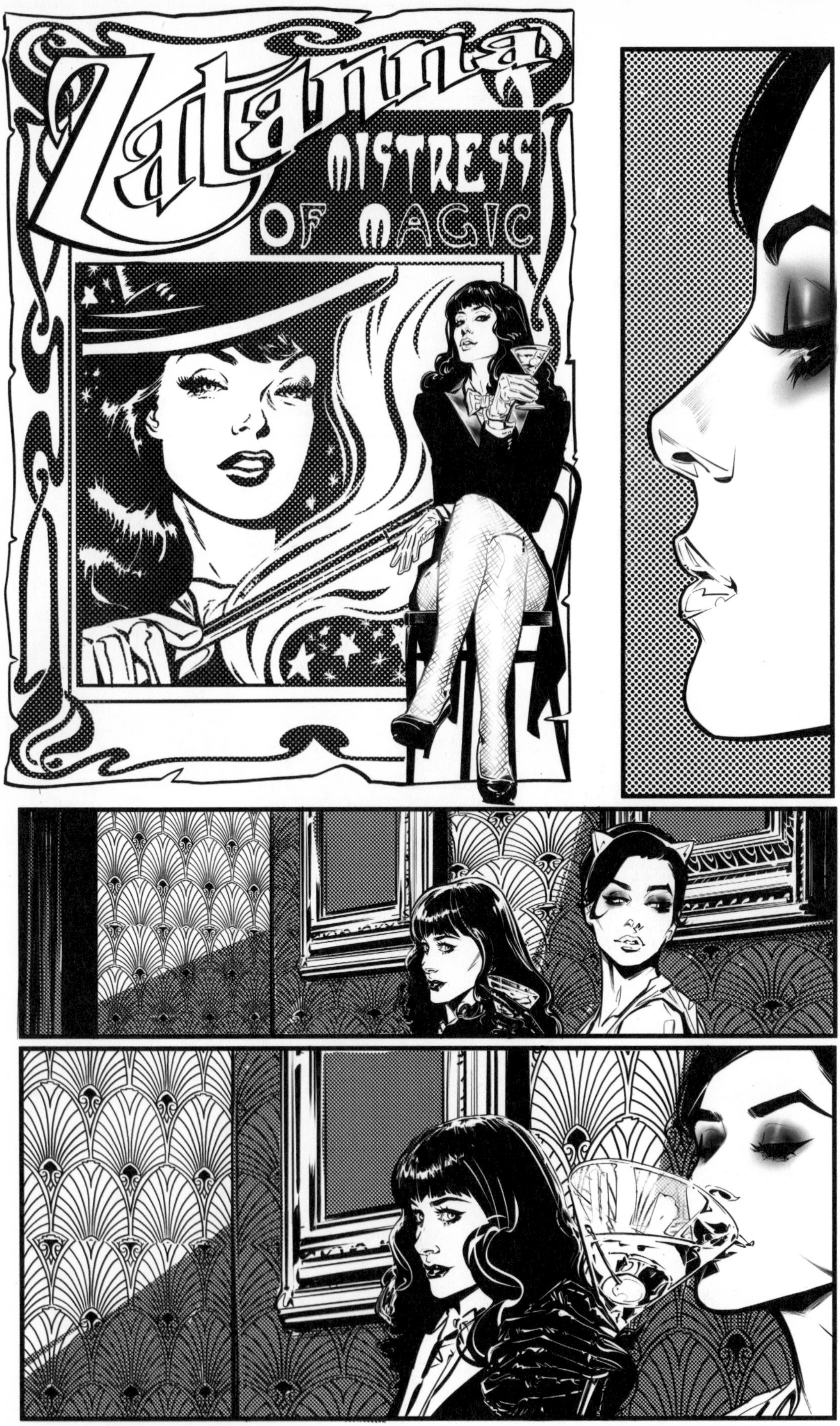
Zatanna
MISTRESS
OF MAGIC

***Catwoman* #18** page 1 line art by Joëlle Jones

"The rare comic-book 'event' that lives up to its own hype."
–WASHINGTON POST

"Recapturing much of the original's unique visual flavor."
–IGN

BATMAN: THE DARK KNIGHT: MASTER RACE

FRANK MILLER with
BRIAN AZZARELLO,
ANDY KUBERT and KLAUS JANSON

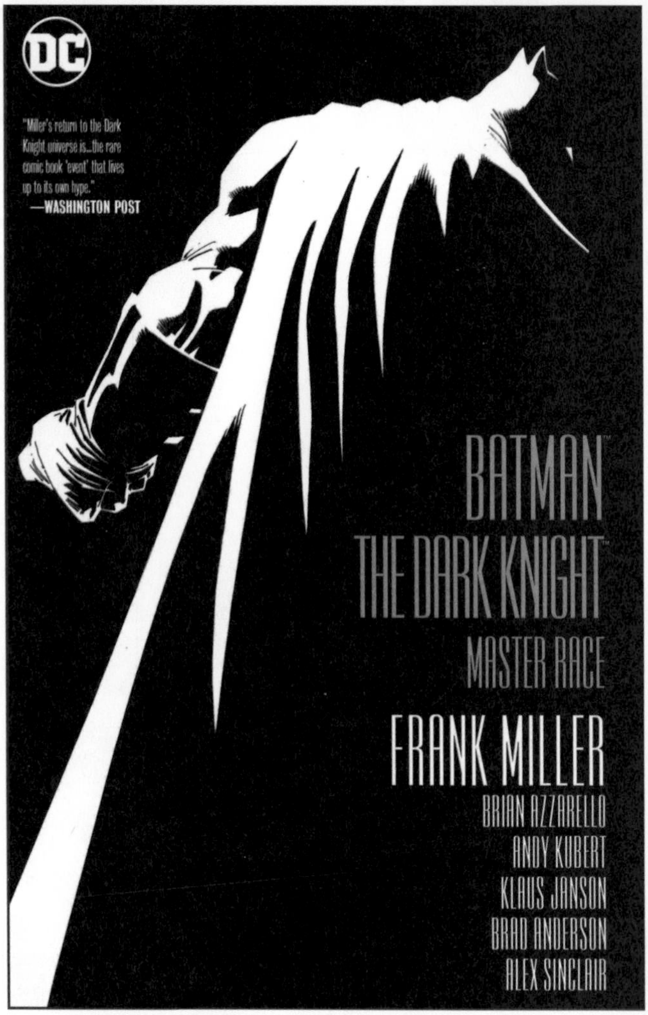

DC
"Miller's return to the Dark Knight universe is...the rare comic book 'event' that lives up to its own hype."
—WASHINGTON POST
BATMAN
THE DARK KNIGHT
MASTER RACE
FRANK MILLER
BRIAN AZZARELLO
ANDY KUBERT
KLAUS JANSON
BRAD ANDERSON
ALEX SINCLAIR

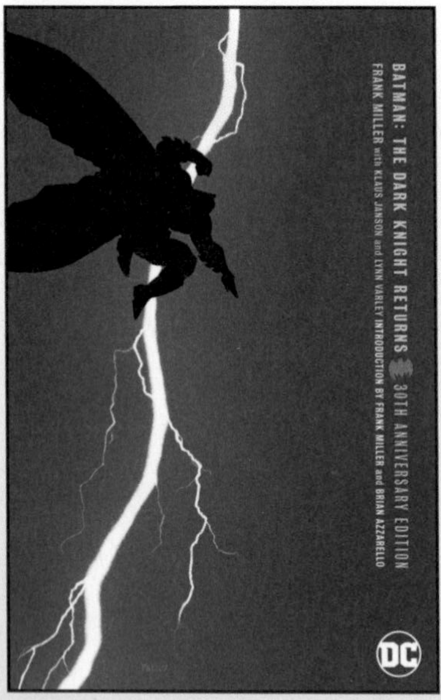

BATMAN: THE DARK KNIGHT RETURNS 30TH ANNIVERSARY EDITION
FRANK MILLER with KLAUS JANSON and LYNN VARLEY INTRODUCTION BY FRANK MILLER and BRIAN AZZARELLO
DC

BATMAN: THE DARK KNIGHT RETURNS

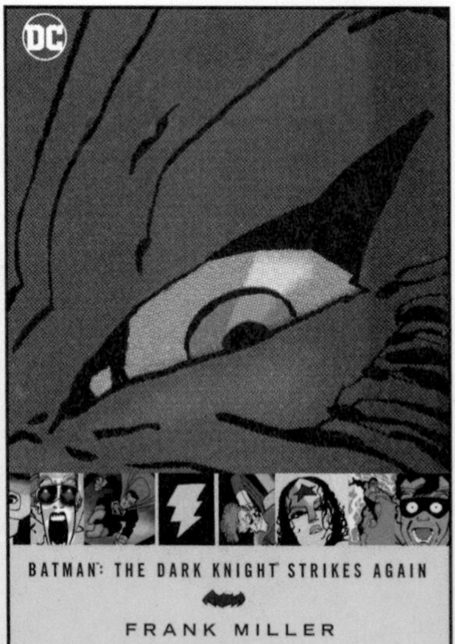

DC
BATMAN: THE DARK KNIGHT STRIKES AGAIN
FRANK MILLER
and LYNN VARLEY

BATMAN: THE DARK KNIGHT STRIKES AGAIN

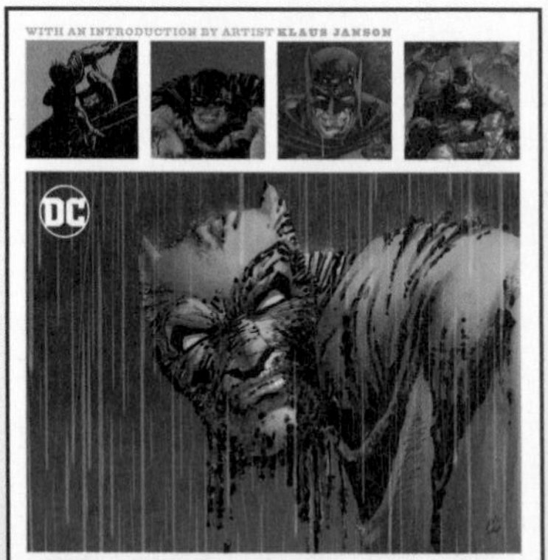

WITH AN INTRODUCTION BY ARTIST KLAUS JANSON
DC
BATMAN
THE DARK KNIGHT
MASTER RACE
THE COVERS
DELUXE EDITION

BATMAN: THE DARK KNIGHT: MASTER RACE : THE COVERS

Get more DC graphic novels wherever comics and books are sold!